Occasional Publication Number 22

# Northern Lakes and Rivers

W.C. Mackay
Editor

A publication of the
Boreal Institute for Northern Studies
1989

Copyright © 1989   Boreal Institute for Northern Studies

All rights reserved.

ISSN 000680303
ISBN 0-919058-67-1

Published by:
Boreal Institute for Northern Studies
The University of Alberta
Edmonton, Alberta
Canada  T6G 2E9
Telephone (403) 492-2919
Electronic mail:  BINS @ UALTAMTS
FAX:  (403) 492-1153
Telex:  037-2979

Cover photo: W.C. Mackay

# Northern Lakes and Rivers

W.C. Mackay, Editor

# Table of Contents

Introduction .................................................................................. 5

Physical Aspects of Northern Freshwater Systems ................................ 6

Stream Flow in the NWT ................................................................ 7

Modelling Snow Transport, Snowmelt and Meltwater
Infiltration in Open, Northern Regions ............................................... 8
D.M. Gray, J.W. Pomeroy and R.J. Granger

Ice Formation on Northern Rivers .................................................... 23

Ice Break-Up on Northern Rivers: The Liard River as an Example ............. 24
T.D. Prowse

Hydrology of Mackenzie Delta Lakes ................................................. 43
Philip Marsh

Freeze-Up and Break-up of Ice Cover on Small Arctic Lakes ..................... 56
Ming-ko Woo and Richard Heron

Biological Processes in Northern Freshwater Systems ........................... 63

Limnology of Arctic Lakes ............................................................. 64

Ecology of Pill Clams (Pisidium, Bivalvia) with Focus on
Adaptations to Northern Winters.
A Short Review of Studies in Scandinavian Lakes and Rivers .................... 66
Ismo J. Holopainen

Growth, Feeding and Reproductive Biology of Freshwater Fish
in Northern Canada ....................................................................... 75
W.C. Mackay

Fish Assemblages in Small Boreal Lakes ............................................ 93
W.M. Tonn and C.L.K. Robinson

Infectious Pancreatic Necrosis Virus in Arctic Char Populations
in the Mackenzie Delta Region ....................................................... 106
T. Yamamoto

# Introduction

This volume focuses on the major physical and biological processes which operate in lakes and rivers in northern regions. Ice and snow dominate all aspects, both physical and biological, of these systems, since they are ice covered for much of the year. The papers included here examine a range of topics from the accumulation of snow, formation and break-up of ice cover to the effects of low oxygen levels on inverterates and the structure of fish communities in small northern lakes.

The physical processes which are significant to northern freshwater start on the land before water enters lakes or rivers. The processes involved in freeze-up and break-up in lakes and rivers have an over riding importance to all aspects of these systems. There is marked seasonal and year to year variation in the quantity and quality of runoff.

Much of the circumpolar north is underlain by permafrost and the ground in more southerly boreal regions is frozen for several months each year. In addition all winter precipitation occurs as snow, which is not distributed uniformly over the landscape and accumulates preferentially in some areas as a result of wind action. During spring snow melt occurs over a very short period of time resulting in a rapid flux of water through freshwater systems at that time.

Ice dominates lakes and rivers at high latitudes. Freeze-up generally occurs rapidly. Rivers freeze in fundamentally different ways than lakes. The formation of frazil ice and its accumulation in rivers can result in very thick ice under some conditions.

While water temperatures under ice cover do not drop below 0°C the water is separated from direct contact with air for long periods of time. The implications of this isolation are profound both in terms of confining volatile pollutants to the water and in terms of oxygen depletion or accumulation of other gases. Polynyas, predictable areas of open water in the winter, are well known in arctic marine systems but they also occur in large rivers providing sites for gas exchange between the water and the atmosphere and also a site of access to the water for air breathing animals.

Break-up is an important and relatively rapid process in northern lakes and rivers. Break-up in northern rivers can result in ice jams, in flooding large areas of land and in erosion of the banks and scouring of the channel. shore. The processes involved in ice break-up have profound effects on physical and biological processes in lakes and rivers in the north. Physical effects such as predictable formation of ice dams in certain locations have implications for human settlements and engineering projects as well as providing special habitat for wildlife.

Biological processes are dominated by the effect of low thermal input, long period of ice cover, short growing season, and low levels of oxygen during the winter. Low water temperatures limit nutrient use, growth rate and production of new biological material. The organisms which are most successful in northern freshwater have adaptations to low teperatures and to low oxygen levels in winter. Northern ecosystems are characterized by a small number of species which have much longer generation time than the same species or their counterparts further south.

# Physical Aspects of Northern Freshwater Systems

Northern freshwater systems are dominated by ice and the processes of freezing and thawing. Ice forms in a number of different ways in northern systems, each type of ice has unique properties which impose constraints on the functioning of aquatic systems, particularly during freeze-up and break-up. The nature of the crystal structure of ice can affect now light penetrates it and the properties it will show during spring melt.

The formation of ice in fall is more rapid and uniform on lakes than in running water. Freeze-up in running water alters the flow of rivers and streams by reducing the cross sectional area of the channel. In addition, due to the turbulent nature of lotic systems (flowing water) the mechansims of freezing are different from those which operate in lentic systems (still water). An important feature of freeze-up in running water is the formation of fazil ice, tiny ice crystals which are found thoughout the water as a result of turbulance. The presence of frazil ice and its aggregation in running water results in the formation of ice pans, anchor ice, and ice dams.

## Snow accumulation and melt

The dynamics of water movement through northern aquatic systems are considerably different than in southern climates. The reasons for these differences are the long periods during the winter when precipitation accumulates on the frozen land and the rapid melting in spring which occurs over frozen soil or permafrost which is often not permeable to water.

Runoff in northern regions is very sporatic. During winter, precipitation accumulates on the surface of the land as snow. However snow accumulation is not uniform because of the action of wind. There is no runoff during winter, when spring arrives melting occurs rapidly. The flow of water through northern systems is usually greatest in spring as a result of rapid snow melt.

## Break-up

The break-up of lakes and rivers in the north is quite different. Break-up of rivers and streams is rapid and dramatic while the disappearance of ice from lakes progresses much more slowly.

Ice on lakes melts from the bottom up and from the edges toward the centre and finally from around the boundaries of ice crystals. Melting around the outside of lotic systems results in a band of water around the outside of lakes which is considerably warmer than the water under the ice. This band of open water provides a warm microhabitat for many aquatic organisms early in the growing season.

Break-up of rivers is assisted by runoff from the land. Once break-up is initiated in rivers the flow of water is markedly different than during the rest of the year. This is a result of the formation of temporary ice dams in river channels and the accumulation of water behind them. The rapid rise in water level which results from the daming of river channels and from increased volumes of water moving through the system flushes ponds and shallow lakes near major river channels and in deltas providing nutrients for these systems and accelerating break-up in them as well. Break-up in north flowing rivers starts in the south and progresses to the north. This accelerates the appearance of open water at the downstream end and in the deltas of major rivers.

Runoff, water which is exported from the land, is the difference between precipitation and evaporation. Although precipitation is generally low in northern Canada 24% of Canada's runoff comes from the NWT and 4.5% from the Yukon. One explanation for this is that evaporation is much lower in the north than in southern regions. Thus a much higher proportion of total precipitation occurs as runoff in northern than in southern Canada.

# Stream Flow in the NWT

## Summary of Presentation by Dr. Arleigh Laycock

Runoff occurs when water input from precipitation exceeds loss via evapotranspiration. In southern regions mean July air temperature is a good indicator of the extent of evapotranspiration.

In the Baker Creek Basin near Yellowknife the flows observed can be explained taking into account undercatch. Measured evapotranspiration is substantially less than that predicted using models developed for southern systems. In northern streams in general flow is much larger than previously predicted because actual evapotranspiration is much less than previous predictions. This results in a larger runoff than previously predicted. There is also severe undercatch in terms of precipitation. An avenue of water entry into northern systems that is not taken into account in the water balance models that have been used is entry through direct condensation of water on surfaces of vegetation, soil and rock. This can be an important source of water in the north.

Taking into account the low evapotranspiration in the north predicted water yield is 17% larger than previous estimates. The eastern arctic islands have a water yield which is three times that of the mainland. The difference, using revised evapotranspiration estimates in the western arctic are not so great. In the Yukon glaciers are very high yield areas. Water yields predicted by the Inland Waters Directorate for the NWT, Yukon and arctic islands is 688,024,000 $Dm^3$ while that predicted from revised estimates of evapotranspiration by Laycock is 1,070,000,000 $Dm^3$.

Canada has about 9% of world stream flow. The NWT and Yukon have 24 and 4.5% respectively of the total Canadian stream flow. (see Laycock, New Canadian Encyclopedia). The NWT has two to three orders of magnitude more water per capita than other regions of Canada.

# Modelling Snow Transport, Snowmelt and Meltwater Infiltration in Open, Northern Regions

### D.M. Gray, J.W. Pomeroy and R.J. Granger
Division of Hydrology, University of Saskatchewan
Saskatoon, Saskatchewan, Canada

**Abstract**

This paper discusses the processes of snow transport (accumulation and distribution), snowmelt and meltwater infiltration into frozen soils as they affect snowcover runoff in northern regions. Physically-based models for describing these processes are presented and applied to shallow snow-covers of the open, grassland region of western Saskatchewan.

## Introduction

A lack of understanding of the processes affecting snowcover runoff has been a limiting factor to the development of water management models for northern Canada. Mathematical models of snowcover runoff provide a tool for developing engineering design criteria for, and an understanding of, the hydrology of the Northern environment.

Throughout a large part of northern Canada snow constitutes the major source of fresh water, comprising on average from 40 to 70% of the annual precipitation. Meltwater derived from the snowcover finds beneficial uses as a domestic supply, for replenishing soil water reserves for plant growth, for recharging groundwater supplies and lakes, and as a habitat for water-fowl and other wildlife. Adversely, direct runoff may cause flooding and erosion and impede transportation, exploration and development.

Runoff calculations require consideration of all the major components of the hydrologic cycle, namely; precipitation, evaporation/evapotranspiration, interception, infiltration and groundwater flow. Unfortunately, within a single paper it is impossible to discuss all the factors and processes affecting each component in detail. Hence this paper focuses on three processes important to the development of a snowmelt runoff model for northern regions. These are snow transport (accumulation and distribution), snowmelt, and meltwater infiltration to frozen soils. Special emphasis is placed on the development of physically-based models that may be used to describe these processes. Modelling schemes are presented and illustrated using the results from studies conducted in the prairie region of central Canada. It is anticipated that the physics of the processes, as well as many of the findings, will be broadly applicable to open landscapes in the North.

**Snow Transport**

Reliable information on the amount and distribution of snow water over an area is central to good forecasts of the rates and volumes of runoff from snowmelt. These data establish the "potential" runoff volume and have a direct effect on the depletion patterns of snowcover over various terrain, melt and runoff rates, source areas of runoff and the area of a watershed contributing flow to a stream channel. Hydrologists are well aware of the problems in streamflow forecasting in flat areas with poor surface drainage development due to the variable nature of the "Contributing Area." Large areas of a watershed may not contribute flow to an outlet due to a lack of snow and large volumes of depressional storage. Generally the size of the "contributing area" tends to increase with increases in snowcover depth and antecedent moisture.

The accumulation of a snowcover is not a straight-forward process, as fallen snow undergoes redistribution by the wind. Steppuhn and Dyck (1974) have shown in the sub-arctic Mackenzie river valley and semi-arid western Saskatchewan that snow distribution patterns over surfaces of similar aero-dynamic characteristics tend to be similar. However, these simple relationships do not account for the effects of varying wind directions and speeds, upwind snowcover and terrain, and sublimation of water vapor from blowing snow crystals on snow transport rates and erosion/deposition patterns. Thus, the distribution of a snowcover cannot be reliably-predicted using only measured snowfall quantities and indices of terrain roughness. For purposes of estimating snowcover accumulation over various vegetation and terrain surfaces, an understanding of the aerodynamics and mechanics of snow transport is required. The phenomenon is complex, thus to predict snow accumulation this knowledge must necessarily be compiled in a mathematical simulation of erosion and deposition processes over a winter. Integration of the physics of blowing snow into a model of snow transport broadens the geographic and functional applicability of the model and provides insight into the behaviour of the phenomenon. While this is not the only viable approach, the lack of suitable data bases for calculating snow transport in northern regions limits the accuracy of empirical models.

Falling snow tends to have a uniform distribution in the lower atmosphere, thus under conditions of low windspeed and open terrain the flux of snow is entirely downward and the resulting snowcovers are quite uniform. However, when windspeeds near the surface exceed a "threshold velocity for horizontal movement of snow particles, snow can be eroded from the surface and appreciable upward and horizontal fluxes occur. The process can be modelled using a control volume of equal horizontal dimensions and some height z (see Fig. 1) and a mass balance to determine the erosion/deposition rate. That is:

$$Q_e = Q_{out} - Q_{in} + dn/dt + F_z \qquad .1$$

where:

$Q_e$ = erosion rate (if negative the deposition rate),

$Q$ = horizontal mass flux of blowing snow in and out of the control volume,

$dn/dt$ = sublimation rate of blowing snow within the volume, and

$F_z$ = vertical flux of snow (if positive upward flux) at height z.

*Two-dimensional, Fully-developed Flow*

Consider the transport of snow under the fully-developed flow conditions which exist in the centre and down-wind portion of an aerodynamically-uniform terrain such as a coastal or glacial lake-bed plain. For fully-developed transport the horizontal snow flux entering the control volume (as in Fig. 1) equals that leaving the volume. In this case the snow surface erosion/deposition rate equals the change in mass of snow in the control volume via either vertical transport or sublimation. The horizontal transport flux determines to some extent the vertical transport and sublimation rates.

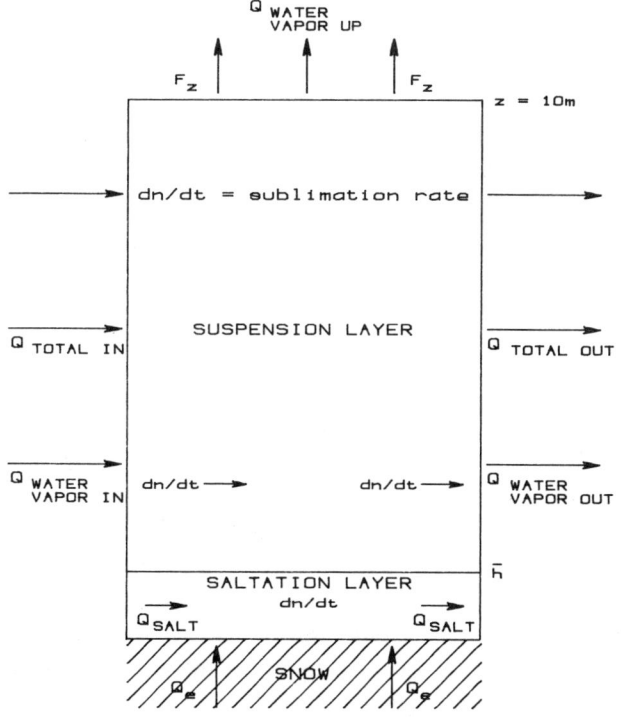

Figure 1   Control volume illustrating the snow and water vapor fluxes in blowing snow. From Gray et al., 1987.

*Horizontal Flux*

Horizontal transport of snow by the wind is somewhat analogous to wind and water transport of sediment. Saltation transport occurs within a few centimeters of the surface with suspended transport above this layer. Saltating snow particles bounce along the surface, colliding inelastically with the surface crystal matrix and sometimes ejecting particles from this surface. The mass flux of saltating snow per unit width perpendicular to the flow direction is directly related to the energy of the wind available to transport the particles. The condition where the energy at the snow surface equals that required to overcome the cohesive forces between surface snow crystals and the energy losses due to inelastic collisions during particle ejection is referred to as the transport threshold and the wind-speed as the threshold windspeed.

Physically-based transport equations for the mass flux of saltating particles ($Q_{salt}$) based on Bagnold's 1941 and 1973 works have been developed by Pomeroy and Male (1987b) and Schmidt (1986) and take the form:

$$Q_{salt} = \rho_{salt} \bar{h} \bar{u}_p \qquad .2$$

where:

$\bar{h}$ = mean height of saltating particle trajectories (-0.01 m),

$\rho_{salt}$ = drift density (mass density of saltating snow in the atmosphere)

and,

$\bar{u}_p$ = mean saltating particle velocity.

The saltating drift density is a function of the difference between the frictional force (shear stress) exerted on the snow by the wind and that exerted at the transport threshold. This frictional force is a function of the square of the windspeed and the logarithm of the aerodynamic roughness of the surface. The mean saltating particle velocity is found by extending the vertical profile of windspeed (a logarithmic profile) to the midpoint of the mean particle trajectory height. It is a function of the windspeed and logarithm of the aerodynamic surface roughness.

For a constant surface roughness the energy available for saltation increases with the cube of the windspeed less an amount expended in shattering snow-crystals from the pack and lost in inelastic rebounds. For a constant windspeed it decreases with the logarithm of the surface roughness. Generally, for older wind-hardened or ice-glazed snow, more energy is expended in shattering cohesive surface bonds and less lost during rebound. The converse is true for fresh snow of low density.

Blowing snow above a few centimeters in height travels in suspension. Turbulent transfer theory describing this mode of transport has been developed by Budd (1966) from Antarctic data and operationalized by Pomeroy and Male (1987b). The mass flux of suspended snow per unit width perpendicular to the flow direction is a function of the windspeed, surface roughness, snowfall rate and drift density. For a smooth snowfield not undergoing snowfall, the suspended mass flux up to 10-m height is roughly 1/10th the saltating flux at low windspeeds (7 m/s) and increases to over 1/2 the saltating flux at higher windspeeds (18 m/s).

The sum of saltating and suspended mass fluxes equals the horizontal flux of blowing snow which for a smooth snowfield of uniform cohesion has a distribution that varies with height and windspeed as shown in Fig. 2. The data show a large decrease in the horizontal flux with height, suggesting most transport is within 1 m of the surface (10 m for extreme conditions). The effects of differing threshold conditions and windspeeds on the total horizontal snow flux up to 10 m are shown in Fig. 3 in which the flux over a smooth snowfield is plotted against the 10-m wind speed, $u_{10}$. Differing threshold windspeeds result in a wide variation of fluxes at a given wind-speed, especially when these fluxes are low. This effect is less pronounced when the fluxes are high. The horizontal mass flux can be calculated by noting the threshold windspeed for drifting, ambient windspeed and the aerodynamic surface roughness and using procedures compiled by Pomeroy and Male (1987a, b). Windspeed is routinely monitored at most climatological stations and the surface roughness can be estimated from the geometry and type of

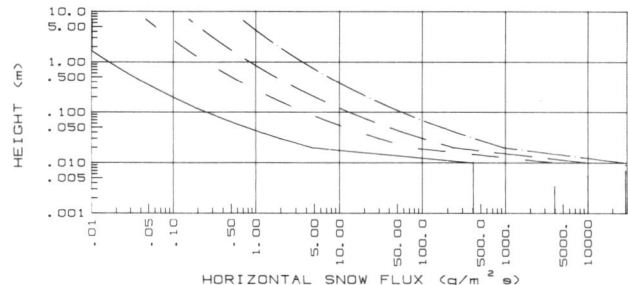

Figure 2  Vertical profiles of the horizontal mass flux of blowing snow. From Gray et al., 1987

- - - - -  $u_{10}$ = 5 m/s,
- - -  $u_{10}$ = 7.5 m/s,
———  $u_{10}$ = 10 m/s,
—·—·—  $u_{10}$ = 15 m/s.

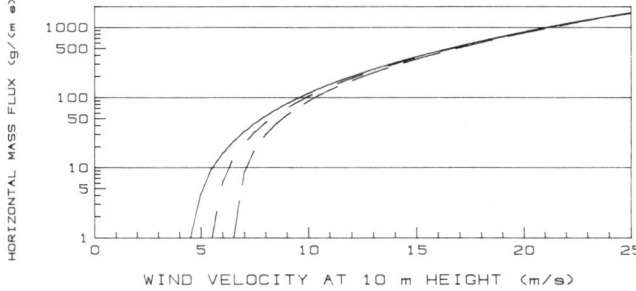

Figure 3  Horizontal mass flux of blowing snow to a height of 10 m. From Gray et al., 1987.

- - - - -  threshold $u_{10}$ = 4.5 m/s,
- - -  threshold $u_{10}$ = 5.5 m/s,
———  threshold $u_{10}$ = 6.5 m/s.

exposed surface vegetation using the techniques of Lyles and Allison (1976) and Lettau (1969).

## Vertical Flux

The vertical mass flux of snow at some height, is a function of the mass density of snow in the atmosphere and the terminal fall velocity of snow particles at that height (Pomeroy and Male 1987b). The terminal fall velocity of snow particles depends on the degree of atmospheric turbulence, the saltating drift density and the size of falling snow particles. Vertical fluxes of blowing snow at a height of 10 m for non-snowfall conditions are of the order of 0.25 mm of snow water per day for a windspeed ($u_{10}$) of 10 m/s and 5.8 mm of snow water per day for a windspeed ($u_{10}$) of 20 m/s. In open regions snow transported above 10 m has little likelihood of deposition before it is completely sublimated. During heavy snowfalls the upward flux of eroded surface snow particles is negligible compared to the downward flux of falling crystals. For this case the vertical flux can be considered equal to the snowfall rate.

## Sublimation Rate

Sublimation from blowing snow can be a significant hydrologic loss. The sublimation rate can be calculated using an involved heat and mass transfer equation developed by Schmidt (1972) and modified by Lee (1975). Its magnitude depends primarily on the drift density, air temperature and humidity. For example, the sublimation rate from a quantity of blowing snow increases 25 fold when the temperature increases from −35° to −1°C. Sublimation can amount to over 20 mm of water equivalent per day for conditions of relative humidity < 50%, temperature > −12°C, windspeed > 20 m/s.

## Erosion Rate

For fully-developed flow the erosion rate is the sum of the vertical mass flux at height z and the sublimation rate of blowing snow below this height. It should be noted that all of the snow eroded under these conditions is unavailable for re-deposition and may be considered a water loss from the snowcover. In an arctic blizzard with no snowfall the fully-developed erosion rate can exceed 40 mm of water per day (approximately equivalent to 200 mm of wind-packed snow).

## Two-dimensional, Developing Flow

Developing flow exists where changes in windspeed, snowpack conditions or aerodynamic surface roughness have caused the horizontal flow through the control volume to differ from the flow conditions at the top and/or bottom of the volume. As a result, the incoming and outgoing horizontal mass fluxes become unequal. This can result in erosion/deposition rates several orders of magnitude different from those expected for fully-developed flow. Takeuchi's (1980) data document the downwind development of the blowing snow horizontal flux from a riverbank onto a snowfield. Pomeroy and Male (1987a) found the shapes of the horizontal profiles could be approximated by a hyperbolic function and it can be used to determine developing fluxes downwind of the boundary of any surface roughness change. The function is:

$$Q_L = c_L(Q_{fd} - Q_i) + Q_i \qquad .3$$

where:

$Q_L$ = mass flux (horizontal, vertical or sublimation rate) at the horizontal coordinate L of interest,

$Q_{fd}$ = fully-developed flux, and

$Q_i$ = the initial flux at the boundary.

The distance coefficient $c_L$ is found as:

$$\begin{aligned} c_L &= (Q_L - Q_i)/(Q_{fd} - Q_i) \\ &= 0.50\{[\tanh[4((L - L_i)/(L_{fd} - L_i)) - 2]] + 0.50 \qquad .4 \end{aligned}$$

where:

$L_i$ = horizontal coordinate at the boundary, and

$L_{fd}$ = horizontal coordinate at which fully-developed flow is re-established.

For Takeuchi's experiment $(L_{fd} - L_i)$ is approximately 300 m, reflecting possible effects of turbulent wakes downwind of riveredge vegetation, In Saskatchewan, $(L_{fd} - L_i)$ of approximately 10 m have been observed over smooth snowfields downwind of fields of standing grain stubble. If there are no effects from turbulent wakes, then $(L_{fd} - L_i)$ decreases logarithmically with aerodynamic roughness. The length of turbulent wakes depends on the difference in roughness at the boundary, Mellor (1965) suggests wakes up to 50 m long, downwind from a 2 m high snow fence. When the roughness change is small, such as that from a snowfield with exposed moss and pebbles to a smooth snowfield, the length of wake is negligible.

Figure 4a shows the variation in horizontal flux downwind from a boundary. Note, the fluxes and distances were calculated by Eqs. 3 and 4 from Takeuchi's data and normalized for $Q_{fd}$ and $L_{fd}$. Normalized values of Takeuchi's data are also plotted. An illustration of the variation of $Q_e$, the erosion rate, is shown in Fig. 4b. This is calculated using mass balances (Eq. 1) conducted in "control" volumes spaced incrementally from $L_i$ to $L_{fd}$ where the fluxes and increments are calculated using Eqs. 3 and 4 from fully-developed fluxes. Note that for horizontal fluxes which increase from the boundary a zone of scouring develops, while for decreasing flow a zone of enhanced deposition develops.

Measurements of wind flow over tundra polygons in the Mackenzie Delta by Gray et al.

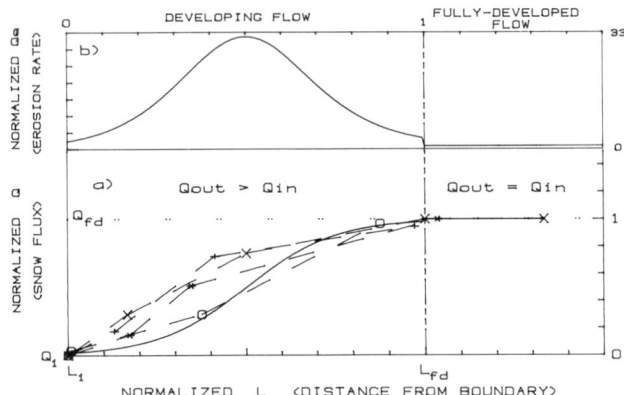

Figure 4 a) Horizontal development of blowing snow flux from a boundary. Normalized values of Takeuchi's (1980) data are plotted:

0 —— 0 $u_1$ = 8.7 m/s, $L_{fd}$ = 200 m;
+ —— + $u_1$ = 8.4 m/s, $L_{fd}$ = 170 m;
X —— X $u_1$ = 7.2 m/s, $L_{fd}$ = 300 m;
* —— * $u_1$ = 5.2 m/s, $L_{fd}$ 290 m.

Solid line represents modelled increase including wake effects (Pomeroy and Male. 1987a).

b) Horizontal transect of erosion rate from a boundary. Normalized values for $Q_{fd}$ = 100 g/ms, note that the maximum $Q_e$ is over 30 times greater than the fully-developed erosion rate. From Gray et al., 1987.

(1974) show that flow is rarely fully-developed in this region. While snow deposition quantities could be calculated for gullies and valleys incised into arctic plains, the calculation of snow erosion rates around a hill or in mountainous terrain involves complex applications of aerodynamic theory. It is expected that coupling of physically-based snow transport models (to calculate incoming snow flux) with deposition models (to calculate snow drift shape) such as those by Schmidt and Randolph (1981) will lend answers to more complex snow accumulation questions. Ultimately one can envision mathematical simulations of snow transport and accumulation which use windspeeds, local vegetation heights, topography and recent local meteorology to determine: the deposition of snow water on various terrain, the quantities of snow available for accumulation as drifts around engineering structures and the amount of snow water lost by sublimation.

## Snowmelt

### Energy Equation

Because snowmelt involves the phase change from ice to water the physical framework used in calculating this quantity is the energy equation. The energy available for melting a unit volume of snowcover ($Q_m$) is given by the expression:

$$Q_m = Q_{sn} + Q_{ln} + Q_h + Q_e + Q_g + Q_a - du/dt \qquad .5$$

where:

$Q_{sn}$ = net short-wave radiation flux absorbed by the snowcover,

$Q_{ln}$ = net long-wave radiation flux at the snow-air interface,

$Q_h$ = convective or sensible heat flux between the air and the snow surface,

$Q_e$ = flux of latent energy (evaporation, sublimation, condensation) at the snow-air interface,

$Q_g$ = flux of energy across the snow-ground interface by conduction,

$Q_a$ = advective energy flux (rain, other external sources), and

$du/dt$ = rate of change in internal (stored) energy per unit time.

The amount of melt can be calculated from Eq. 5 by the expression:

$$M = Q_m/(\rho h_f B) \qquad .6$$

where:

M = depth of snowmelt,

$\rho$ = density of water,

$h_f$ = latent heat of fusion, and

B = thermal quality of snow or the fraction of ice in a unit mass of wet snow.

For normal conditions, $h_f$ = 333.5 kJ/kg and $\rho$ = 1000 kg/ms. Hence, Eq. 6 can be reduced to:

$$M = Q_m/(3335\ B), \qquad .7$$

in which B is usually taken in the range 0.95-0.97. M is in cm when all other terms in Eq. 5 are in $kJ/m^2$.

As shown by Granger (1977) when advective fluxes are negligible, net radiation and the transfer of sensible heat govern the melt of shallow snowcovers of open, grassland regions. Generally, at the beginning of "active" melt of a complete snowcover net radiation is the dominant flux, whereas later in the sequence energy supplied from both sources may share equal importance. Only in cases where the exchange is dominated by energy transferred from a large, stagnant, slow-moving warm air mass or derived over patchy snowcover conditions will simple procedures, such as the temperature index approach commonly applied to forested, mountainous regions, give reasonable estimates of melt. In open areas the relative amounts of energy available for melt from radiative and convective sources vary widely from day to day and net radiation and ambient air temperature frequently show poor correlation.

Often, the possibility of using an energy balance approach for calculating snowmelt is negated by the lack of available data, particularly radiation measurements. This limitation is especially serious in northern regions. In the discussion below, an attempt is made to demonstrate that it may be possible to obtain estimates of daily net radiation of sufficient accuracy for water management models from readily-measured meteorological variables.

*Net Radiation*

Net radiation is the sum of the net short-wave flux absorbed by the snowcover ($Q_{sn}$) and the net long-wave flux at the surface ($Q_{ln}$), i.e.,

$$Q_N = Q_{sn} + Q_{ln}. \qquad .8$$

Davies (1965, 1967) and Davies and Idso (1979) have shown from analyses of both daytime and nighttime values of net radiation that over bare and vegetated surfaces $Q_{sn}$ is the dominant flux and plots of $Q_N$ and $Q_s$ the incident short-wave flux — are remarkably linear with high correlation coefficients. These findings suggest that variations in albedo or the mean reflectance of vegetative surfaces during summer are small and do not vary widely under clear-sky conditions. Further, Davies and Buttimor (1969) noted that the linear association could also be applied to sky conditions when the incoming long-wave radiation is not constant.

Figure 5 shows a plot of measured values of $Q_N$ and $Q_{sn}$, observed at the Bad Lake Climatological Station located in western Saskatchewan during periods of "Melt" and during the "Postmelt" period immediately following the disappearance of the seasonal snowcover. $Q_N$ are daily values from a Funk (Middleton) net radiometer and $Q_{sn}$-values were calculated as the difference between incoming ($Q_s$) and reflected ($Q_r$) short-wave radiation measurements from upright and inverted Kipp solarimeters. The best-fit equation of the line is:

$$Q_N = -0.371 + 0.522\, Q_{sn} \qquad .9$$

which has a correlation coefficient of 0.89 and a standard error of estimate of 1.39 MJ/m²–d with $Q_N$ and $Q_{sn}$ are in MJ/m²–d. Considering the high degree of association between the variables (despite the fact $Q_{sn}$ was calculated as the difference between two point measurements); the sensitivity of a snowmelt runoff model to varying inputs of $Q_N$ will vary with the system,

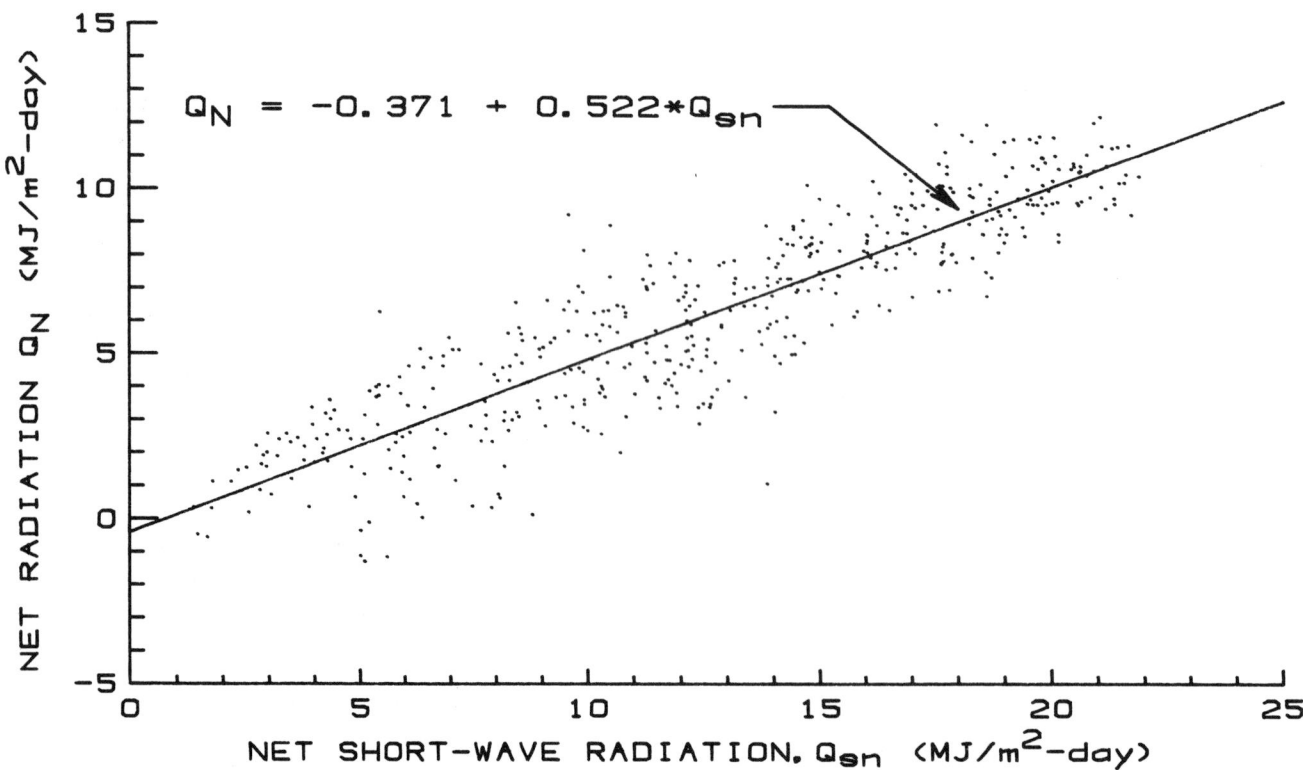

Figure 5  Relationship between daily net radiation and net short-wave radiation during Melt and Postmelt periods, 1972-1985 inclusive, Bad Lake, Saskatchewan. From Gray et al., 1987.

and that 1 MJ/m²–d of energy applied to ice at 0°C will produce approximately 3 mm of melt, it is assumed the estimates of $Q_N$ given by Eq. 9 will satisfy many operational requirements.

*Incident Short-wave Radiation*

Equation 9 requires an estimate of the net short-wave flux, which can be obtained from the expression:

$$Q_{sn} = Q_s(1-A), \qquad .10$$

where A is the albedo. Numerous investigators (Penman 1948; Mateer 1955; Brutsaert 1982) have shown that $Q_s$ can be related to either the clear-sky insolation ($Q_o$) or the extraterrestrial radiative flux ($Q_A$) and the sun-shine ratio (n/N) by simple linear equations of the form:

$$Q_s = Q_o(a + b(n/N)) \text{ or } Q_A(A + B(n/N)) \qquad .11$$

in which the coefficients a, A, b and B are evaluated from measured data and n/N is the ratio of the number of bright sunshine hours (for example, as measured by a sunshine recorder) (n) to the number of possible hours of sunshine (N). Equation 11 has the advantage of simplicity; once the values for the coefficients have been assigned only a measurement of "n" is needed for a solution because $Q_o$, $Q_A$ and N are fixed in time and geographical location. Use of the clear-sky insolation as input to the equation is amenable for snowmelt calculations because models have been developed that allow partitioning $Q_o$ to direct beam and diffuse components. This partitioning allows one to account for the effect of slope on the energy received. Two expressions that are useful for this calculation are those proposed by Garnier and Ohmura (1970) and List (1968). The relationship between the ratio of $Q_s$ and $Q_o$ — calculated by these procedures — for the Bad Lake station for the months of Feb. – Mar. inclusive is plotted as a function of n/N in Figure 6. The relationship is

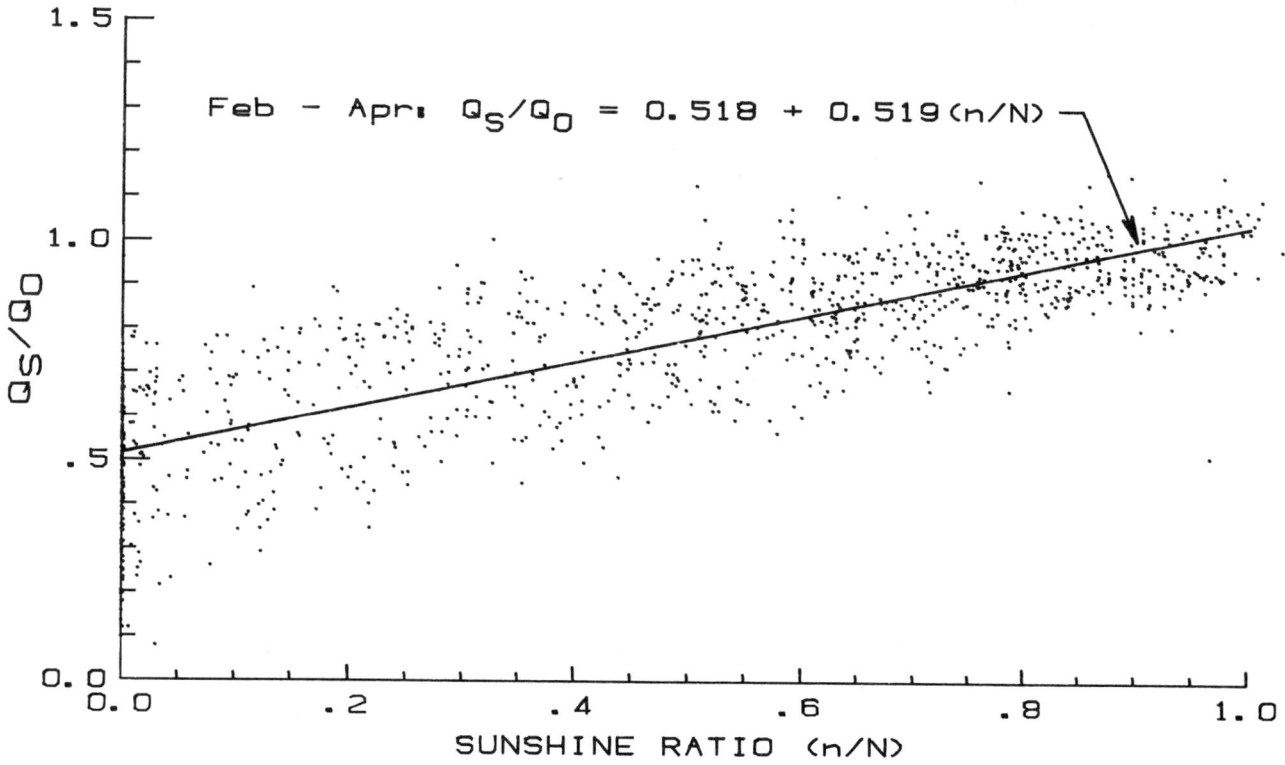

Figure 6  Relationship between ratio of measured daily global radiation to the calculated clear-sky, short-wave radiation and sunshine ratio for the months Feb.-Apr. inclusive at Bad Lake, Sask., 1972-1985. From Gray et al., 1987.

described by the equation:

$$Q_s/Q_o = 0.518 + 0.519 n/N, \quad .12$$

which has a correlation coefficient of 0.81 and a standard error of estimate of 0.12. Note, the calculation of $Q_o$ is based on a transmissivity coefficient for the earth's atmosphere of p = 0.85. The magnitude of p will change with the time of the year and with geographical location.

*Albedo*

Equation 10 also requires knowledge of the albedo of the snow surface. Because this parameter is not routinely-measured it is often evaluated from tables using the physical characteristics of the snowcover such as colour, ripeness, wetness, age, impurity content and other properties.

From examination of the depletion in albedo with time during late winter and early spring it was observed that when the effects of snowfall and melt events were neglected the decrease tends to follow an orderly pattern in each of the "Premelt," "Melt" and "Postmelt" periods (see Fig. 7) (Gray et al. 1986a). During Premelt, the albedo decreases gradually with time at a relatively constant rate due to metamorphic processes. Average annual daily depletion rates in the period, assumed to start Feb. 1st of any year, were measured in the range 0.004 – 0.009/d with an average of 0.0061/d.

During Melt the change in albedo is largest and most rapid. This is attributed to changes in the structural properties of a snowcover brought about by meltwater, radiation penetrating to the ground surface and the development of patchy snowcover. Gray et al. (1986) found that during continuous ablation of a shallow snowcover the rate of depletion is of the order of 0.071/d. On average, a snowcover on the Prairies disappears in 5-8 days.

During Postmelt, when the ground is bare, the albedo can be taken as equal to 0.17.

An algorithm of the model has been written and modified to account for albedo changes during the transition period, e.g. Premelt to Melt, and those caused by snowfall and interrupted melt events. Also built into the routine are procedures for establishing the "start" of melt based on measured ambient air temperature and calculated net radiation. Figure 8, taken from Gray and Landine (1987), compares the measured and a simulated albedo for a high snow year — 1974 (Fig. 8a) with a depth of snowcover at the start of melt of ~46 cm and for a low snow year, 1980, with an initial snow depth of ~9 cm (Fig. 8b). It can be noted that the agreement between the two curves is reasonable and it is expected that the calculated albedos would give acceptable estimates of $Q_{sn}$.

Values of the net short-wave flux, calculated by Eq. 9 using Eq. 12 and simulated albedo, ($Q_{snc}$) were compared to measured net short-wave ($Q_{snm}$) for 61 days of melt recorded over 6 years. This analysis showed a mean difference in ($Q_{snc} - Q_{snm}$) of 0.18 MJ/m² and standard deviation in individual values of 2.72 MJ/m². For 1974 and 1980, the values were -0.035 and 2.34 MJ/m², respectively.

In summary, it is suggested that a simple, practical model for calculating the daily net radiative flux required in snowmelt calculations is close to development. The same can not be said about procedures that may be used to estimate the sensible heat flux.

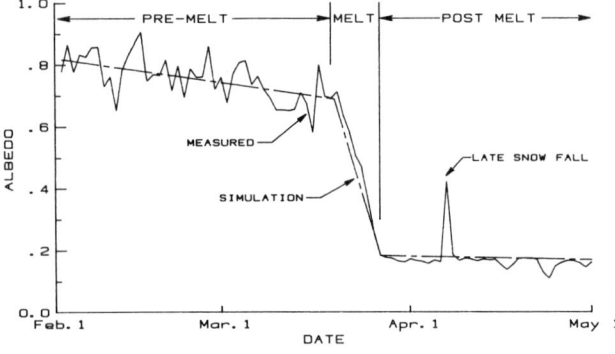

Figure 7  Schematic of the variation in albedo of a Prairie snowcover with time during Premelt, Melt and Postmelt periods. From Gray et al., 1987.

## Snowmelt Infiltration into Frozen Soil

Meltwater generated by a snowcover is destined either to infiltrate the underlying soil, evaporate or to run off. Whether one's interest is

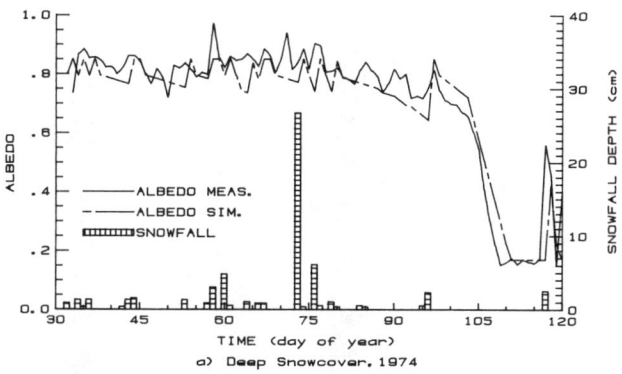

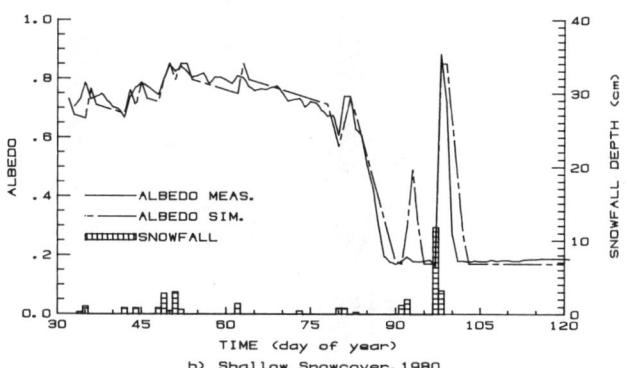

Figure 8　Comparison of measured and simulated albedo depletion curves for Bad Lake, Saskatchewan: (a) 1974, deep snowcover; (b) 1980, a shallow snowcover. From Gray et al., 1987.

in determining volumes or rates of runoff, an understanding of the infiltration phenomenon is essential because it is the major process governing the apportionment of the meltwater to runoff.

Meltwater infiltration at northern latitudes usually involves water entering frozen soils. The process is governed by the complex phenomenon of coupled heat and mass transfer through porous media and is affected by many factors such as the hydrophysical and thermal properties of the soil, the soil moisture and temperature regimes, the rate of release of water from the snowcover, and the energy content of the infiltrating water. In the absence of major structural deformations e.g., cracks or other macro-pores, the most important hydrophysical property of a frozen soil governing its ability to absorb and transmit water is its frozen moisture content. The existence of an inverse relationship between infiltration and the frozen soil moisture content has been demonstrated or postulated by many investigators. For example, Fig. 9 (after Granger et al. 1984) shows this trend for medium to fine-textured, frozen prairie soils. A point of interest is "degree-of-saturation" the 0-300 mm soil layer reaches from snowmelt infiltration. Generally, the higher the initial moisture content at the time of melt, the higher the degree-of-saturation following melt. The line enveloping the points can be described by the expression: $\theta_L = 0.60 + 0.40\ \theta_p$, in which $\theta_L$ and $\theta_p$ are the saturation limit and premelt moisture content, respectively expressed as the degree of pore saturation in units of $mm^3/mm^3$. When considered together with the finding that the average depth meltwater penetrates a frozen *prairie* soil is of the order of 300 mm (Granger et al. 1984); it can be demonstrated that the infiltration potential of these soils is limited and small. For example, infiltration to a soil having a porosity of 50% by volume and a premelt moisture content near the wilting point of 15% by volume would not likely exceed about 63 mm. This would be the equivalent water content of a 25-cm depth of snowcover having a density of 250 $kg/m^3$.

Implicit in the consideration of the effects of thermal properties on infiltration is the definition of what constitutes a frozen soil. For example, findings reported by several Soviet investigators suggest that soils frozen to depths less than 500 – 600 mm may have infiltration characteristics similar to those of unfrozen soils, and as such could be viewed as being only "partially-frozen."

Although much progress has been made in modelling the phenomenon, infiltration into frozen soils must still be estimated from empirical equations or simple, physically-based relationships in solving large-scale water management problems. Recent studies (Granger et al. 1984; Gray et al. 1985a, 1986b) have led to the development of a semi-empirical model describing snowmelt infiltration to frozen soils. The model is based on a comprehensive field study of infiltration to frozen soils in the Dark

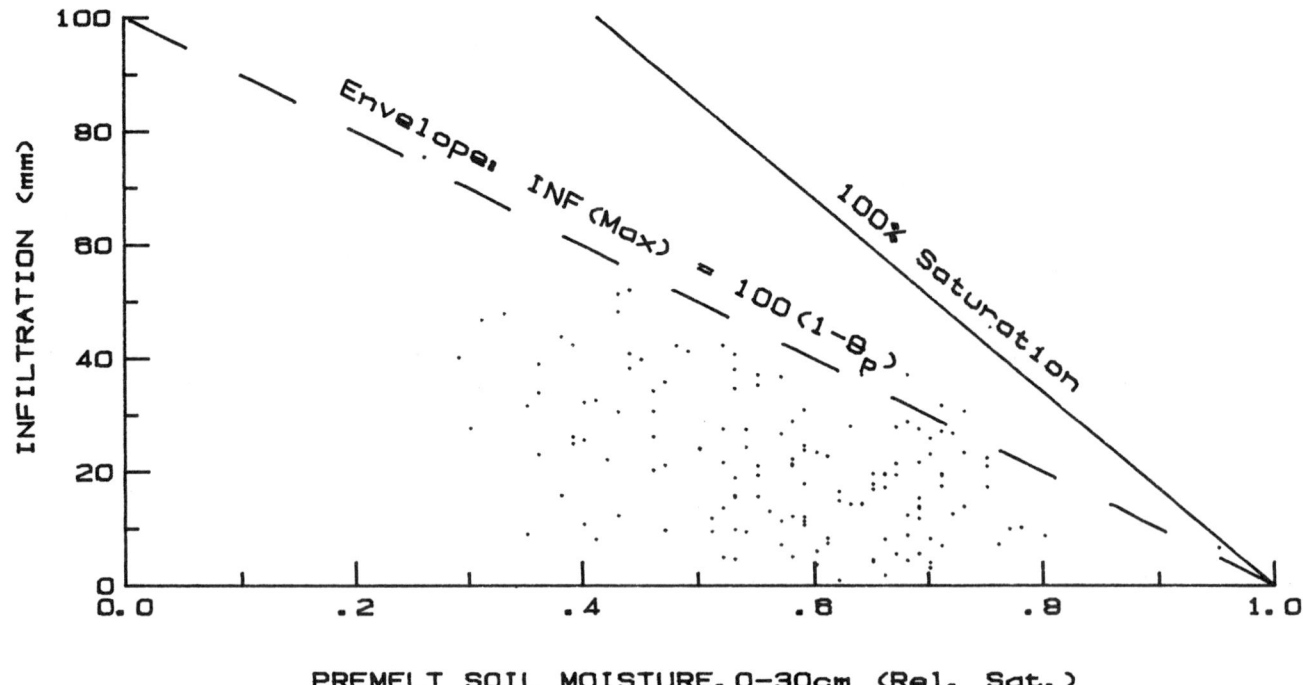

Figure 9   Scatter diagram of infiltration (INF) plotted against premelt frozen water content of the 0-30 cm soil layer ($\theta_p$) expressed as the relative degree of saturation (Rel. Sat.). From Grey et al., 1987.

Brown and Brown soil zones of west-central Saskatchewan, and on the results of infiltration studies under similar climatic regions of the USSR reported in the literature. The model assumes that frozen mineral soils may be grouped into three broad categories with regard to their infiltration potential, namely: Restricted, Limited and Unlimited (see Fig. 10).

- Restricted infiltration is impeded by an impermeable layer, such as an ice lens at the soil surface or within the soil near the surface. For practical purposes the amount of meltwater infiltration can be assumed to be negligible and most of the snow water goes to direct runoff and evaporation.
- Limited infiltration is governed primarily by the snowcover water equivalent and the frozen water content of a shallow layer of soil, 0-300 mm.
- Unlimited dry heavily-cracked clays, coarse dry sands or other soils that have a large number of large, air-filled, non-capillary pores or macropores at the time of melt. Most or all of the snow water will infiltrate.

For medium to fine-textured, uncracked frozen soils to which entry of meltwater is not impeded by ice layers (i.e.: the Limited case) snowmelt infiltration (INF), can be estimated from the snowcover water equivalent (SWE) and the premelt moisture content ($\theta_p$) by the equation:

$$\text{INF} = 5(1-\theta_p)\text{SWE}^{0.584} \qquad .13$$

in which INF and SWE are in mm and $\theta_p$ is the degree of pore saturation in $mm^3/mm^3$. The equation has a correlation coefficient of 0.85 and a standard error of estimate of 5.5 mm. Figure 10b is a graphical presentation of the model.

Such a simple model of infiltration to frozen soil can be applied to a broad spectrum of water-related management problems where snowmelt and frozen soils are involved. To agriculturalists the model provides a useful tool for the planning of sensible snow management practices (trapping wind-transported snow) for

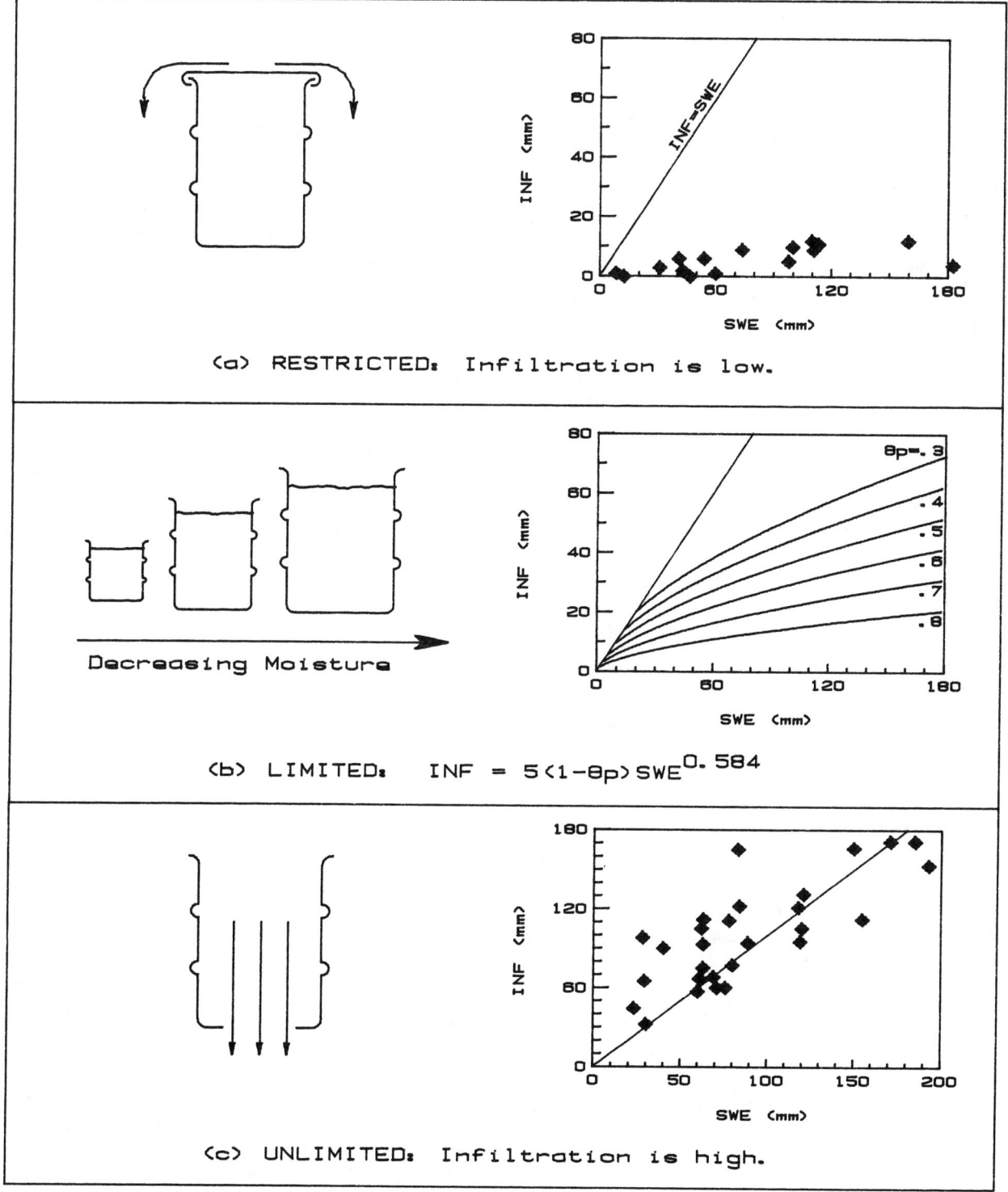

Figure 10  Snowmelt infiltration model for frozen Prairie soils: (a) Restricted, (b) Limited and (c) Unlimited. After Gray et al., 1987.

augmenting soil water reserves needed for crop production in dryland farming areas (Gray and Granger 1985; Gray et al. 1986c; Granger and Gray 1986). The model has also been successfully applied to the problem of simulating streamflow from snowmelt (Gray et al. 1985a, 1985b). When interfaced with the U.S. National Weather Service River Forecasting System (NWSRFS) and the U.S. Army Corps of Engineers" Streamflow Synthesis and Reservoir Regulation System (SSARR) and applied to synthesizing flow on a prairie watershed much closer agreement was obtained between the observed and simulated hydrographs with the infiltration model than with the original system. At its present stage of development the model must still be considered as "first-generation." However, because it is simple, has a physical base and does not require a large data base, it should in the interim find favor as a useful tool for water managers dealing with snowmelt and frozen soils.

## Summary

This paper discusses the processes of snow transport (accumulation and distribution), snowmelt and meltwater infiltration to frozen soils. Physically-based models for describing these processes in open, grassland regions are presented and applied to shallow snowcovers of west-central Saskatchewan.

Estimating snowcover accumulation over various terrain surfaces requires an understanding of the aerodynamics and mechanics of snow transport. Techniques for modelling the phenomenon using a mass balance to determine the erosion/deposition rate of a "control" volume are discussed. For fully-developed, two dimensional flow the total horizontal flux of blowing snow varies with height and most transport occurs within 1 m of the surface. The effects of differing threshold conditions and windspeeds on flux are illustrated.

Sublimation from blowing snow can be a significant hydrologic loss which is greatly affected by air temperature. For example, the sublimation rate increases 25 fold with an increase of temperature from -35° to 1°C.

The problem of modelling snow transport for two-dimensional, developing-flow conditions is outlined.

Practical methods of estimating the daily net radiative flux are presented. It is shown that during melt of a shallow, prairie snowcover, net radiation and net short-wave radiation are linearly related with a high correlation coefficient. The incident net short-wave flux can be estimated from the clear-sky insolation, sunshine hours and snowcover albedo. A model for simulating the depletion in albedo of shallow snowcovers which are not subject to frequent mid-winter melt events is described. It is shown that the decrease with time can be approximated by three line segments having different slopes and encompassing the periods of Premelt, Melt and Postmelt. Implementation of the routine requires a procedure for establishing the "start" of the Melt period. This is accomplished by an algorithm which makes use of daily inputs of net radiation, maximum air temperature, threshold temperature and snowfall and snowcover depths. Close agreement between "simulated" and "measured" albedo depletion of different snowcovers during the period from Feb. 1st to the disappearance of the seasonal snowcover is demonstrated.

Comparisons between net short-wave fluxes calculated from empirically-derived clear-sky radiation, sunshine hours and simulated albedo with "measured" values for 61 days of Melt recorded over a 6-year period showed a mean difference of 0.18 MJ/m$^2$ and a standard deviation in individual values of 2.72 MJ/m$^2$.

The phenomenon of meltwater infiltration to frozen soils is discussed and a simple, physically-based model for describing the process is presented. The model is based on the concept that frozen soils may be grouped into three broad categories with respect to their infiltration potential. Unlimited -cracked or highly porous soils containing a large number of macropores that are capable of infiltrating most of the snow water; Limited -the infiltration potential of a soil depends primarily on the snowcover water equivalent and the ice/water content of the soil layer, 0-300 mm at the time of melt; and Limited — a soil containing an impermeable layer on or near the surface that inhibits infiltration. An empirical equation relating infiltration to the snowcover water and ice/water content of the 0-300 mm soil layer is given.

**Acknowledgements**

The writers wish to acknowledge the financial support provided the different projects by the Natural Sciences and Engineering Research Council of Canada, the Research Management Division, Alberta Department of the Environment; and the Farmlab Program, Saskatchewan Department of Agriculture. Special thanks are directed to Mr. P.G. Landine for his assistance in data analysis and preparation of the graphics.

**References**

Bagnold, R.A.
1941 The Physics of Blown Sand and Desert Dunes. Methuen, London. 265 p.
1973 The nature of saltation and of "bed-load" transporting water. Proceedings of the Royal Society of London A, 332:472-504.

Budd, W.F.
1966 The drifting of non-uniform snow particles. Studies in Antarctic Meteorology, American Geophysical Union Antarctic Research Series, 9:59-70.

Brutsaert, W.
1982 Evaporation into the Atmosphere. D. Reidel Publishing Company, London, England, 229 p.

Davies, J.A.
1965 The use of Gunn-Bellani distillator to determine net radiative flux for West Africa. Journal of Applied Meteorology, 4:547-549.
1967 A note on the relationship between net radiation and solar radiation. Quarterly Journal of the Royal Meteorological Society, 93:109-115.

Davies, J.A. and D.H. Buttimor
1969 Reflection coefficients and net radiation at Simcoe, Southern Ontario. Agricultural Meteorology, 6:373-386.

Davies, J.A. and S.B. Idso
1979 Estimating the surface radiation balance and its components. In Modification of the Aerial Environments of Crops (B.J. Barfield and J.F. Gerber, eds.). American Society of Agricultural Engineers, St. Joseph, MO. pp. 183-210.

Garnier, B.J. and A. Ohmura
1970 The evaluation of surface variations in solar radiation income. Solar Energy, 13:21-24.

Granger, R.J.
1977 Energy exchange during melt of a prairie snowcover. M.Sc. Thesis, Department of Mechanical Engineering, University of Saskatchewan. 122 p.

Granger, R.J., D.M. Gray and G.E. Dyck.
1984 Snowmelt infiltration to frozen prairie soils. Canadian Journal of Earth Sciences, 21(6)996-677.

Granger, R.J. and D.M. Gray
1986 Combined subsoiling and snow management for drought attenuation. In Proceedings of the Canadian Hydrology Symposium No. 16-1986, Drought: The Impending Crisis, National Research Council of Canada, Associate Committee on Hydrology, pp. 213-225.

Gray, D.M. and R.J. Granger
1985 Snow management practices for increasing soil water reserves in frozen Prairie soils. In Watershed Management in the Eighties (E. Bruce Jones and Timothy J. Ward, eds.). American Society of Civil Engineers, pp. 256-263.

Gray, D.M. and P.G. Landine
1987 Albedo model for shallow prairie snowcovers. Canadian Journal of Earth Sciences (submitted for publication).

Gray, D.M., D. Erickson and F. Abbey
1974 Energy studies in an arctic environment. Report No. 74-18, Environmental-Social Committee, Northern Pipelines Task Force on Northern Oil Development, Information Canada, No. R57-10/1974, Ottawa, ON. 60 p.

Gray, D.M., J.W. Pomeroy and P.G. Landine
1986a  Development and performance evaluation of energy balance snowmelt models. Final Report for Research Management Division, Alberta Environment, Edmonton, AB, Research Agreement RMD 83-34B, 67 p.

Gray, D.M., J.W. Pomeroy and R.J. Granger
1987  Prairie snowmelt runoff. Proceedings of Canadian Water Resources Association, Saskatoon, SK, October, 1986 (in press).

Gray, D.M., P.G. Landine and R.J. Granger
1985a  Simulating infiltration into frozen prairie soils in streamflow models. Canadian Journal of Earth Sciences, 22(30)464-472.

Gray, D.M., P.G. Landine and G.A. McKay
1985b  Forecasting streamflow runoff from snowmelt in a Prairie environment. In Proceedings of the 7th Canadian Hydrotechnical Conference, Canadian Society of Civil Engineers, 1A:213-231.

Gray, D.M., R.J. Granger and P.G. Landine
1986b  Modelling snowmelt infiltration and runoff in a Prairie environment. In Proceedings of the Symposium: Cold Regions Hydrology, American Water Resources Association, pp. 427-438.

Lee, L.W.
1975  Sublimation of Snow in Turbulent Atmosphere. Unpublished Ph.D. Thesis, University of Wyoming, Laramie, WY. 162 p.

Lettau, H.
1969  Note on aerodynamic roughness-parameter estimation on the basis of roughness-element description. Journal of Applied Meteorology, 8:828-832.

List, R.J.
1968  Smithsonian Meteorological Tables. 6th Edition.

Lyles, L. and B.E. Allison
1976  Wind erosion: the protective role of simulated standing stubble. Transactions American Society of Agricultural Engineers, 19:61-64.

Mateer, C.L.
1955  A preliminary estimate of average insolation in Canada. Canadian Journal of Agricultural Science, 35:579-594.

Mellor, M.
1965  Blowing snow. Cold Regions Science and Engineering, Part III, Section A3C. Cold Regions Research and Engineering Laboratory, U.S. Army Materiel Command, Hanover, NH.

Penman, H.L.
1948  Natural evaporation from open water, bare soil and grass. Proceedings of the Royal Society A, 193:120-145.

Pomeroy, J.W. and D.H. Male
1987a  Physical modelling of blowing snow for agricultural production. In Proceedings of the Snow Management for Agriculture Workshop. Swift Current, SK. July, 1985. (in press)
1987b  Wind transport of seasonal snowcovers. In Seasonal Snowcover: Physics, Chemistry, Hydrology. NATO Advanced Study Institute Series, D. Reidel Publishing Co., Dordrecht, Netherlands. (in press)

Schmidt, R.A.
1972  Sublimation of wind-transported snow — A model U.S. Forest Service Rocky Mountain Forest and Range Experiment Station Research Report, RM-90, Fort Collins, CO. 24 p.
1986  Transport rate of drifting snow and the mean windspeed profile. Boundary Layer Meteorology, 34:213-214.

Schmidt, R.A. and K.L. Randolph
1981  Predicting deposition of blowing snow in trenches from particle trajectories. Proceedings of the 49th Western Snow Conference, St. George, UT. pp. 34-42.

Steppuhn, H. and G.E. Dyck
1974  Estimating true basin snowcover. In Advanced Concepts and Techniques in the Study of Snow and Ice Resources. National Academy of Sciences, Washington, DC. pp. 314-318.

Takeuchi, M.
1980  Vertical profile and horizontal increase of drift-snow transport. Journal of Glaciology, 26(94):481-492.

# Ice Formation on Northern Rivers

## Summary of Presentation by Dr. R. Gerard

Freeze-up of rivers occurs in predictable patterns starting from the edges and moving in toward the center of the channel as this boarder ice grows. The crossectional area of a river or stream is reduced as ice is formed thus water level must rise if the volume of water passing downstream remains constant.

An important component of freeze-up in rivers is frazil ice, small, plate-like (1 mm diameter with a thickness about 1/50 the diameter), crystals of ice which form in running water. Frazil ice crystals are "sticky" as they grow and are well mixed in the water column by the current. These crystals are sticky because they are growing and can attach to one another to form slush which grows into ice-pans. In rivers where flow is tranquil the boarder ice grows in toward the center of the river and ultimately the ice-pans will lodge against boarder ice in predictable locations so that the river or stream is completely ice covered in that location. Then the ice-pans build up back upstream forming a continuous sheet of ice. The progression of boarder ice formation is a function of the frazil pan activity. Freeze-up on rivers of this type occurs only after lodgement. The ice-pack has to build back upstream for complete freeze-up to occur. Pack build up and thus freeze-up occurs quite quickly on rivers such as the North Saskatchewan but on faster flowing rivers such as the Nelson River in northern Manitoba the ice-pack has to become very thick (up to 12 m in the Nelson River) before lodgement will occur so freeze-up of the river can take many weeks. Under rapid flow regimes anchor ice may be formed from frazil ice produced in super cooled water (super cooling may only be 1/100°C). Under these conditions frazil ice sticks to whatever it touches, including the stream bed. Eventually the stream bed will be coated with ice giving it a pale appearance. There have been suggestions that fish could suffocate on frazil ice crystals.

Initial ice cover on running water can be thick or thin but there is normally growth in thickness of the ice cover downward during the winter. This ice is usually called dark ice, it is clear but appears dark from above. Dark ice is composed of very large ice crystals whoes size increases with depth. If the bed is shallow the ice may reach the bed right across the stream or river channel and block flow. The water then floods out on top of the ice and freezes to form *aufeis*. Aufeis is white and has an amorphous structure. Most of the flow however would likely be through the stream bed in late winter when ice cover becomes very thick and water levels are low.

Open areas such as in fast moving water will produce frazil ice as long as they remain open. The frazil ice will then be deposited on the bottom of the ice cover downstream perhaps forming an ice dam. Engineering impacts of freeze-up ice dams.
1. Delay freeze-over by weeks or even months.
2. Can remove ice over long reaches of a river.
3. Stage goes up as a function of ice thickness
4. Maintains open water down stream from dam and modifies natural *polynas*. Polynas are areas which stay open during the winter.

Their location is usually predictable, particularly around islands. The number of polynas is a function of island frequency (0.2 × island frequency).

Ice dams change depths, velocity and flow fluctuations in lentic systems. The most important effects of ice dams is probably not the ice itself but the creation of open water areas.

# Ice Break-Up on Northern Rivers: The Liard River as an Example

T.D. Prowse
National Hydrology Research Institute
Environment Canada
11 Innovation Blvd.
Saskatoon, Saskatchewan
S7N 3H5

## Abstract

The major hydromechanical and hydrothermal processes which control ice break-up on northern rivers are reviewed. The Liard River, one of the more intensely studied northern rivers, is used as the primary example. Break-up of the Liard is especially significant because it "triggers" break-up of the Mackenzie River, Canada's longest river and one of the world's largest ice-covered rivers. According to combinations of river discharge and ice strength, six years of data on break-up are classified into thermal and mechanical events. Mechanical events produce the most dramatic form of break-up, characterized by break-up fronts moving at speeds in excess of 5 m s$^{-1}$ and the formation of ice jams, 4-8 m thick and 10-22 km long. The results of an equilibrium jam analysis for the development of a jam stage-discharge relationship are reviewed and suggestions for future research needed to achieve flood-damage reduction on northern rivers are presented.

## Introduction

River ice break-up can be a spectacular process, capable of modifying the biologic, geomorphic and hydrologic regimes of rivers and severely affecting man's related activities. The annual cost in Canada of ice jams alone has been estimated by Atkinson (1973) to be $31,000,000 (1983 dollars, see Prowse 1985a). The most dramatic and potentially damaging break-ups occur on northward flowing rivers or rivers in which break-up first occurs in the headwaters and then moves progressively downstream, following a downstream warming created by prevailing weather patterns. Examples within northern Canada include the Yukon and Mackenzie, which are characterized by break-ups originating in southern regions and advancing into the colder higher latitudes, and rivers such as the Liard, Peace and Athabasca which have headwaters in the Cordillera and then flow into the colder continental interior. The "warm to cold" pattern of break-up poses the most severe ice jamming and flooding problems because the spring flood wave is always having to push against a downstream ice cover. A much less dramatic form of break-up occurs on rivers which flow in a direction opposite to that of climatic warming. On south flowing rivers, for example, south to north warming allows ice clearance to work progressively upstream, thereby reducing the probability of ice jamming.

Although break-up has often been considered to occur at a single point in time, usually in relation to the first sustained movement of the ice cover, the entire break-up period is a continuum of often lengthy processes which first ablate, then fracture and finally convey the ice cover downstream. Assuming that the break-up period can be bracketed by the first signs of ice deterioration and the time that the river becomes clear of floating ice, the mean duration of river ice break-up on Canadian rivers is 15.7 days (data from 102 rivers with >10 year record; unpublished data, Atmospheric Environment Service), although it can vary from as little as a few days to over a month. The duration of break-up is especially important to many northern communities because it often means a period of isolation without conventional transport by water or ice road.

Given that this conference has a multi-disciplinary theme of "Knowing the North," the objective of this paper is to describe in layman's terms the major hydromechanical and hydrothermal processes which characterize break-up on northern rivers. The Liard River, one of the more intensely studied northern rivers, will be used as the primary example. More detailed reviews of river ice can be found in Ashton (1985) and Michel (1971) and a catalogue of case studies concerned with ice break-up on North American rivers in Petryk (1984, 1985).

## Site Description of Liard River

### Physical setting

The break-up of the Liard River is especially significant because it "triggers" that of the Mackenzie River, Canada's longest river and one of the world's largest ice-covered rivers. Upstream of the Liard confluence, break-up of the Mackenzie River is primarily dependent on flow out of Great Slave Lake. Although southern tributaries, such as the Athabasca, Hay, Peace and Slave rivers contribute to the Northerly flow of water, discharge from these basins is heavily damped by the stabilizing effects of Great Slave Lake (MacKay and Mackay 1973a). Hence, break-up in the upstream portions of the Mackenzie River usually occurs later and is less spectacular than the break-up produced by the rapid spring runoff from the unregulated Liard catchment.

Draining an area of 277,000 km², the Liard is the largest tributary of the Mackenzie River downstream of Great Slave Lake. From its headwaters in the Cordillera, the Liard flows in a generally south-east direction until it meets the Fort Nelson River at Nelson Forks (Fig. 1). From Nelson Forks, the Liard heads north-eastward across the plains of the Interior Plateau to its confluence with the Mackenzie River at Fort Simpson, NWT, a distance of approximately 430 km. Other major tributaries along the route include the Birch, Petitot, Poplar, and South Nahanni rivers. During the ice-covered season, the Liard River contributes less than 20% of the Mackenzie River flow, although this percentage increases to between 25 and 35% during break-up and to over 45% in late May, after most floating ice has cleared (Prowse 1984).

### Spring Climate

Upstream of Nelson Forks, the Liard River divides into a northern (upper Liard River) and southern (Fort Nelson River) catchment. As shown in Figure 1, much of the upper Liard River basin lies above 900 m and could be classed as alpine, whereas a large proportion of the Fort Nelson River Basin is lowland. The difference in elevation between the two catchments is reflected in their spring temperatures. The mean April air temperature at Watson Lake in the upper Liard catchment is -0.6°C but that for Fort Nelson is +1.6°C.

In early spring, the southerly headwaters of the Nelson River are influenced largely by warm Pacific air masses, while the downstream and more northerly reaches of the Liard are affected by the colder more continental climate of the interior plains. A gradual influx of the warm westerly air replacing colder Arctic air produces a downstream gradient in springtime warming (Anderson and Fogarasi 1981). The gradient is apparent in mean April air temperatures which decrease by 1.8°C between Fort Nelson and Fort Liard, then by a further 1.3°C to Fort Simpson at the river mouth.

Snowmelt in the Liard catchment usually occurs first in the upstream tributaries of the Fort Nelson River and produces a corresponding rise in discharge. Rainfall in the spring months tends to be relatively low, and thus runoff is primarily snowmelt-generated (Anderson and Fogarasi 1981). Figure 2 illustrates long term, mean discharges for the Fort Nelson River, three points on the Liard River and the Mackenzie River at Fort Simpson, during the April-May break-up period. Strong temporal differences are readily apparent in the onset of spring runoff among the stations. On average, discharge on the Fort Nelson River begins to rise appreciably after the first week in April, followed by less

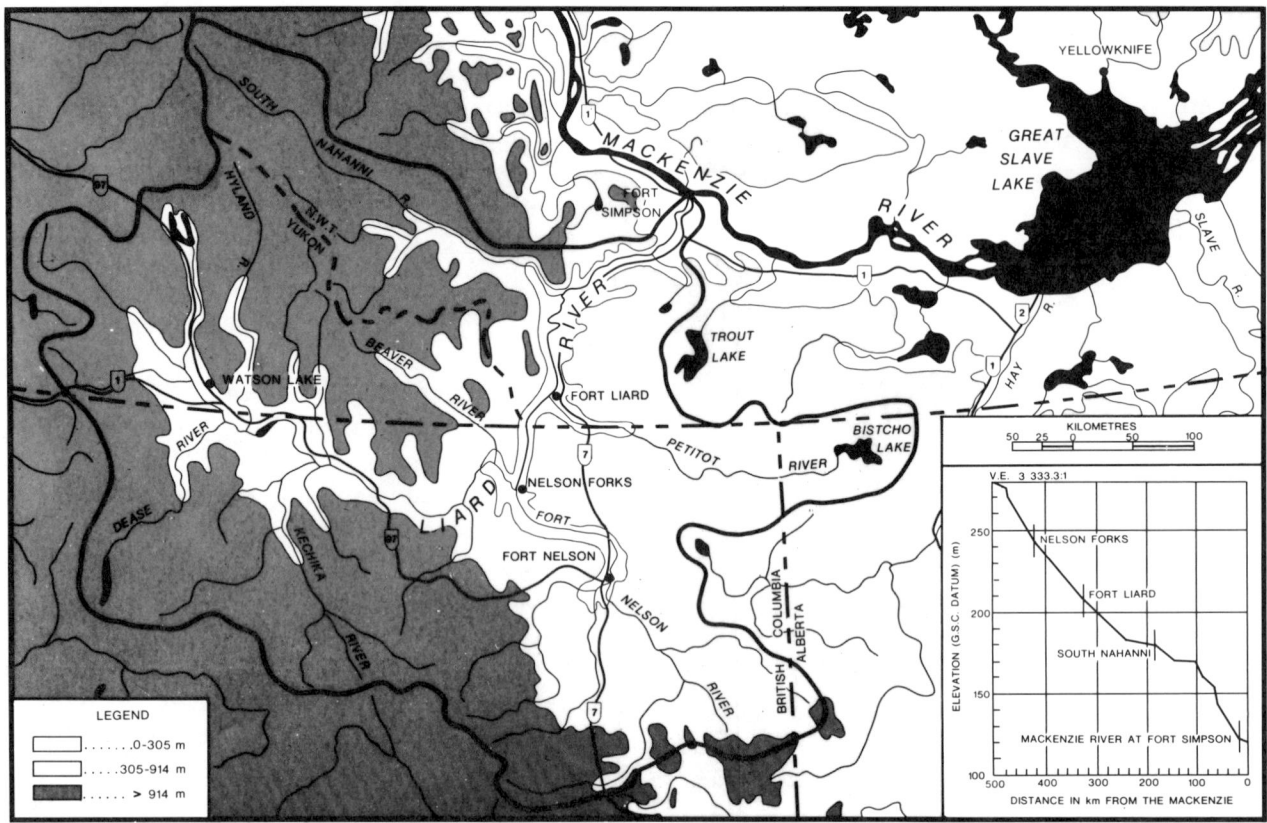

Figure 1    Liard River basin. River slope is shown in the inset (after Parkinson and Holder 1982).

pronounced rises in the lower reaches of the Liard River, as evidenced at Fort Liard and the river mouth. In contrast, that from the portion of the Liard River upstream of Nelson Forks does not begin to increase noticeably until late in April.

*Break-up pattern*

The large scale pattern of ice clearance on the Liard River is typical of most northward flowing rivers in which break-up originates in the headwaters and then progressively moves downstream. Figure 3 shows the mean isochrones of river ice break-up compiled from a 5-year record of 27 stations (Anderson and Fogarasi 1981). As illustrated, break-up usually occurs in the upper portions of the Fort Nelson catchment prior to April 20 and then passes downstream, reaching the Liard River mouth soon after May 10. Notably, break-up in the upper portions of the Liard catchment is retarded. For example, both Watson Lake in the upper Liard and Fort Liard, 100 km downstream of Fort Nelson, lie on the May 5 isochrone. Ice from the upper Liard is usually not part of the initial break-up front which passes down the Liard River, but rather comes down as a second wave of floating ice, sometimes even after ice clearance has continued into the Mackenzie River (Prowse 1984).

**Break-up Processes**

Break-up processes are reviewed under four major headings: pre-break-up, break-up, ice jams and, water levels and discharge. The pre-break-up section contains generic descriptions of processes that are typical of most northern

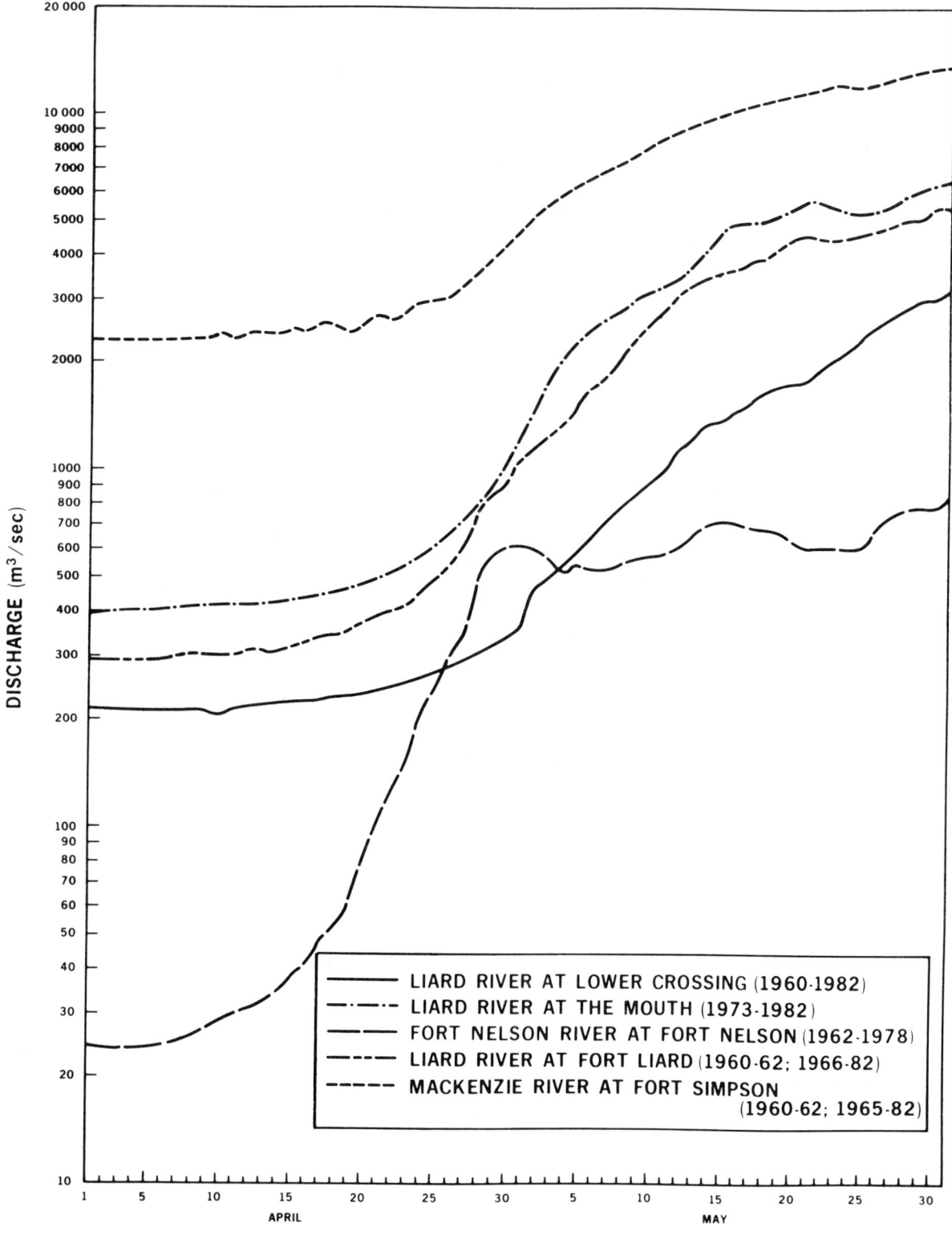

Figure 2 Mean daily discharge during break-up. Length of records shown in brackets. "Liard River at lower crossing" refers to lower crossing of the Alaska Highway, 59°24'N 126°05'W. (from Prowse 1984; Water Survey of Canada, unpublished data)

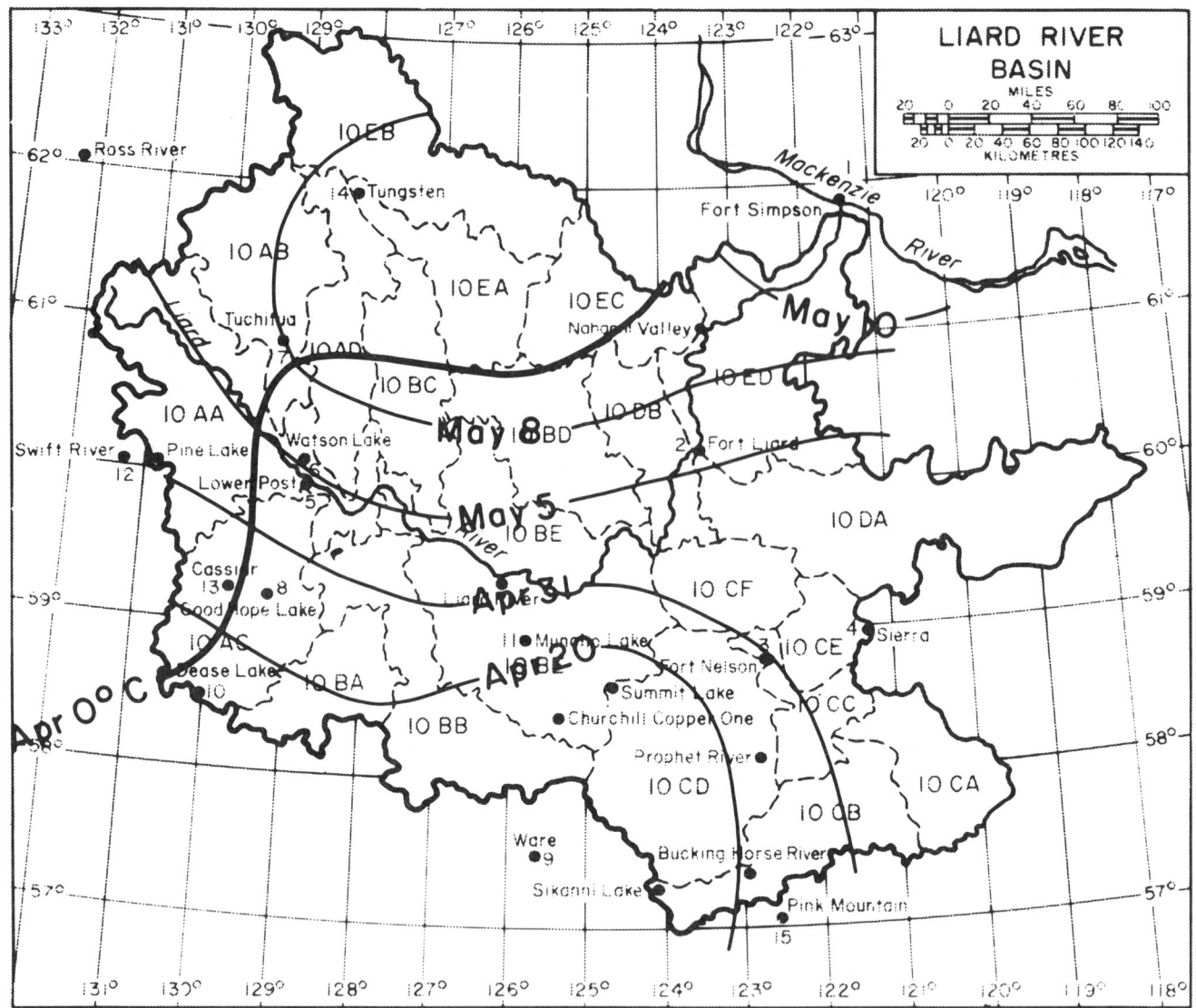

Figure 3  Mean isochrones of river ice break-up (1973-1977) and mean April 0°C isotherm. (from Anderson and Fogarasi 1981).

rivers. This section forms part of a review of river ice processes being prepared for the National Research Council of Canada (NRCC), Working Group on River Ice Jams. More site-specific data about the Liard River are used to illustrate the processes involved with break-up advance and ice jamming. Information has been extracted from a number of research papers and case studies including: Anderson (1982), Parkinson (1982b), Parkinson et al. (1981), Parkinson and Holder (1982), Prowse (1984, 1985b, 1986a,b) and Sherstone (1981).

*Pre-break-up*

During the pre-break-up period, even before air temperatures rise above freezing, snow on the river ice and on land begins to melt under the influence of solar radiation. The onset of spring melt advances the break-up process in two ways. Firstly, snowmelt runoff produces increases in discharge, velocity, and water levels and secondly, heat exchanges at both the snow-air and ice-river water interfaces result in melt of the river snow and ice cover, decreasing both its thickness and mechanical strength.

Although the transfers of sensible and latent heat by convection and conduction, and radiative heat are all important to the thermal ripening and the melting of ice, it is radiation which can produce the largest and most dramatic changes in the mechanical strength of an ice cover. During the early spring, most heat supplied to the ice surface is consumed in the process of melt. Beginning with a fresh snowcover, much of the incoming short wave radiation is reflected from the surface. However, as the surface snow ages and ripens, the albedo decreases thereby allowing a larger percentage of the income radiation to penetrate into the underlying ice and snow. Once the snow cover is totally eliminated and the underlying ice sheet becomes exposed, radiative losses due to reflection may still be quite large if the top of the ice sheet is comprised of relatively opaque "white ice" forms (see Adams 1976 and Michel 1971 for description of ice types). However, once the relatively transparent layers of columnar black ice become exposed, significant amounts of short wave radiation can penetrate deep within the ice sheet.

Much of the light attenuated within black ice is absorbed at inter-crystalline boundaries; zones where there is a concentration of impurities deposited during the freeze-out process. Radiation absorbed in these zones causes a localized warming and an eventual melt of the crystal perimeters, a process termed "candling." The low structural integrity of this ice is apparent in Fig. 4 which depicts the disintegration of a thermally weakened ice sheet. For comparison, a more competent ice sheet is shown fracturing in Fig. 5.

During the pre-break-up period. melt may also occur at the base of the ice sheet. Although the temperature of the river water may only be a fraction of a degree above freezing, high flow velocities promote a rapid transfer of heat to the ice cover. From a study of pre-break-up conditions on the Liard River, Marsh and Prowse (1987) found that the hydrothermal heat transfer to the ice cover increased from approximately 10 W m$^{-2}$ one week before break-up to almost 100 W m$^{-2}$ immediately preceding break-up. The dramatic increase was largely

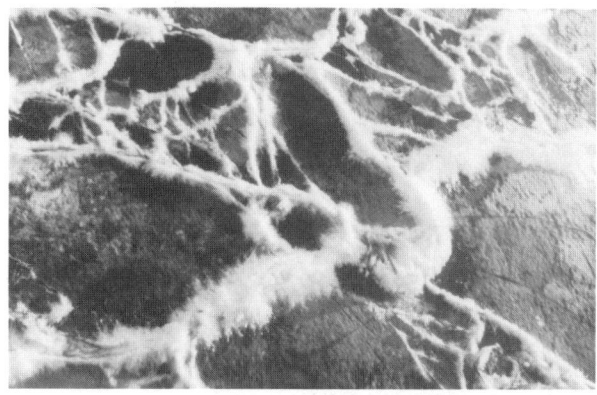

Figure 4   Break-up of thermally decayed black ice sheet. Individual black ice crystals are being extruded at floe boundaries.

Figure 5   Break-up of competent ice sheet.

ascribed to a rise in water temperature associated with break-up advance (Fig. 6). The water to ice heat transfer can be further increased by the formation of ice ripples (Fig. 7) which increase subsurface turbulence and the related heat transfer coefficient. For example, Ashton and Kennedy (1972) and Gilpin et al. (1980) found that heat transfer was 50 to 60% greater for rippled ice surfaces than for smooth ice.

During the pre-break-up phase, the above hydrothermal processes may result in the appearance or increase in size of open water zones, thinning of ice in snow free sections and a decrease in the load of snow on the river.

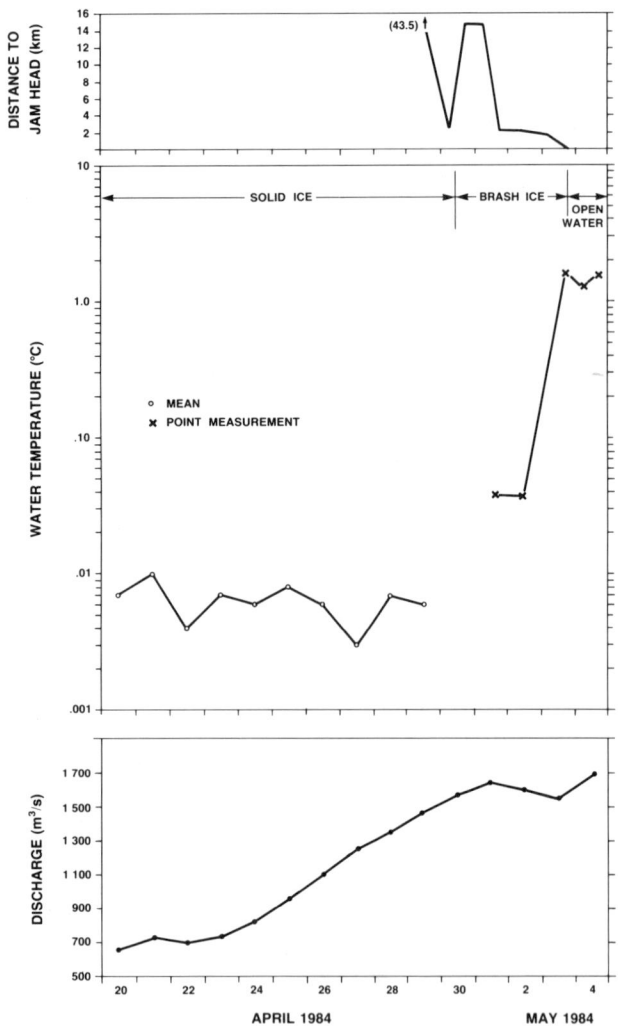

Figure 6   Water temperature and discharge associated with break-up and advance (from Marsh and Prowse 1987).

However, from the point of view of break-up the most important feature of this period is the increase in river flow which increases both water levels and downstream forces applied to the ice cover. In response, the ice begins to crack in patterns determined by its nonuniform thickness, strength and bonds to the banks and bed.

As the ice cover is buoyed by the rising water, it is essentially subjected to an upward loading. In many cases, the ice sheet first rises along near-vertical "hinge cracks" that formed either

Figure 7   Ice ripples formed by thermal erosion at the base of an ice sheet.

from ice shoving during freeze-up or from the vertical failure of the ice sheet during the winter recession in water levels (Fig. 8). Although the centre portion of the ice sheet may rise, strips of ice on the bank-side of the hinge crack remain frozen to the bed and become inundated with river water and runoff from adjacent slopes. The term "shore lead" is often used to describe the accumulation of water along the banks.

For all unregulated rivers, the pre-break-up phase will normally develop to at least the above conditions. With further warming, the shore ice will completely melt or detach from the shore material. Similarly, the central portion of the ice sheet will detach from the banks and, with the increase in river width resulting from rising water levels, begin to shift within the channel. This is often the period when transverse cracks (Fig. 9) have been reported to appear. Tensile stresses caused by bending are the most probable mechanism of fracture (Beltaos 1985).

While the major stem of the river remains largely ice covered, ice from smaller tributaries, which are more quickly affected by snowmelt runoff, drives down to accumulate at the tributary junction with the main stem (Fig. 10a). In other small tributaries where runoff is rapid yet the ice cover remains intact, often frozen directly to the bed, water may flow over the ice and directly on to the main ice sheet (Fig. 10b). At the end of the pre-break-up phase, hydro-mechanical and hydrothermal action may have

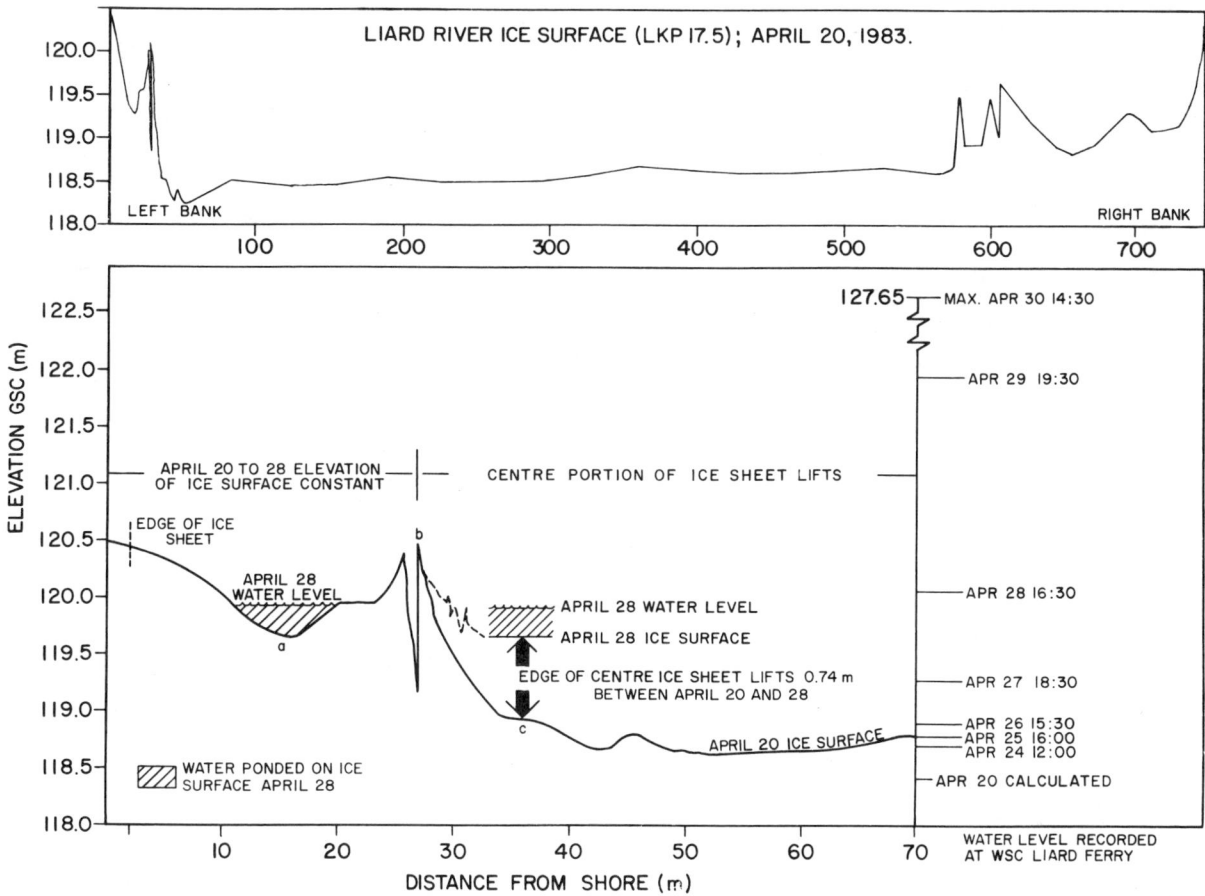

Figure 8  Ice life along a hinge crack. Upper diagram shows entire river cross-section with hinge cracks at both banks. A large scale view of the left bank hinge crack is shown in the bottom diagram. Note the rise of the centre ice sheet between April 20 and April 28 and inundation of the shore fast ice. (from Prowse 1984).

created open water zones, primarily at rapids sections and near tributary mouths, but most of the river remains covered by a substantial ice cover.

*Break-up*

Although break-up has effectively occurred at a number of specific sites (e.g., high velocity reaches) in the above discussion, it is just being initiated at the larger river scale. This next stage, which has been aptly referred to as the "drive" (Michel 1971), is characterized by the continued increase in discharge as snowmelt accelerates but may also be marked by interruptions to flow created by ice jams. The drive stage can best be illustrated by considering two extremes in break-up conditions, "premature" or "mechanical" and "over-mature" or "thermal."

The two classifications refer to specific combinations of river discharge and ice strength, both of which are largely determined in the pre-break-up period. In the thermal case, which most closely approximates break-up conditions on lakes, spring discharge remains small while the ice sheet melts and is thoroughly weakened by thermal exchanges. This type of situation usually occurs in years or regions,

Figure 9  Transverse crack formed in otherwise intact ice sheet.

where the winter snow accumulation is small and makes only limited and gradual contributions to spring runoff. Eventually the ice sheet will weaken to a state where it can easily be carried downstream even under low flow conditions. The term "drive" barely applies in a situation of over-mature break-up.

For the pre-mature case, conditions are reversed to include a strong, competent ice cover which may still be strongly attached to the shore, and a large, spring flood wave that is usually created by rapid and extensive snowmelt, sometimes augmented by rainfall. With rising discharge, the downstream forces become sufficient to rupture and dislodge the intact ice sheet driving it downstream. Initiation of this phase is often characterized by large hummocks or debacles formed by compressive forces between large ice sheets. Figure 11 illustrates the formation of a large hummock where two ice sheets have come into contact over a shoal. Note the extent of bending in the intact ice sheet at the upstream base of the hummock.

Prowse (1986a) notes that both thermal and mechanical break-ups have occurred on the Liard River between 1978 and 1984. Mechanical break-ups were the most common, occurring in all years except 1980 and 1984. The downstream advance of a mechanical break-up was dominated by a sequential, downstream progression of a localized zone of ice fracturing and ice clearance which took from 4 to 8 days to travel

Figure 10a  Ice jam formed at tributary mouth against intact ice sheet of larger order river.

Figure 10b  Ice and water from break-up of tributary spilling onto the intact ice sheet of larger-order river.

Figure 11  Hummock formed by downstream forces of advancing break-up front (background). Flow is from left to right. Note binding of ice sheet at the upstream end of the hummock. Exposed portion of ice sheet is approximately 0.7 m thick.

Figure 12  Rapid fragmentation of ice sheet associated with advance of mechanical break-up front. Note water spilling onto intact ice sheet.

from Nelson Forks to the Liard River mouth (0.6 – 1.2 m s$^{-1}$). In these years, the ice cover displayed little evidence of thermal decay or mechanical weakening before the arrival of the break-up front. Other than shore leads, zones of open water were generally restricted to large shoal areas or high velocity reaches. Most tributaries were ineffective in cutting open water channels into the main ice sheet and instead either jammed at their mouths or spilled ice and water out onto the surface of the Liard ice cover.

Within many reaches, the break-up zone rapidly advanced along a single front at which the intact ice sheet was fractured — almost pulverized — into small diameter floes such as those shown in Fig. 12. The front was followed by a large mass of this fractured ice, which extended tens of kilometres upstream, and finally by the leading edge of open water. The rate of advance of these break-up fronts often exceeded normal open water velocities. In the 1983 break-up, for example, the break-up front approached the Liard River mouth at an average velocity (measured over an 18 km distance) of just over 5 m/s (Prowse 1984). Similar velocities have been observed on other large northern Canadian Rivers (Doyle 1977; Doyle and Andres 1978; Gerard 1975; Gerard et al. 1984; Parkinson 1982a) and have generally been ascribed to surges resulting from the failure of upstream ice jams.

The ice clearance patterns associated with the 1980 and 1984 thermal break-ups differed considerably from those of the other five years. Although a general downstream progress in ice clearance occurred on a basin-wide scale, more locally the advance of break-up was relatively haphazard. In many instances, a number of break-up fronts were simultaneously active within different portions of the river. Many of the break-up fronts had been initiated by flow in high velocity zones or by flow from major tributaries. The ease with which contributing flow could fracture and move the ice cover was partly dependent on the amount of prior thermal weakening of the ice. Even the structure of the advancing fronts differed from those in Fig. 12. Most were comprised of very large diameter floes and only at a considerable distance upstream of the front was the ice cover finally reduced to small brash ice. In some locations the ice sheet almost melted in situ (Fig. 13).

A major factor controlling the pattern of break-up was the degree of pre-break-up thermal decay. A simple measure of the amount of atmospheric heating can be obtained from a surrogate heat index, such as degree days. Table 1

Figure 13  In situ thermal decay ice sheet during thermal break-up.

lists the number of accumulated degree days (ADD; °C) from April 1 to the day of break-up for the years 1978 to 1984 at Fort Simpson. The relatively high degree of atmospheric heating of the ice cover which occurred prior to break-up in 1980 and 1984 is reflected in ADD totals of +149 and +71 for these two years of thermal break-up. The other five years of mechanical break-up produced only negative ADD totals, ranging from -174 to -56.

Table 1  Accumulated degree days (Celsius) from April 1 to day of break-up (from Prowse 1986a)

| Break-up year | Date | Accumulated degree days* | Discharge (m³/s)† |
|---|---|---|---|
| 1978 | May 03 | -61.7 | 2270 |
| 1979 | May 11 | -174.2 | 900 |
| 1980 | May 02 | +149.1 | 1700 |
| 1981 | May 07 | -73.0 | 2800 |
| 1982 | May 09 | -55.7 | 1000 |
| 1983 | Apr 29 | -48.3 | 1450 |
| 1984 | Apr 29 | +70.8 | 1460 |

\* Meteorological data from Fort Simpson Airport, 2 km from the Liard River WSC station.
† Mean daily discharge.

## Ice Jams

As is the case for most northern rivers, ice jams are a regular feature of the Liard River break-up. Based on observations via aerial reconnaissance and satellite imagery (Fig. 14), Sherstone (1981) concluded that the highest frequency of jamming occurs on the lower Liard in a 25-km reach approximately 100 km upstream of the river mouth and in the lower 60 km of the river. One particular location, at the confluence of the Liard and Mackenzie Rivers, has also been identified by MacKay and Mackay (1973b) to be a site of recurrent and often spectacular ice jamming. Ice jams at the Liard River mouth are typical of jams that form on rivers which flow into lakes or into other rivers that break-up later. Unlike ice jams which tend to form randomly, for example at irregular intervals and locations in the vicinity of channel restrictions or low velocity reaches, the river mouth or delta type of ice jam regularly develops at approximately the same location. This is apparent in Fig. 15 which shows the regular position of the ice jam toe (downstream end) across the Liard River mouth. Table 2 summarizes the dimensions of these jams, which range in length from 9.5 to 22.1 km and in area from 10.0 to 22.8 km².

Despite the regularity in location and similarity in area, the jams differed in other important characteristics, such as surface composition, thickness and effect on water levels. As noted by Prowse (1986a), these differences are largely related to the type of break-up which lead to jam formation. First, consider the surface composition. In years of mechanical break-up, the ice jam toe was often comprised of small diameter floes butting against a relatively intact ice cover; a physical situation resembling that of the moving break-up front in Fig. 12. Furthermore, almost the entire surface area of all the mechanical jams consisted of small diameter brash ice. In contrast, the toe and upstream portions of the thermal jams were dominated by large floes some of which bridged the entire river cross-section. The relative lack of small diameter brash ice in the thermal jams is indicative of the absence of a dynamic break-up front that was present in the mechanical break-ups.

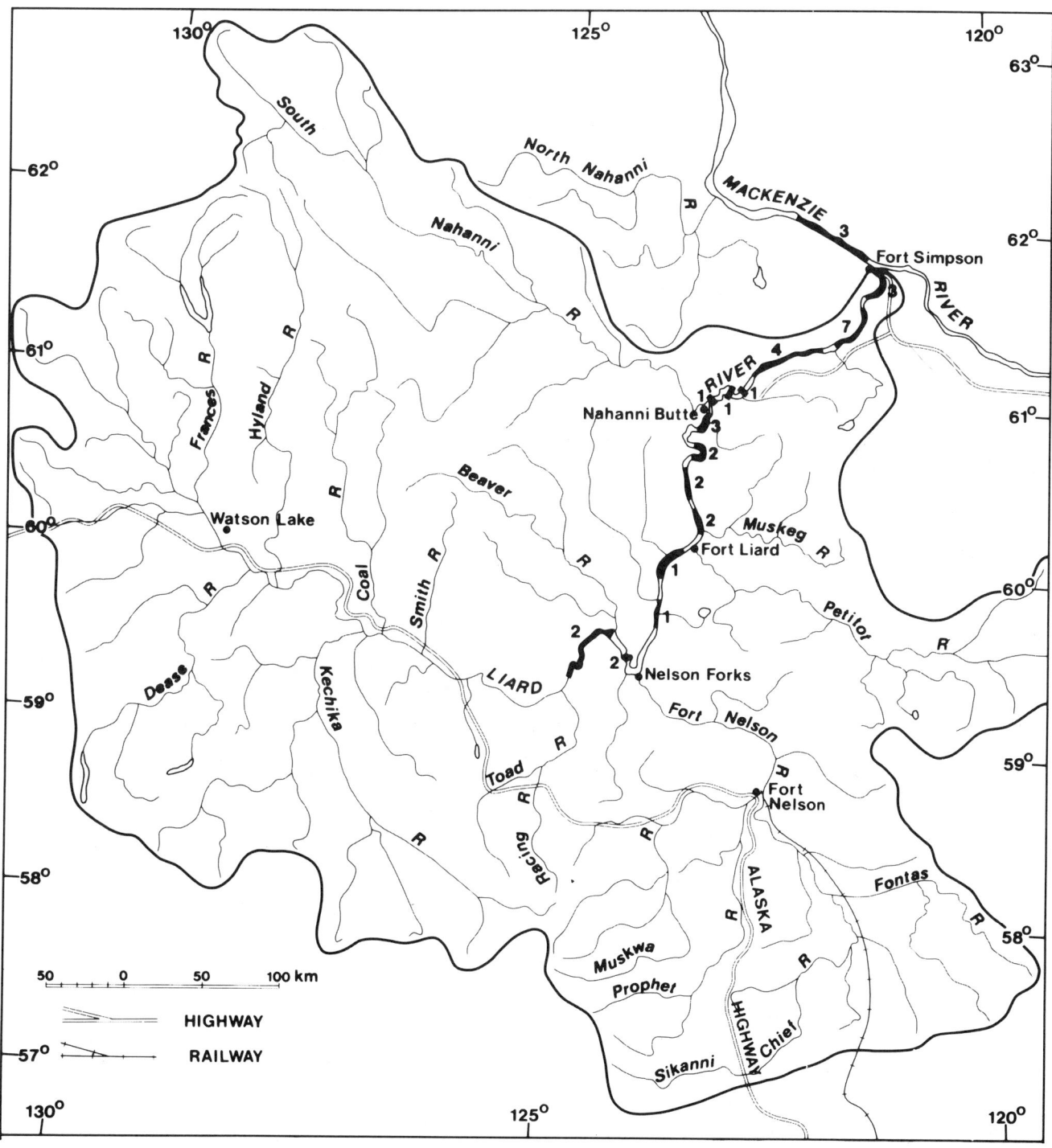

Figure 14  Location and frequency of ice jamming observed from satellite over the period 1973-1978 (from Sherstone 1981).

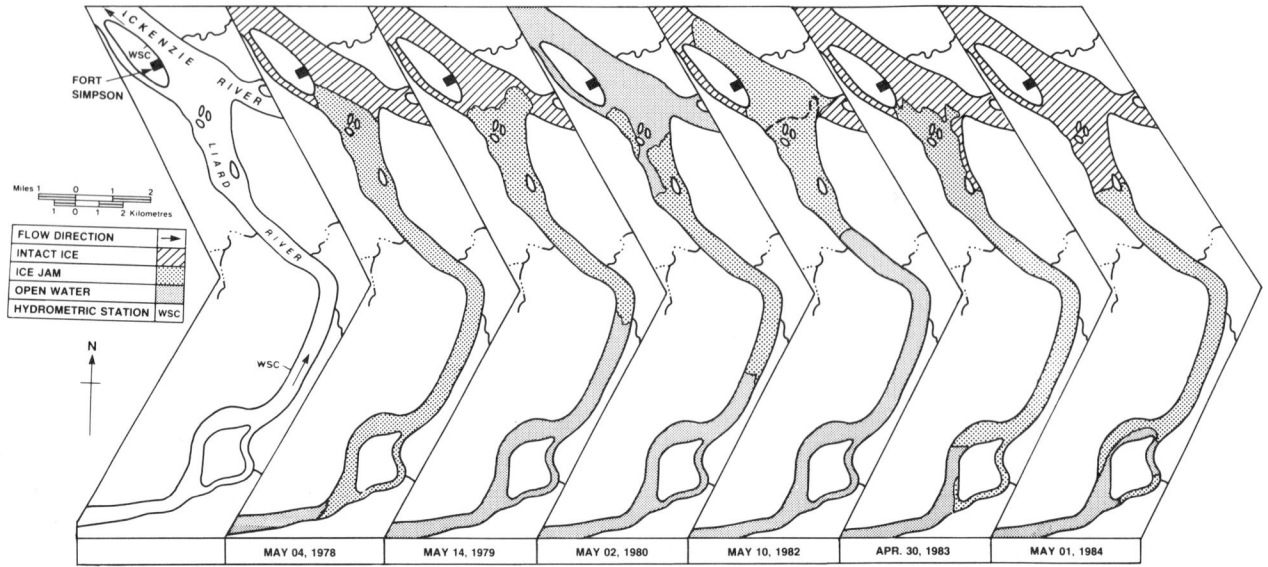

Figure 15  Position of ice jams at the Liard River mouth (from Prowse 1986a).

Table 2  Ice jam characteristics (from Prowse 1986a).

| Year | Date | Length (km)* | Area (km²)† | Discharge (m³/s)** |
|------|--------|------|------|------|
| 1978 | May 04 | 22.1 | 22.8 | 3110 |
| 1979 | May 14 | 12.1 | 11.7 | 1850 |
| 1980 | May 02 |  9.5 | 10.0 | 1700 |
| 1982 | May 10 | 17.8 | 10.8 | 1500 |
| 1983 | Apr 30 | 19.1 | 19.2 | 1750 |
| 1984 | May 01 | 11.0 | 13.1 | 1680 |

\* measured along the centre of the ice covered channel
† excluding areas of open water and mean daily discharge
\*\* mean daily discharge

Figure 16  Shear walls remaining after ice jam release, Liard River mouth.

There are also distinct differences in the thickness of the ice accumulations. Although in situ measurement of jam thickness is nearly impossible considerable information has been gathered about the vertical dimensions of shear walls which Calkins (1983) and Beltaos (1983a) suggest as surrogate measures of jam thickness In years of mechanical break-up, shear walls ranging from 4-8 m remained along the banks of the ice-jam reach (Anderson 1982; Parkinson et al. 1981; Prowse 1984, 1986b; Sherstone 1981). Figure 16 shows the height of such walls recorded during the 1983 mechanical event. Much smaller shear wall heights characterized the 1980 and 1984 thermal events. Within some zones the walls reached a height of 2-2.5 m but, over much of the reach, remnant shore ice was only the thickness of the original ice sheet.

Based on the surface area and thickness information obtained for the 1983 ice jam, which was classed as a large event, Prowse (1986a) estimated the ice volume within the jam to be $64.4 \times 10^6$ m³. In terms of ice contained within the pre-break-up ice cover, this represents only 19%

of the ice downstream of Nelson Forks, or approximately the lower 89 km of the river. This distance is even less than the 150 km which the break-up front travelled in the 24 hr period preceding the ice jam event. Thus, even within one day, almost 40% of the pre-break-up ice cover was either stranded on the shores, melted during downstream travel or was sufficiently fragmented to pass under the jam. More importantly, the results suggest that recent large events, as exemplified by the 1983 jam, have developed from only a limited amount of the total available ice supply. Much longer ice jams could therefore be expected to develop given hydrologic and meteorologic conditions more favourable to the rapid downstream transport of ice. More generally, high ice losses can be expected for long river reaches with many tributaries, whereas much smaller losses are typical of shallow, steep rivers where the ice-contributing area is small (U.S. Army 1982).

Marsh and Prowse (1987) point to the significance of hydrothermal melt in removing ice during the break-up period. Figure 6 shows the rapid rise from near 100 W m$^{-2}$ immediately prior to break-up, to over 10,000 W m$^{-2}$ following fragmentation and subsequent jamming of the ice. Hydrothermal melt has also been shown by Prowse and Marsh (1985) to be important in the ablation of the 1983 ice jam at the Liard mouth, which decreased in length from approximately 23 km to only 6 km within a five day period (Fig. 17).

The dramatic rise in hydrothermal heat flow which accompanies ice break-up is due not only to the rough subsurface enhancing the water-ice heat transfer but also to a rise in water temperature. Given the same meterological conditions, the greatest rise in water temperature should occur during mechanical break-ups in which upstream reaches have been largely cleared of floating ice thereby permitting uninterrupted heating of the flow. Reduced heating and lower temperatures will prevail in thermal break-ups which leave upstream zones of alternating ice cover and open water.

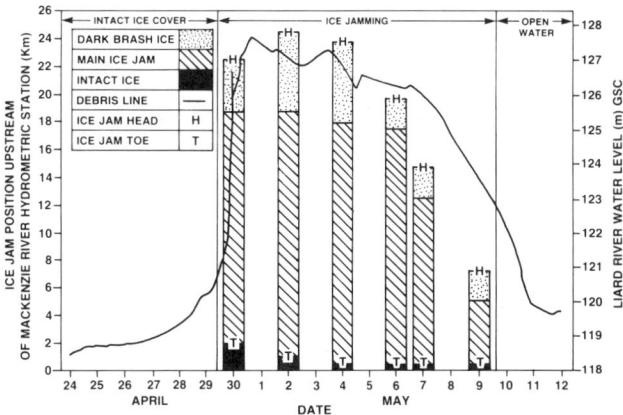

Figure 17  Shrinkage or ice jam due to thermal decay (after Prowse and Marsh 1985). Note rapid decline in water levels associated with the decrease in jam length.

*Water Levels and Discharge*

Water stage data have been collected near the Liard River mouth by the Water Survey of Canada since 1972. As for most northern rivers, numerous gaps exist in the record because of frequent ice damage to recording instruments during the break-up period. However, since 1978 special efforts have been made to record maximum stage produced by ice conditions. Table 3 lists the maximum stages during both the open water and ice conditions periods for the years 1978-84. Notably, except for 1984, all annual maximum stages were measured during the period of river ice break-up and not during the open water period.

Based on evidence from aerial photographs and field surveys, the high stage in these years can be directly attributed to conditions created by ice jams at the Liard River mouth. Given the location of the Liard hydrometric station relative to the ice jams (Fig. 15), the stage records are considered to be representative of conditions found within the upper portions of the ice accumulation or slightly upstream of the jam head (upstream end of ice accumulation). Characteristics of the jams provided in Table 2 and Fig. 15 refer to the same day as, or at most one day after, the recording of the respective maximum water levels.

As evident in Table 3, there is a noticeable difference in water levels between thermal and mechanical break-ups. The 1980 and 1984 ice jams produced relatively low water levels of 121.38 and 122.19 m above mean sea level (amsl), while the maximum stage from the other five jams ranged from 125.15 to 128.20 m amsl. All other factors being equal, this contrast in water levels between mechanical and thermal break-up jams can be largely explained by differences in ice jam thickness and subsurface roughness. The thermal jams are not only thinner but the subsurface roughness of the large floes is small relative to that of heavily fragmented ice. The combined effect of a low ice thickness to flow depth ratio and small subsurface roughness presents a much smaller resistance to flow through the jam section than that of the thick, rough ice accumulations typical of the mechanical ice jams. The higher the flow resistance, the higher the backwater levels will be for a particular discharge.

Discharge, however, also varied among jams. Inspection of Table 3 reveals that, even when comparing years of mechanical break-ups, different water levels occurred with similar flows. These variations can be partly explained by differences in physical conditions of the mechanical jams, but the situation is complicated by the quality of discharge information (Prowse et al. 1986). During break-up, ice conditions are so variable that no consistent relationship can be established between stage and discharge. To circumvent this problem, a standard practice used on northern rivers is to estimate *mean daily* discharge figures by extrapolating flow data from upstream ice-free sites to the downstream ice-affected reaches. Allowances are made for flow travel time and hydrometerological events such as snowmelt and rainfall. However, a major drawback of this approach is the difficulty in accounting for rapid fluctuations in flow and water levels which occur on time frames of much less than one day. Hence, mean daily discharge figures are of limited use for analyzing break-up water levels.

One method by which maximum water levels can be estimated for ice jams which form under a range of flow conditions is offered by the theory of wide channel equilibrium jams (Pariset et al. 1966; Uzuner and Kennedy 1976; Beltaos 1983a). Prowse 1986a) used this technique for analyzing the Liard River jams. Assuming that equilibrium jams formed at different levels of discharge would have similar physical characteristics, the stage-discharge curve in Fig. 18 was developed. Also shown is a stage-discharge relationship based on a simplified

Table 3 Annual maximum water levels during ice and open water conditions (from Prowse 1986a)

| | Ice Conditions | | | Open Water | | |
|---|---|---|---|---|---|---|
| Year | Date | Stage (m amsl) | Discharge ($m^3/s$)* | Date | Stage (m amsl) | Discharge ($m^3/s$)† |
| 1978 | May 03 | 125.25 | 2270 | June 11 | 120.89 | 6116 |
| 1979 | May 14 | 125.15 | 1850 | July 07 | 123.66 | 13300 |
| 1980 | May 01 | 121.38 | 1550 | June 12 | 121.35 | 7130 |
| 1981 | May 07 | 128.20 | 2800 | May 31 | 122.89 | 11500 |
| 1982 | May 10 | 126.91 | 1500 | May 21 | 123.65 | 12900 |
| 1983 | Apr 30 | 127.65 | 3971 | June 05 | 121.86 | 8400 |
| 1984 | May 01 | 122.19 | 1640 | June 12 | 122.61 | 10900 |
| Mean | 1978-1984 | 125.24 | 1909 | — | 122.42 | 10035 |

\* mean daily discharge except 1983 which is an instanteous value
† instantaneous discharge

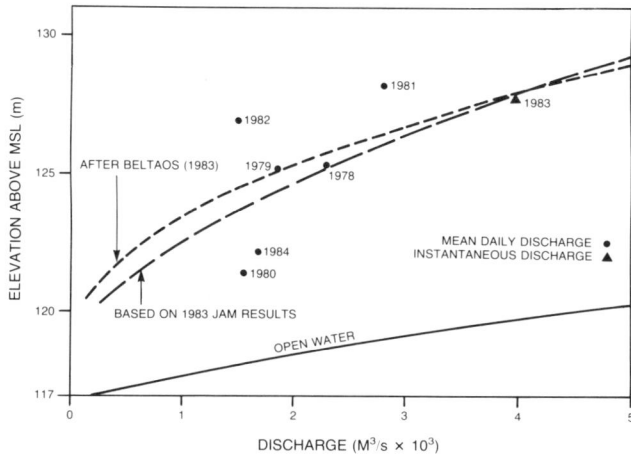

Figure 18  Open water and ice jam stage-discharge relationships for the Liard River mouth. (from Prowse 1986a).

method described by Beltaos (1983a). Although both approaches predict dramatic increases in stage of approximately 4-8 m above those which would result from equivalent discharge under open water conditions, neither curve forms an upper envelope to all the ice jam events. However, only the 1983 event is plotted using an instantaneous discharge. The remaining points are referenced to mean daily discharge figures. Much greater discharge may have been responsible for the observed jam stages and could result in the events falling on or below the ice jam rating curves. The major obstacle to using the equilibrium jam theory for predicting both the magnitude and frequency of high stages on northern rivers is simply the lack of useable discharge information.

## Discussion

As an introduction to break-up on northern rivers, the above material was structured as a sequence of processes from the early stages of melt to ice-clear conditions. There are, however, numerous gaps in our understanding of break-up processes, some simply due to the lack of relevant, quantitative field data. In recognition of this, the NRCC Working Group on River Ice Jams has developed a set of guidelines for river ice monitoring programs (Prowse 1985a) and for the extraction of break-up data from existing hydrometric records (Beltaos 1983b). To improve our ability to deal with river ice problems, there is also a range of specific research needs which should be addressed. The following details a few of the more pressing of these.

One of the most important changes which occurs during the pre-break-up period is the decrease in the ability of an ice cover to resist downstream forces. Although the general effect of the major heat flows on the structural integrity of an ice sheet are known, a technique does not yet exist to accurately predict changes in ice strength from standard meterological variables. Moreover, the importance of internal ice strength relative to other factors that determine the overall cover stability, such as attachment to the banks, remains unknown. The ability to predict changes in ice strength will also allow the forecasting of the overall severity of break-up, as evidenced by the strong contrasts between mechanical and thermal break-ups on the Liard River.

In the past few years, significant advances have been made in our understanding of some of the large-scale fracturing processes which accompany break-up but questions remain about what controls the rapid fragmentation of ice associated with mechanical break-up fronts. More generally, research should be focussed on explaining the surge-stall behaviour of break-up advance. Surges are thought to be released by the sudden failure of upstream ice jams to produce rapidly moving break-up fronts, but little is known about the conditions leading to jam failure or those that dampen the downstream passage of the surge and eventually lead to stalling of the break-up front and formation of another jam. Explanation of the stalling behaviour is a key to forecasting the initiation of jams that form more randomly in time and space than the delta-type of jam, as described for the Liard River mouth.

One of the more readily justifiable reasons for conducting research on river ice is the high damage costs which result from backwater flooding created by ice jams. Since the mid-1960's, the theory of equilibrium jams has evolved as an effective tool for predicting the maximum stage which would result from ice jams under varying discharge. However, the development of frequency-stage curves for ice jams has been thwarted by the inability to accurately calculate the frequency and magnitude of discharge which leads to jam formation. A number of approaches have been suggested for improving the measurement of discharge during the break-up period (Prowse et al. 1986) but improvement of the forecasting of break-up discharge will require a number of major research advancements. First, a model of break-up advance will have to be developed based on an improved understanding of the surge-stall behaviour of break-up. In conjunction, a flow routing model also needs to be developed which takes into account the large and rapid fluctuations in discharge which characterize the surge-stall style of break-up. In order to provide input to these two models, they will have to be interfaced with existing snowmelt and runoff models. It should then be possible to predict the downstream passage of flow under break-up conditions and, with existing ice jam-stage models, predict potential flooding. Frequency predictions of stage will, however, still require probability estimation of jam formation and runoff magnitude.

Given the complexities of developing and linking the above models, development of stage-frequency curves for break-up conditions should be considered a long term objective but one that is essential if effective flood damage reduction is to be achieved on northern rivers.

## References

Adams, W.P.
1986   A classification of process and form for freshwater ice. The Musk-Ox, 18, pp. 99-111.

Anderson, J.C.
1982   Liard and Mackenzie River ice break-up, Fort Simpson Region, NWT, 1982. Report for Water Resources Division, Indian and Northern Affairs Canada, Ottawa, Ont. National Hydrology Research Institute, Environment Canada, 37 p.

Anderson, J.C. and S. Fogarasi
1981   The hydroclimatic setting of the Liard River basin spring flood. In: Spring Break-up, Mackenzie River Basin Study report, Supplement 3. Mackenzie River Basin Committee, (Canada). pp. 4-48.

Atkinson, C.H.
1973   Problems and economic importance of ice jams in Canada. Seminar on ice jams in Canada, Edmonton, Alberta, May 1973, NRC Tech. Memo. No. 107, pp. 1-16.

Ashton, G.D. (Ed.)
1985   River and lake ice engineering. Water Resources Publications, Littleton, Colorado.

Ashton, G.D. and J.F. Kennedy
1972   Ripples on underside of river ice covers. ASCE Journal of the Hydraulics Division, 98(HY9), pp. 1603-1624.

Beltaos, S.
1983a   River ice jams: Theory, case studies and applications. ASCE Journal of Hydraulic Engineering, 109(10), pp. 1338-1359.
1983b   Guidelines for extraction of ice-break-up data from hydrometric station records. Draft report. Working Group on River Ice Jams, Subcommittee on Hydraulics of Ice Covered Rivers, Associate Committee on Hydrology, National Research Council of Canada.
1985   Initial fracture patterns of river ice cover. NWRI report 85-139, Hydraulics Division, National Water Research Institute, Environment Canada, Burlington, Ont.

Calkins, D.J.
1983   Ice jams in shallow rivers with floodplain flow. Canadian Journal of Civil Engineering, 10(3), pp. 538-548.

Doyle, P.F.
1977   1977 break-up and subsequent ice jam at Fort McMurray. Report SW-77/01, Transportation and Surface Water Engineering Division, Alberta Research Council, Edmonton, Alta., 25 p.

Doyle, P.F. and D.D. Andres
1978  1978 break-up in the vicinity of Fort McMurray and investigation of two Athabasca River ice jams. Report SWE-78/05. Transportation and Surface Water Engineering Department, Alberta Research Council, Edmonton, Alta., 44 p.

Gerard, R.
1975  Preliminary observations of spring ice jams in Alberta Proceedings of the International Association of Hydraulic Research, International Symposium on Ice Problems, Hanover, NH, pp. 261-277.

Gerard, R., T.D. Kent, R. Janowicz, and R.D. Lyons
1984  Ice regime reconnaissance, Yukon River, Yukon. Canadian Society for Civil Engineering Proceedings, Cold Regions Specialty Conference, Edmonton, Alta., pp. 1059-1073.

Gilpin, R.R., T. Hiarata, and K.C. Cheng
1980  Wave formation and heat transfer at an ice-water interface in the presence of a turbulent flow. Journal of Fluid Mechanics, 99, pp. 619-640.

MacKay, D.K. and J.R. Mackay
1973a Locations of spring ice jamming on the Mackenzie River, NWT Report 73-3, Hydrologic Aspects of Northern Development, Glaciology Division, Water Resources Branch, Department of the Environment, Ottawa, Ont., pp. 237-257.
1973b Break-up and ice jamming of the Mackenzie River, NWT. Report 73-3 Hydrologi aspects of Northern Development, Glaciology Division, Water Resources Branch, Department of the Environment, Ottawa, Ont., pp. 117-237

Marsh P. and T.D. Prowse
1987  Water temperature and heat flux to the base of river ice covers. Cold Regions Science and Technology (in press).

Michel, B.
1971  Winter regime of rivers and lakes. Cold Regions Science and Engineering Monograph (III-B1a, Cold Regions Research and Engineering Laboratory U.S. Army, Hanover, New Hampshire.

Pariset, E., R. Hausser, and A. Gagnon
1966  Formation of ice covers and ice jams in rivers. ASCE Journal of the Hydraulics Division, 92(HY6), pp. 1-25.

Parkinson F.E.
1982a Water temperature observations during break-up on the Liard-Mackenzie River system. Workshop on the Hydraulics of Ice Covered Rivers, Edmonton, Alta., National Research Council of Canada, pp. 261-295.
1982b Liard-Mackenzie winter regime study, observations of 1982 break-up. Report LHL-868 for British Columbia Hydro and Power Authority, Vancouver, B.C. Lasalle Hydraulic Laboratory Ltd.

Parkinson, F.E., G.K. Holder, and S.M. Kirby
1981  Liard-Mackenzie winter regime study, observations of 1981 break-up. Report LHL-823 for British Columbia Hydro and Power Authority, Vancouver, B.C. Lasalle Hydraulic Laboratory Ltd.

Parkinson, F.E. and G.K. Holder
1982  Liard-Mackenzie winter regime study, final report. Report LHL-830 for British Columbia Hydro and Power Authority, Vancouver, B.C. Lasalle Hydraulic Laboratory Ltd.

Petryk, S.
1984  Case studies concerned with ice jamming: a compilation of descriptions from contributors. 3rd Workshop on the Hydraulics of River Ice, June 1984, Fredericton, New Brunswick, pp. 113-126.
1985  Casebook on ice jams. Draft report. Working Group on River Ice Jams, Subcommittee on Hydraulics of Ice Covered Rivers, Associate Committee on Hydrology, National Research Council of Canada.

Prowse, T.D.
1984  Liard and Mackenzie River ice break-up. Fort Simpson Region, NWT, 1983. Report for Water Resources Division, Indian and Northern Affairs Canada, Ottawa, Ont. National Hydrology Research Institute, Environment Canada, 73 p.

1985a   Guidelines for river ice data collection programs. Draft report. Working Group on River Ice Jams, Subcommittee on Hydraulics of Ice Covered Rivers, Associate Committee on Hydrology, National Research Council of Canada.

1985b   Hydrometerological conditions prevailing during the 1984 river ice break-up, Fort Simpson region, NWT. Report for Water Resources Division, Indian and Northern Affairs Canada, Ottawa, Ont., National Hydrology Research Institute, Environment Canada, 30 p.

1986a   Ice jam characteristics, Liard-Mackenzie rivers confluence. Canadian Journal of Civil Engineering, 13 (in press).

1986b   1985 break-up and ice jam observations, Liard and Mackenzie Rivers near Fort Simpson, NWT. Report for Water Resources Division, Indian and Northern Affairs Canada, Ottawa, Ont., National Hydrology Research Institute, Environment Canada, 31 p.

Prowse, T.D. and P. Marsh
1985   Hydrothermal decay of ice jams. Proceedings of the 42nd Eastern Snow Conference, Montreal, Quebec, pp. 272-276.

Prowse, T.D., J.C. Anderson, and R.L. Smith
1986   Discharge measurement during river ice break-up. Proceedings of the 43rd Eastern Snow Conference, Hanover, New Hampshire, (in press).

Sherstone, D.A.
1981   Ice break-up in the Liard basin. In: Spring break-up, Mackenzie River Basin Study report, Supplement 3. Mackenzie River Basin Committee (Canada). pp. 49-123.

Uzuner, M.S. and J.F. Kennedy
1976   Theoretical model of river ice jams. ASCE Journal of the Hydraulics Division, 102(HY9), pp. 1365-1383.

U.S. Army.
1982   Ice engineering. Engineer Manual No. 1110-2-1612, Department of the Army, US Army Corps of Engineers, Washington, D.C.

# Hydrology of Mackenzie Delta Lakes

Philip Marsh
National Hydrology Research Institute
Environment Canada
11 Innovation Blvd.
Saskatoon, Saskatchewan
S7N 3H5

## Abstract

The Mackenzie Delta is dominated by a vast number of lakes which occur throughout its entire 200 by 165 km extent. These lakes play a significant role in the delta ecosystem. They affect the distribution of permafrost, support large populations of fish, waterfowl and mammals, and provide storage for water, sediment, and pollutants. The hydrologic regime of these lakes is the driving force for this complex, productive ecosystem.

From a hydrologic point of view all lakes are dominated by the Mackenzie River spring flood, but variations in the sill elevation separating the lakes and main river channel produce significant differences in lake regime. Low sill-elevation lakes experience a continuous inflow and outflow of water throughout the summer. Moderate sill-elevation lakes are flooded once per year at most, and the highest sill-elevation lakes are flooded only every few years.

The water balance of the low sill-elevation lakes is dominated by channel discharge, while other water balance components take on added significance in the higher sill-elevation lakes. In these high sill-elevation lakes, evaporation is greater than summer precipitation and without flooding they experience a negative water balance and would eventually disappear.

Further work is required to improve our understanding of the linkages between the hydrologic regime of these lakes and the flora and fauna, in order to be able to predict the environmental impact of future development in the Mackenzie Basin. This includes, but is not limited to, the effect of flow regulation and the introduction of pollutants.

## Introduction

The Mackenzie Delta is the largest active delta in Canada and is also one of the most northerly (Fig. 1). Despite its latitude (67° 30'N to 69° 30'N), it is a very productive ecosystem with large populations of fish, mammals, and waterfowl, and with the treeline close to its most northerly limit. The richness of this northern alluvial ecosystem is related to the complex relationships between a number of physical and biological processes (Peterson et al. 1981). The main driving force is the Mackenzie River which introduces large amounts of water (Marsh 1986), energy (Findlay 1981), and sediment to the Delta (Peterson et al. 1981).

As development proceeds in the Mackenzie Basin, the relationships between water, sediment, energy, and the flora and fauna may be disturbed with potentially severe consequences. In order to predict and to minimize the environmental impact of ongoing or future developments, it is necessary to understand the processes linking the physical and biological portions of the ecosystem. The initial link in this complex ecosystem, the hydrological cycle, is the subject of this paper.

The following sections present a generalized discussion of lakes in the Mackenzie Delta. This includes a description of the physical characteristics of lakes, the processes controlling those physical conditions, and finally the hydrological regime of a variety of lakes.

## The Mackenzie Delta

The Mackenzie Delta is approximately 200 km long, 65 km wide (Fig. 1) and covers an area of 12,000 km$^2$. Mackay (1963) provides the most complete description of the physical environment of the Mackenzie Delta region. The Mackenzie River, the largest in Canada draining 1.6 million km$^2$, is the primary source of water to the delta. It has a mean annual discharge of 9,600 m$^3$/s and a maximum monthly discharge of 21,900 m$^3$/s in June (Mackenzie River above Arctic Red River, Environment Canada 1980). The Arctic Red River and the Peel River also provide significant flow to the Mackenzie Delta with mean annual discharges of 145 and 776 m$^3$/s respectively (Environment Canada 1980).

The major hydrologic event of the year is the spring break-up in mid May. At this time the air temperature at Inuvik rises above 0°C (Atmospheric Environment Service 1982a), snowmelt and the first deterioration of ice on the Mackenzie River East Channel are initiated, and the water level in the Mackenzie River begins to rise as meltwater from the southern portions of the basin reaches the Mackenzie Delta. Eventually the ice begins to shift, moves downstream and ice jams occur. The river is clear of ice by mid-June. The combination of high discharge and ice jams results in the highest water levels of the year. As floodwater enters the lakes, the ice melts rapidly and the lakes are usually ice free by early to mid-June.

Air temperature falls below 0°C in late September (Atmospheric Environment Service 1982a) and the lakes freeze shortly afterwards. The first permanent ice forms on the Mackenzie River East Channel at Inuvik by October 11 on average, and it is completely frozen by October 19 (Allen 1977).

## Physical Characteristics of Mackenzie Delta Lakes

The tremendous diversity of lakes in the Mackenzie Delta is illustrated in Fig. 2. They vary greatly in size, shape, and channel connection, and cover a significant portion of the delta surface. An analysis of aerial photographs for a typical 70 km$^2$ area south west of Inuvik, NWT showed that 282 lakes covered 50% of the surveyed area, with a lake density of 4.03 lakes per km$^2$. Mackay (1963) found that lakes covered from 5% of the area in the outer delta to 50% of the area in the middle parts of the delta.

Lakes in the delta vary in length from less than a hundred metres up to 8 km. They are larger in the younger, outer portions of the Delta and smaller in the older, upper portions of the Delta (Mackay 1963). In a given location, there are a small number of larger lakes and many small lakes (Fig. 2). Near Inuvik for example, 61 lakes cover 39% of the area while 207 cover only 8% of the area. The relative abundance of large and small lakes is controlled by the combined processes of delta cutoff and levee development described later. The size of the lakes discussed in this paper are given in Fig. 2.

These delta lakes are very shallow. In mid-summer NRC Lake (Fig. 2), has a maximum depth of 1.6 m and a mean depth of 0.88 m., while South Lake (Fig. 2) has a maximum depth of 3.5 m and a mean depth of 1.46 m. The ice cover on these lakes is not as thick as would be expected for lakes at this latitude. In May 1985 for example, the mean ice thickness at NRC Lake was only 0.72 m., leaving a maximum of 0.88 m of unfrozen water beneath the ice.

### Processes Controlling Lake Characteristics

Delta lakes are not static features, but are dynamic components of the ever changing delta floodplain. The following section outlines the major processes controlling lake change within the main body of the delta. It does not include processes operating at the seaward edge of the delta.

**Channel abandonment:** Small delta channels are occasionally cut off from nearby main channels as silting blocks the channel entrance or when a neck of a loop is breached (Mackay 1963). The result is an easily recognized long, narrow lake (Fig. 2). Sedimentation eventually infills the lake, leaving only small lakes (Fig. 3) located in the deepest portions of the original channel. As Gill (1971) noted, these abandoned channels develop and retain a

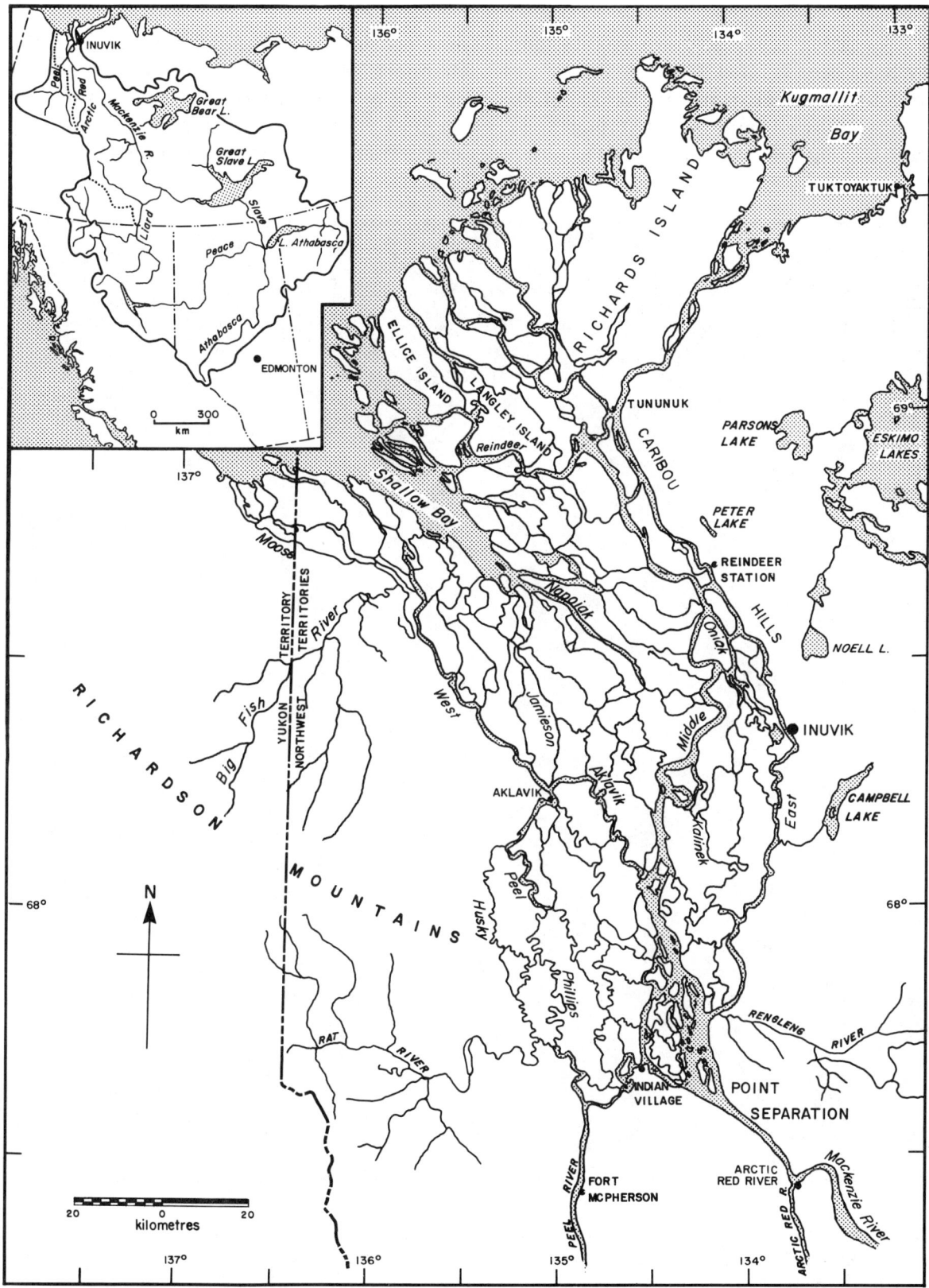

Figure 1    Location map of the Mackenzie Delta. The study area is located 5 km SW of Inuvik.

different vegetation cover and are visible long after they have been infilled.

**Point bar development:** Lakes often develop in the swell and swale topography (American Geological Institute 1974) which develops on the inside edge of migrating river channels (Mackay 1963). These lakes are long, narrow and curved to a radius similar to the original channel bend (Fig. 2). They range in length from tens of metres to a few kilometres.

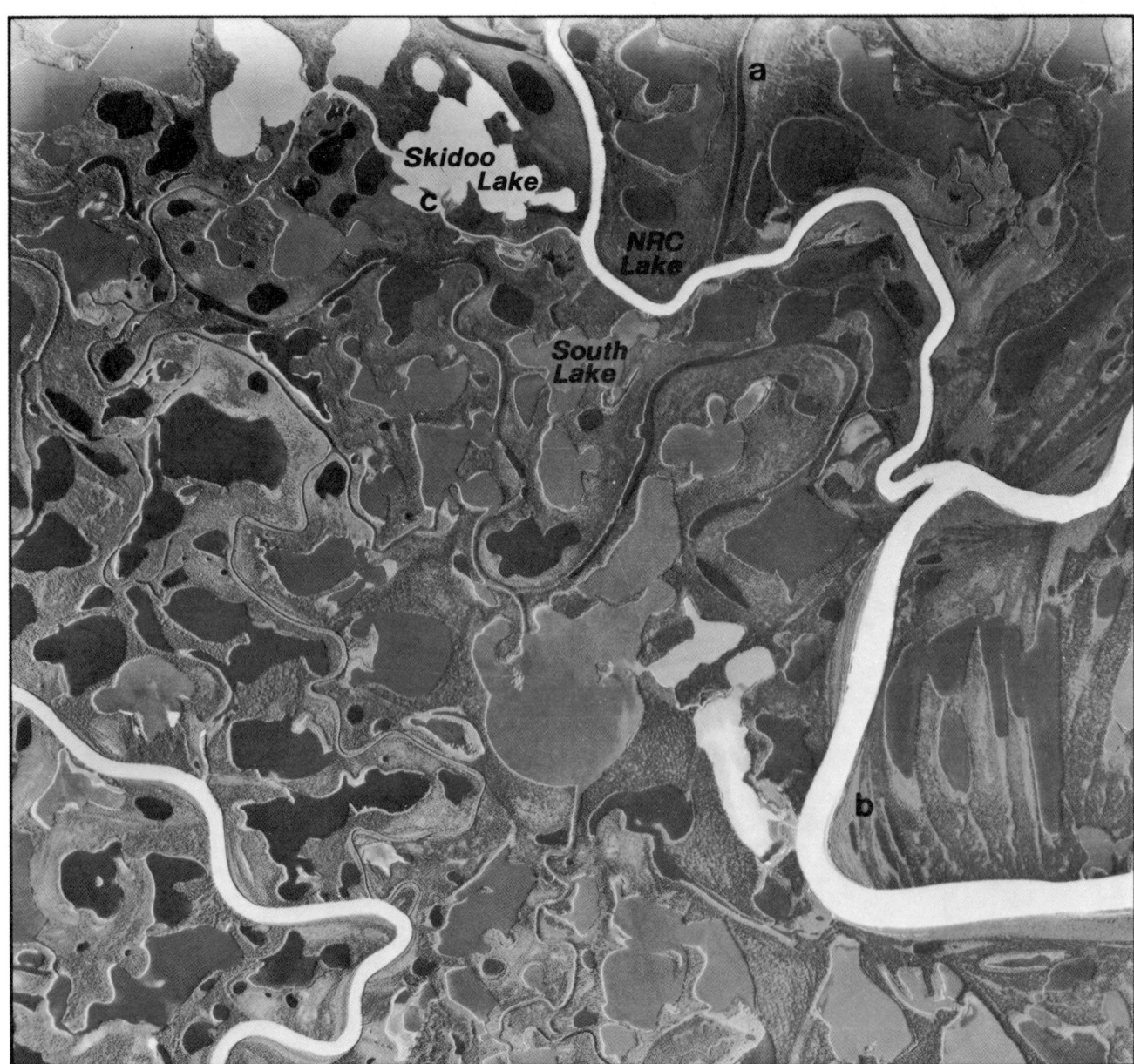

Figure 2   Aerial photograph of the study area showing the three study lakes. Lake sizes are: NRC Lake — .3 km in length and 0.069 km² in area, South Lake — 1.4 km in length and 0.44 km² in area, and Skidoo Lake — 1.2 km in length and 0.51 km² in area. Also shown are lakes formed by channel abandonment (a) and point bar development (b), and a reverse delta (c).

Figure 3   Small lakes formed in an abandoned channel.

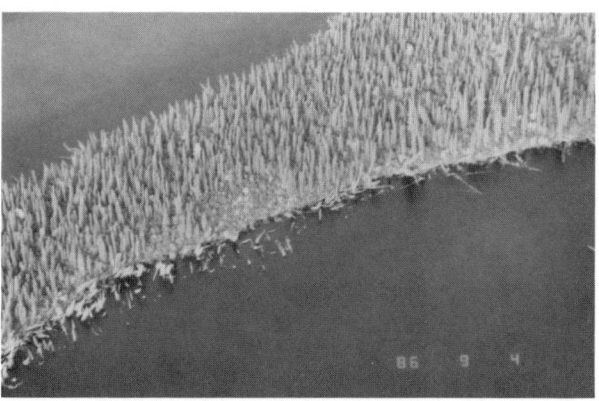

Figure 4   Shoreline retreat due to thermal erosion of a lake bank.

**Thermokarst:** Melting of ice-rich lake banks results in bank slumping and the retreat of the shoreline. In forested portions of the Mackenzie Delta, this process is indicated by trees leaning towards the lake and a large number of trees in the lake (Fig. 4).

**Delta cut-off lakes:** Small deltas form where channels enter lakes (Fig. 2 and 5). Gill (1971) called these reverse deltas. These deltas grow into the lake and eventually cut the original lake into a number of smaller lakes. The result is to increase the number of lakes and to decrease lake size.

**Levee development:** The rate of sedimentation on the Mackenzie Delta floodplain is dependent on the proximity to the river channel. Since the rate of sedimentation is greatest closest to the river channel, interchannel depressions are gradually deepened to form a bowl-shaped basin with a lake in the central low. The levee, which parallels the channel, is normally the highest portion of the basin. These levees are breached in one or two places to form a channel linking the lake to a nearby lake or channel. Figure 6 illustrates a typical levee basin situation.

**Sedimentation:** When sediment laden Mackenzie River water enters a lake, a portion of the suspended load is deposited. Lake to lake variations in amount of sediment deposited are dependent on their proximity to a main channel. This can be seen in Fig. 2 where water with a high suspended sediment concentration is light

Figure 5   Development of a reverse delta into a lake, illustrating the formation of delta cut off lakes.

in colour and water with a low concentration appears dark. Within lake variations depend on the location of inflow channels and lake currents. The rate of sedimentation in Mackenzie Delta lakes, the variation from lake to lake, or the within lake variations are unknown at present.

**Channel migration:** As channels migrate within the Mackenzie Delta (Lapointe 1984) they encroach upon delta lakes (Fig. 7). When the land between the lake and channel is breached, the lake is either drained if it is perched above the channel level, or the lake becomes connected to the river channel if it is near the channel level.

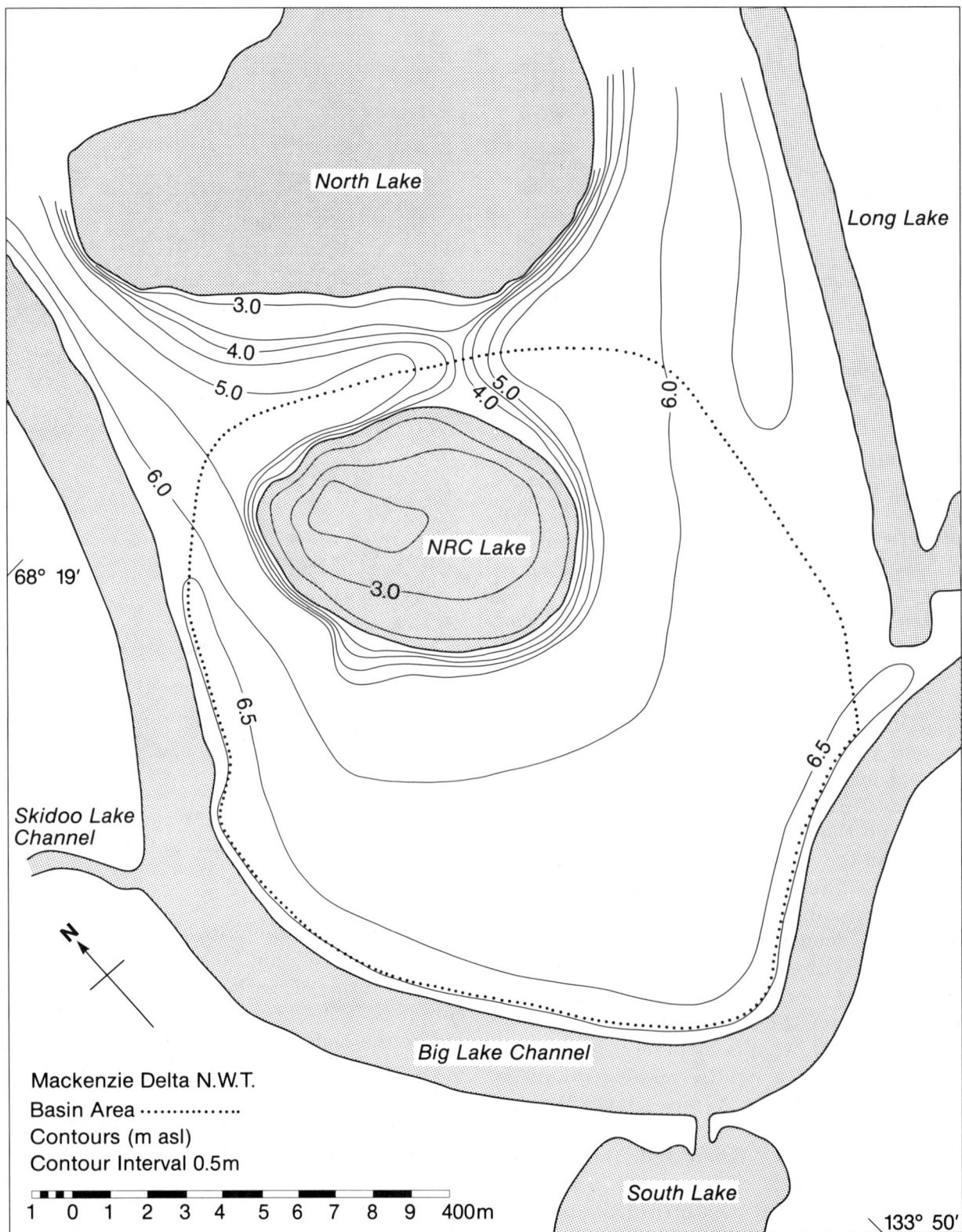

Figure 6  Topographic map of NRC Lake basin. This is a typical example of a levee basin lake.

Figure 7  Channel migration encroaching upon delta lakes. This process is responsible for the destruction of many lakes.

Changes in the physical characteristics of delta lakes are not governed by single processes but by a combination of the above processes and therefore the rate of change of lake characteristics, or the effect of these changes on the utilization of the lake by the flora and fauna.

## Hydrologic Regime of Mackenzie Delta Lakes

### Factors influencing the hydrologic regime

The hydrologic regime of lakes in the Mackenzie Delta is controlled by the water balance components shown in Fig. 8 and given by

(1)   $P + E + Q_o + Q_{in} + Q_{sp} + Q_{sb} + Q_s = ds/dt$

where P is precipitation on the lake surface, E is evaporation from the lake surface, $Q_o$ and $Q_{in}$ are channel discharge into and out of the lake, $Q_{sp}$ and $Q_s$ are suprapermafrost groundwater and surface rill flow from the surrounding basin, $Q_{sb}$ is subpermafrost groundwater flow through the talik beneath the lake, and ds/dt is the change in lake storage. In all cases the terms have positive values when water is added to the lake and negative when removed from the lake. Methods for measuring and calculating the terms in equation 1 are given by Marsh (1986).

The magnitude of P, E, $Q_{sp}$, and $Q_s$ are similar for nearby lakes and the $Q_{sb}$ term is close to zero (Marsh 1986). Channel discharge ($Q_{in}$, $Q_o$) however, varies greatly from lake to lake. It is controlled by the relative height of the Mackenzie River water level and the lake sill, where the sill is defined as the highest elevation along the channel thalweg (Fig. 8). Variations in regime from lake to lake are due primarily to variations in discharge, and therefore related almost entirely to sill elevation.

The sill elevation of lakes varies significantly. Near Inuvik, for example, sill elevations range from less than 2.5 m above mean sea level (amsl) to over 5.5 m amsl, with a modal value of 3.75 m amsl (Fig. 9). The important point is that the distribution of sill elevations is continuous between the low and high extremes (Fig. 9). As a result there is a continuum of regime types. For comparison, typical Mackenzie River water levels are 1.5 m amsl in early spring, 4.5 to 6.5 m amsl during the spring peak, 2.0 to 3.0 m amsl during the summer, and less than 2 m amsl during the fall and winter.

In the following section the hydrologic regime of 4 lakes will be discussed. These are: (1) Skidoo and South Lakes which have sills of less than 2 m amsl, (2) NRC Lake which has a sill of 3.8 m amsl and (3) Dishwater Lake with a sill of over 9 m amsl. Because Dishwater Lake is located about 50 km south west of Inuvik (Bigras 1985), the sill elevation cannot be directly compared to those near Inuvik. However, it has a hydrologic regime similar to lakes near Inuvik with a sill elevation of >6.5 m amsl.

### Hydrologic regime

**Low sill-elevation lakes:** For these lakes, the water level begins to rise in late May when the main channel level overtops the sill. Levels rise rapidly to a peak in early June and then quickly decline (Fig. 10). Over the summer, the overall pattern is for a general decline in level, with small peaks superimposed upon it.

The pattern of channel discharge into and out of these low sill-elevation lakes varies greatly from lake to lake. Lakes with two connecting channels (i.e., Skidoo Lake, Fig. 2) act as a throughflow system. One channel is

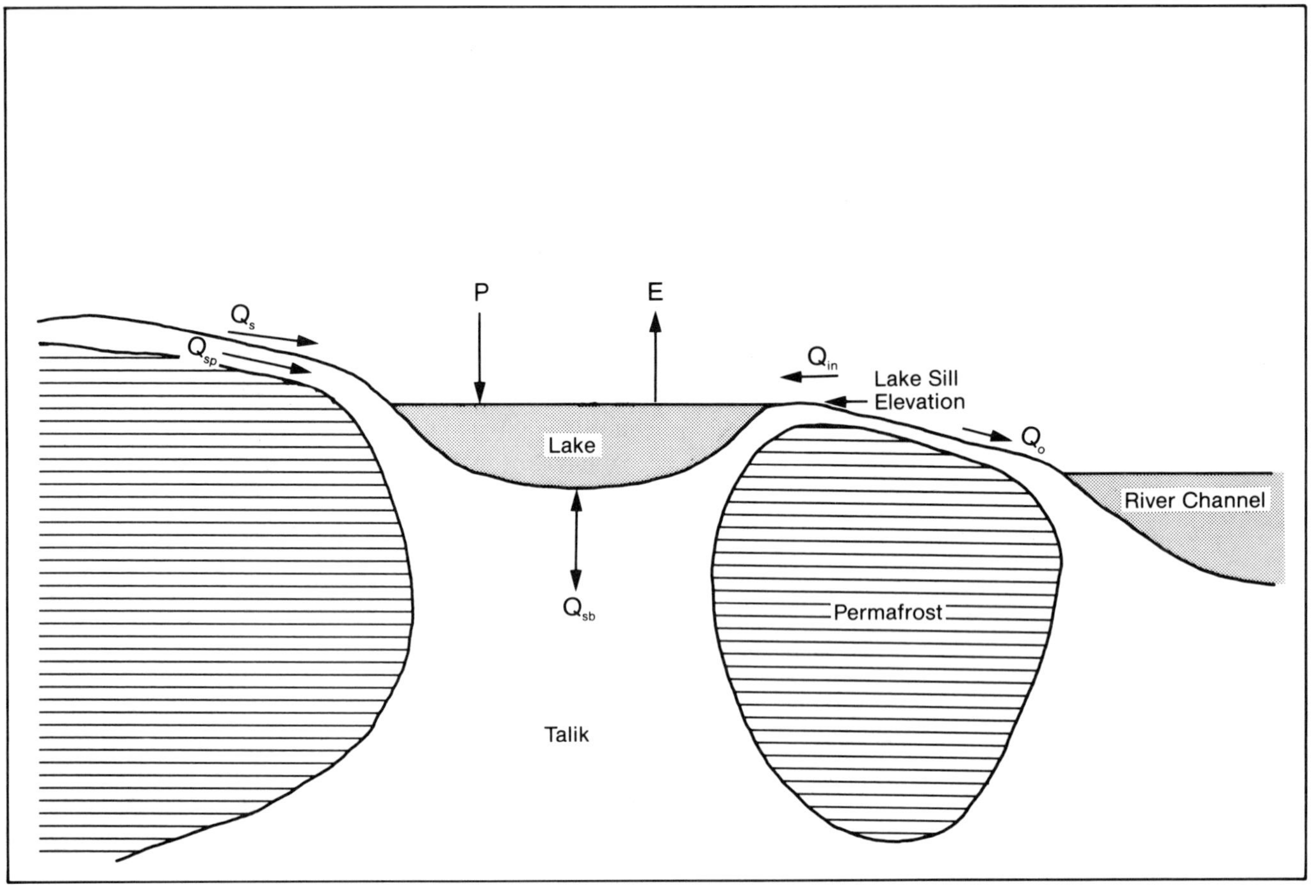

Figure 8   Water balance components for a typical delta lake.

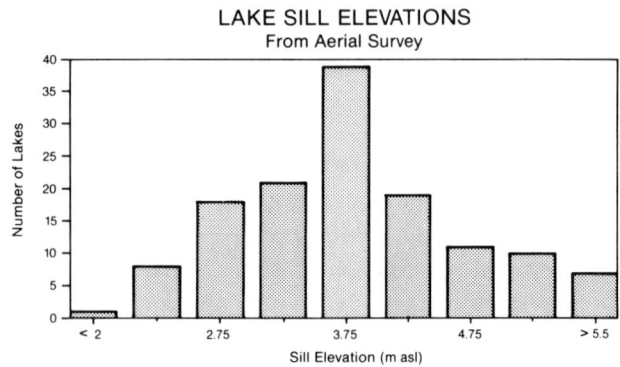

Figure 9   Sill elevations for lakes in the study area. These were obtained by a spring aerial survey of the timing of lake flooding, in conjunction with measured channel water level.

generally flowing into the lake and the other out of the lake, but the flow direction does change (Fig. 10 and 11). The flow direction is dependent on the relative water level of the two main channels feeding the lake system. Lakes with a single connecting channel (i.e. South Lake, Fig. 2) act as a pulsating system with rapid variations in channel discharge (Fig. 10 and 11). The flow direction in this case is controlled by the relative level of the lake and main channel.

The water balance of low sill-elevation lakes is dominated by channel discharge. The other components are of minor importance.

**Moderate sill-elevation lakes:** NRC Lake has a simpler water level and discharge regime than the low sill-elevation lakes (Fig. 12).

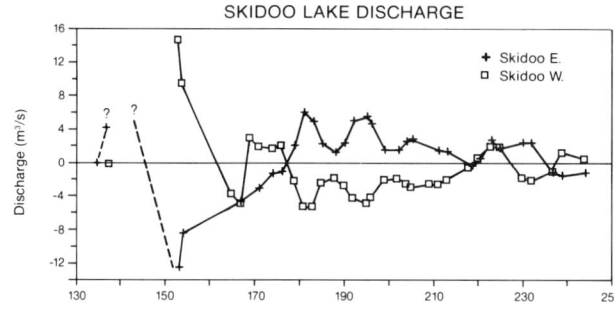

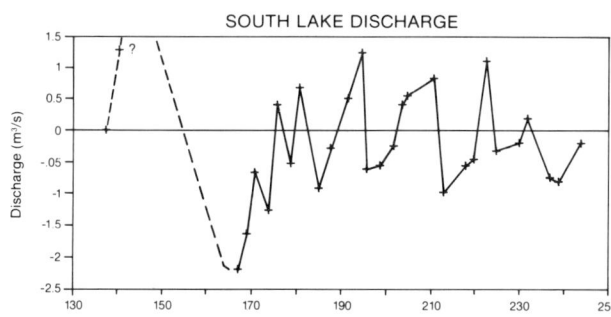

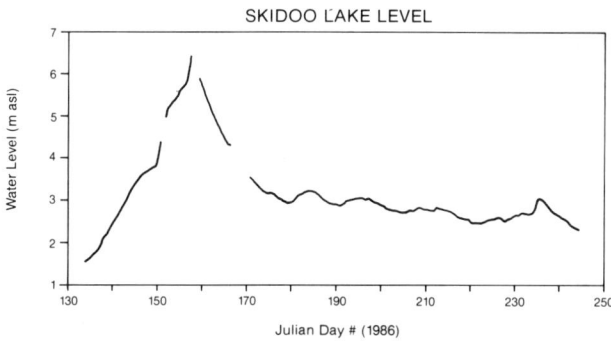

Figure 10  Water level for Skidoo Lake and channel discharge for both Skidoo Lake and South Lake. Note that Skidoo Lake has two channels entering the lake (Fig. 2). Discharge into the lake has a positive value, and out of the lake a negative value.

Water level begins to rise later in the spring, but once the lake sill is overtopped, the water level is similar to the low sill-elevation lakes. After the spring peak, levels decline rapidly until they approach the sill elevation. For the remainder of the summer, levels decrease slowly with only occasional, very small rainfall induced rises. Channel discharge is simply into the lake until

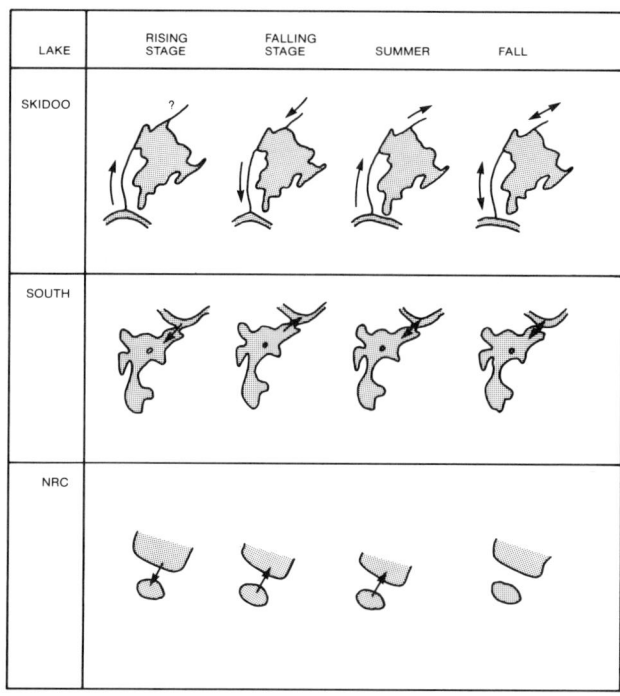

Figure 11  Simplified flow directions for Skidoo, South, and NRC Lakes for the summer of 1986. Arrows indicated flow direction in the channels.

the peak water level is reached, and then out of the lake until discharge ceases when lake level falls below the sill elevation.

The annual water balance of these lakes is dominated by channel discharge, but other components of the lakes water balance take on added importance compared to the low sill-elevation lakes. The water balance of NRC Lake for May to September 1985 (Table 1) may be divided into three distinct intervals with each dominated by a different process. These are: (1) the flooding period when lake level is controlled by the Mackenzie River level (May 21 to June 9), (2) the discharge period when channel discharge out of the lake is controlled by the outlet channel geometry (June 9 to August 4), and (3) the evaporation period when channel discharge has ceased (August 4 to September 1).

During the flooding period, discharge into and out of the lake is very large (Table 1). Snowmelt runoff from the surrounding land ($Q_{sp}$, $Q_s$) was close to zero due to the large

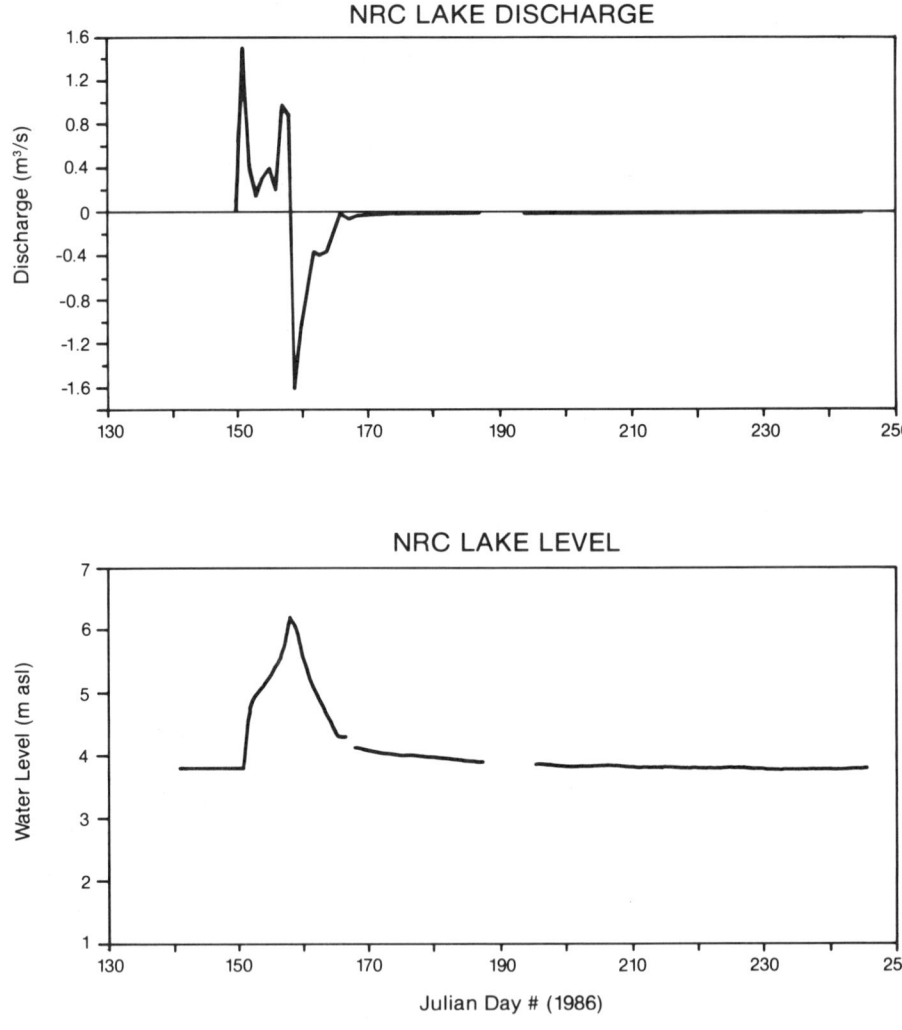

Figure 12  Water level and channel discharge for NRC Lake.

Table 1  **Water balance, NRC Lake 1985. All units are in mm.**

|  | Inputs | | | | | Outputs | | | error |
|---|---|---|---|---|---|---|---|---|---|
| Date | P | $Q_{sp}$ | $Q_s$ | $Q_{in}$ | $Q_{sb}$ | $Q_o$ | E | ds/dt | e |
| May 21 – June 9 | 5 | 0 | 0 | 2578 | 0 | 2113 | 0 | 465 | -5 |
| June 9 – Aug 4 | 22 | 9 | 239 | 0 | 0 | -579 | -185 | -437 | 56 |
| Aug 4 – Sept 1 | 4 | 0 | 0 | 0 | 0 | 0 | -60 | -62 | -6 |
| Total | 31 | 9 | 239 | 2578 | 0 | -2692 | -245 | -34 | 45 |

infiltration capacity of the frozen soils, and lake evaporation was limited by the lake ice cover. Over this period the lake storage term increased.

Over the second period (Table 1), discharge from the lake dominated the water balance. The $Q_{sp}$ and $Q_s$ terms increased as Mackenzie River flood water drained from the surrounding basin. This water was not snowmelt or rainfall runoff. Evaporation was important after the lake ice cover was removed. During this time interval lake storage declined.

After August 4 the lake level fell below the sill, discharge ceased and the land surrounding the basin dried so that $Q_{sp}$ and $Q_s$ fell to zero. The only inputs and outputs were precipitation and evaporation. Evaporation was significantly larger than precipitation and the lake experienced a negative water balance and lake level slowly declined.

Even though it received a large volume of floodwater in 1985, NRC Lake experienced a decline in lake storage over the summer period (Table 1). Mackenzie River floodwater, including $Q_{in}$, $Q_{sb}$, and $Q_s$, was responsible for 2826 mm of water input to the lake. The only other source of water was precipitation on the lake surface which totalled 31 mm. This was less than the 30 year normal of 101 mm for the AES Inuvik Airport weather station (Atmospheric Environment Service 1982b). The only outputs were discharge (-2692 mm) and evaporation (-245 mm). The evaporation is larger than the mean annual lake evaporation of 180 mm reported in the Hydrological Atlas of Canada (Fisheries and Environment Canada 1978) for the Inuvik area. It is interesting to note that the evaporation from NRC Lake in 1985 is greater than the normal summer precipitation and nearly as large as the normal annual precipitation (266 mm) at Inuvik (Atmospheric Environment Service 1982b).

**High sill-elevation lakes:** The sill of these lakes is not overtopped annually, but only during high flood years. Dishwater Lake for example, was last flooded in June 1982 (Bigras 1985) when Mackenzie River water filled the lake basin (Fig. 13). Since June 1982, the lake level has continued to decline at an average rate of 320 mm/year. The water balance of this lake during non-flooding years is dominated by the balance between evaporation and precipitation. Complete water balance data are not available for Dishwater Lake, but the NRC Lake water balance for 1985 can be used to illustrate typical conditions for a high sill-elevation lake. As shown in the previous section, without flooding, the only input is precipitation and the only output evaporation. Since evaporation is greater than precipitation, the lake experiences a strongly negative water balance and as shown for Dishwater Lake (Fig. 13), the lake level declines

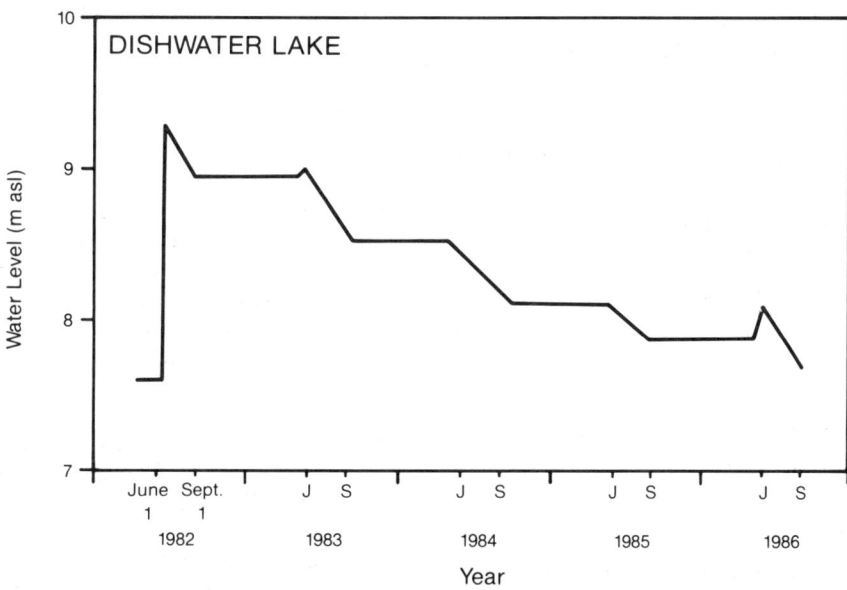

Figure 13 Water level for Dishwater Lake for the period June 1982 to September 1986.

at a steady rate. This will continue until the lake is dry, or it is once again flooded by the Mackenzie River. Without flooding, the lakes would disappear.

## Discussion

As Gill (1971) and Peterson et al. (1981) have emphasized, it is the integrated web of hydrological, fluvial, and biological processes which are responsible for the richness and diversity of the flora and fauna of the delta. However, many of the interrelationships among hydrological conditions and sedimentation, nutrient input, water depth at freeze-up and below the winter ice cover, ice cover melt, water temperature, and biological activity are unknown.

Future development in the Mackenzie River Basin will undoubtedly affect these interrelationships, but the overall impact on the ecosystem is unknown. For example, regulation of the Mackenzie River flow by a dam downstream of Great Slave Lake or on the Liard River, would change the hydrological regime of lakes in the delta. The following are a few concerns:

(1) reduction of discharge during spring break-up would reduce peak water levels in the Delta and decrease the frequency and duration of flooding of the moderate and high sill-elevation lakes. The effect on lake productivity is unknown. In the extreme case, high sill-elevation lakes would not be flooded and would disappear within a few years. Similar problems were encountered in the Peace-Athabasca Delta after the construction of the W.A.C. Bennet Dam in 1968.

(2) Fluctuations in Mackenzie River levels during summer control the movement of water into and out of low sill-elevation lakes. Changes in the Mackenzie regime would upset the natural discharge pattern. The effect on the lakes is unknown.

(3) Lake sill elevations are controlled by the hydrological and sedimentation regime of the connecting channels. Changes in connecting channel discharge may change the sill elevation. The relationships controlling sill elevation are unknown.

(4) The ice cover of delta lakes is removed quickly by the influx of relatively warm flood-water. If the spring flooding regime is altered, the development of open water in the lakes and the warming of the lake water would be delayed. The effect on waterfowl, mammals, and fish is not known.

Future development in the Mackenzie River Basin will also increase the input of pollutants into the river. Many large rivers throughout Canada are used as cheap, convenient "sewers" to carry pollutants to the ocean. Because of the Mackenzie Delta, the Mackenzie River does not provide this "easy" solution. Pollutants in the Mackenzie will be redistributed throughout the delta channel and lake network by the vast system of distributary channels. The number of lakes affected and the residency time of pollutants will depend on (1) the river stage, (2) whether the stage is rising or falling, and (4) the time of year. More information on the hydrological regime of Mackenzie Delta lakes is required in order to estimate the effect on the lakes under different flow conditions.

The Mackenzie Delta is a unique northern ecosystem. The biological richness of this area is significantly affected by the hydrological regime of the Mackenzie River and the delta lakes. To avoid future environmental problems in this area, much research is required not only on the hydrology and the biology of the delta, but also on the interactions between these two processes.

## References

Atmospheric Environment Service
1982a    Canadian climate normals. Vol. 2. Temperature 1951-1980. Environment Canada. 306 pp.
1982b    Canadian climate normals. Vol. 3. Precipitation 1951-1980. Environment Canada. 602 pp.

Allen, G.D.
1977    Freeze-up, break-up and ice thickness in Canada. Atmospheric Environment, Publication CLI-1-77, 185 pp.

American Geological Institute.
1974    Dictionary of geological terms. Anchor Press/Doubleday, Garden City, New York, 545 pp.

Bigras, S.C.
1985 Lake regimes. Mackenzie Delta, NWT, 1981. National Hydrology Research Institute, Internal Report, Environment Canada, Ottawa, 39 pp.

Environment Canada
1980 Historical streamflow summary, Yukon and Northwest Territories. Inland Waters Directorate, Water Resources Branch, Ottawa, 96 pp.

Findlay, B.F.
1981 Natural energy present during the thaw season in the Mackenzie Delta, NWT: A general assessment. In: Mackenzie River Basin Committee, Spring Break-up, Mackenzie River Basin Study Report Supplement 3.

Fisheries and Environment Canada
1978 Hydrological atlas of Canada. Supply and Services Canada, Ottawa, Canada.

Gill, D.
1971 Vegetation and environment in the Mackenzie River Delta, NWT A study in sub-Arctic ecology. University of British Columbia, Ph.D. Thesis, 694 pp.

Lapointe, M.F.
1984 Patterns and processes of channel change, Mackenzie Delta, NWT, 1983-84 progress report. National Hydrology Research Institute, Internal Report, Environment Canada, Ottawa, 52 pp.

Mackay, J.R.
1963 The Mackenzie Delta area, NWT, Geol. Survey of Canada Misc. Report 23, 202 pp.

Marsh, P.
1986 Modelling water levels for a lake in the Mackenzie Delta. Cold Regions Hydrology Symposium, American Water Resources Association, Fairbanks, Alaska, 23-29.

Peterson, L.M. Allison, and R.D. Kabzems
1981 Alluvial Ecosystems. In: Mackenzie River Basin Committee, Mackenzie River Basin Study Report Supplement 2, 129 pp.

# Freeze-Up and Break-up of Ice Cover on Small Arctic Lakes

Ming-ko Woo
Department of Geography
McMaster University
Hamilton, Ontario
and
Richard Heron
Department of Geography
Carlton University
Ottawa, Ontario

## Abstract

Lakes in the Canadian Arctic are ice-covered for eight months or more in each year. The ice growth rate is strongly affected by snow cover and the ice thickness is predictable using heat conduction equations. In the Arctic Islands, maximum thickness reaches 2.5 m in the windswept, snow-free areas. Break-up involves thermal and mechanical processes. At Resolute, NWT, it was found that 40% of ice ablation occurred at the upper ice surface, 10% at the bottom, and the rest involved internal melting of the ice. Once the ice cover has fractured, decay is accelerated by mechanical action, enhanced by a weakening of the ice structure through internal melt. A regional survey showed that larger lakes at higher elevations may retain an incomplete multi-year ice cover throughout several summers. While the process-oriented approach produces superior results in ice prediction, the cost of acquiring the requisite meteorological data may necessitate the usage of empirically based, but simpler, degree-day techniques.

## Introduction

The Canadian Arctic, considered as the area north of the tree-line (Bird 1967) comprises the northern edge of the continental land mass and the Arctic archipelago. This vast area has varied topography ranging from low-lying coastal plains in the northwest, plateaus and rolling uplands, to rugged mountains in the east. The climate is extremely harsh, with permafrost continuously underlying the ground at shallow depths. Snow and ice cover the land surface for 8-10 months in each year.

Numerous lakes occupy this region. These lakes acquire a lengthy seasonal ice cover (Fig. 1). This paper will examine the physical processes leading to the formation and decay of ice on small lakes. The presence of a lake ice cover affects the access to water supplies for many northern communities; and the freezing and thawing of the ice influence the temperature and chemical regimes within lakes which have significant implications upon the aquatic ecology (Hobbie 1975; Rigler 1978).

## Ice Regime

Three broad types of ice may be recognized on small Arctic lakes. Transparent, clear ice, formed by the freezing of lake water due to heat loss, is also known as "black" ice because one can see through this ice to the darker lake water or lake bed. White ice, which is due to the incorporation of snow or ice particles (frazil ice) in the ice cover, appears to be white because it reflects the sunlight. In some lakes, remnants of ice from previous winters can linger on to form multi-year ice which exhibits evidence of partial summer thawing and fracturing.

The ice regime, or the average seasonal pattern of ice cover changes, for several Arctic and subarctic lakes during the course of a winter is shown in Fig. 2. Freezing begins after the air temperature has fallen below 0 C. The mean date of freeze-up is around late September for lakes in the Arctic Islands, but is progressively delayed southward. The duration of an ice cover is shortened, as one moves southward because of late freeze-up and early break-up. Thus, in the Queen Elizabeth Islands, ice cover duration averages about 10 months, and is reduced to 9 months in the Keewatin District (Fisheries and Environment Canada 1978). The shorter freezing season and the less severe winter coldness produce shallower ice in the subarctic. The mean lake ice thickness is 2.0 m in the Queen Elizabeth Islands, 1.8 m in the Keewatin, and 1.1 m in the subarctic.

The ice regime only indicates the long term mean conditions and does not reveal how the lake ice growth and decay respond to the thermal conditions specific to individual years or for particular lakes. To do so, a knowledge of freeze-up and break-up processes is needed.

## Ice Growth Processes

With a prolonged period of darkness, Arctic winters are characterized by tremendous heat losses so that ice growth often proceeds without interruption. The first several snow falls may be incorporated in the ice but with exceedingly low temperatures, a complete ice cover is quickly established. After that, there is little opportunity for the slushing of subsequent snowfalls and "black" ice constitutes a large portion of the ice cover.

Since there is little solar radiation input in winter to complicate matters, winter ice growth can be predicted by heat conduction alone. Heat is conducted from the warm lake water (at approximately 0°C or above) to the cold atmosphere (Fig. 3). As the water temperature falls below the freezing point, ice is formed. Heat loss is retarded by a snow cover on the ice because of the insulating property of snow (i.e. heat conductivity is low). These effects are summarized in the modified Stefan's equation which has frequently been used to predict ice growth in calm waters where heat loss to the cold atmosphere is achieved through heat conduction.

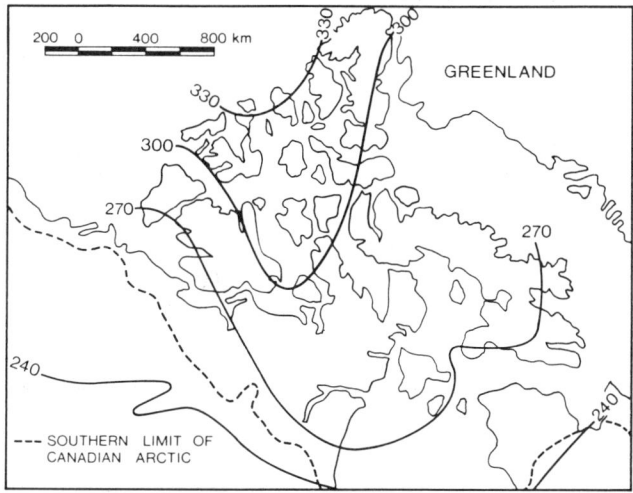

Figure 1   Duration of lake ice cover (in days) in the Canadian Arctic.

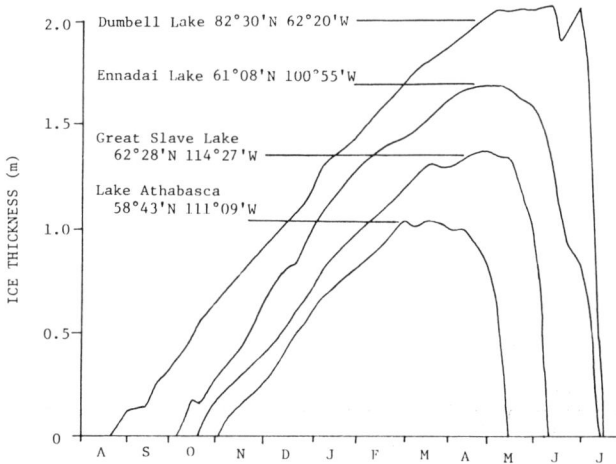

Figure 2   Ice regimes of selected lakes in Arctic and subarctic Canada.

$$\frac{\Delta h_i}{\Delta t} = \frac{(T_w - T_s)}{\rho_i L_f} \left[ \frac{h_i}{K_i} + \frac{h_s}{K_s} \right]^{-1} \quad (1)$$

Here, $\Delta h_i/\Delta t$ is the rate of ice growth, $T_s$ is snow surface temperature, approximated by the air temperature while $T_w$ is the freezing point of water, $h_i$ and $h_s$ are the snow and ice thicknesses, $\rho_i$ is ice density, taken as 910 kg/m³, $L_f$ is the latent heat of fusion, $K_i$ and $K_s$ are the thermal conductivity of ice and snow. Thermal conductivity of snow may be calculated from $k_s = 2.84 \times 10^{-6} \rho_s^2$ where $\rho_s$ is the snow density (Abels 1892).

To demonstrate the efficacy of eq. (1) as a predictor of ice growth, daily air temperature and snow cover data for Resolute, Cornwallis Island, NWT (74°43'N, 94°58'W) was used to estimate daily ice thickness for the winters of 1969-70 and 1971-72. The results are compared to the field measurements of ice thickness made at Char Lake located 2.5 km southeast of the weather station (Schindler et al. 1974). Despite the scatter in the observed data because of changing measurement locations from week to week, the predicted values agree closely with the observed points (Fig. 3). This suggests that the modified Stefan's equation offers a satisfactory approach to ice growth prediction for Arctic lakes.

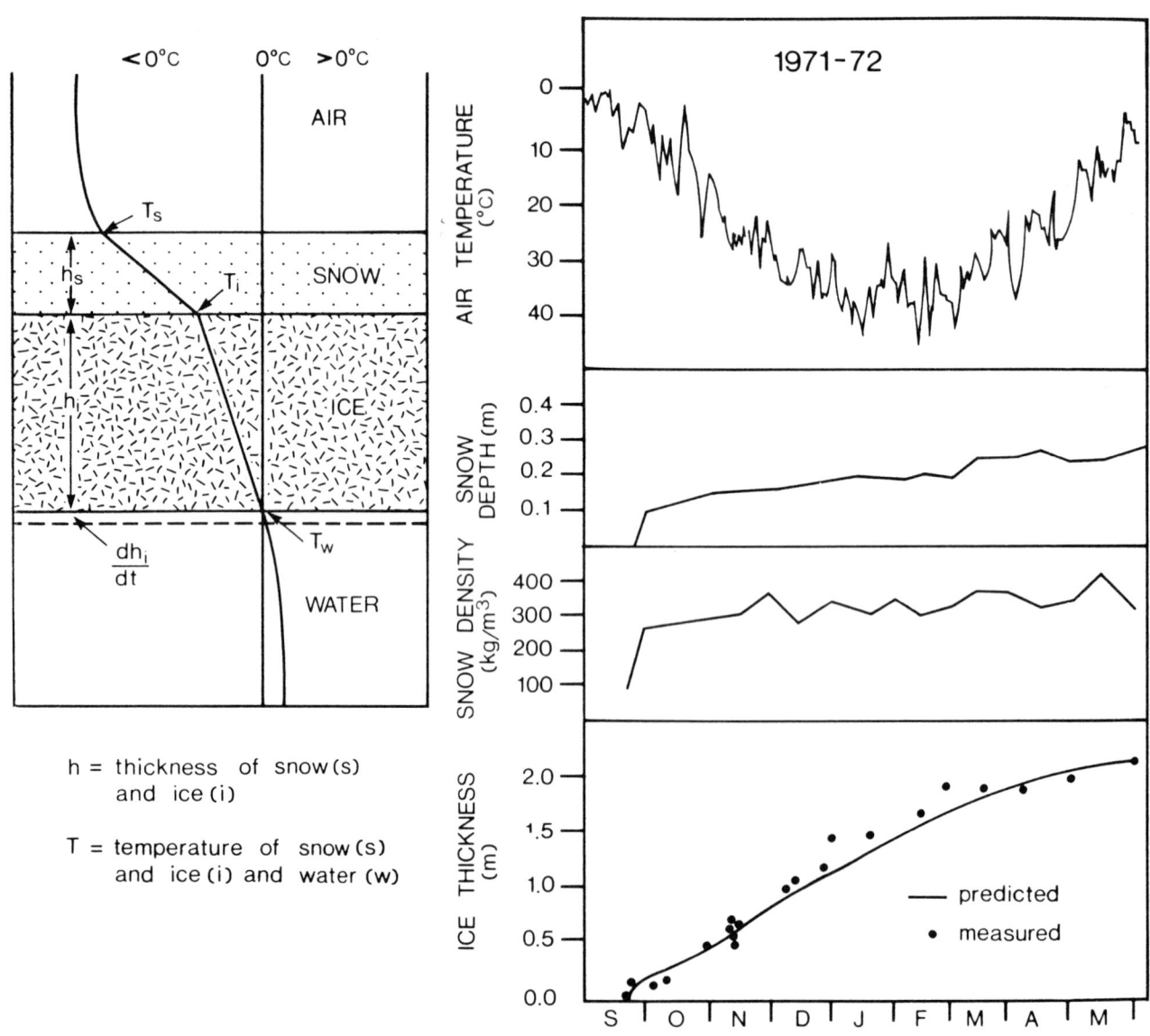

Figure 3  Diagrammatic representation of the Stefan's equation and the application of this equation to predict lake ice thickness for Char Lake, using air temperature and snow data from Resolute.

It is clear from eq. (1) that the depth of snow on the lake ice affects the maximum ice thickness that can be attained in a winter. This has been empirically verified elsewhere (Holtzmark 1965; Muguruma and Kikuchi 1963). Similar results were obtained at the lakes around Resolute. At the end of the 1978-79 winter, for example, the snow-free areas had a maximum observed ice thickness of 2.4 m. Ice thickness dropped to 2.0 m with a 0.2 m snow cover, decreasing further to 1.6 m when the snow depth was 0.5 m.

### Ice Decay Processes

The decay of a lake ice cover is due to melting and mechanical disintegration. Ice melt is controlled by the gains and losses of energy to the ice cover, and melting can be partitioned as follows:

$$M = M_{surface} + M_{bottom} + M_{internal} + M_{lateral} \quad (2)$$

where M denotes the amount of melt, and the subscripts are self explanatory. Figure 4 depicts the various melt components diagrammatically. Surface melt, including sublimation, is governed by the supply of radiation energy at the ice surface, the gains of sensible and latent heat, and the transfer of heat to the ice from rainfall. Internal melt is caused by the penetration of short-wave radiation into the ice. In this regard, white ice reflects more short-wave radiation and there is less radiation penetration (Roulet and

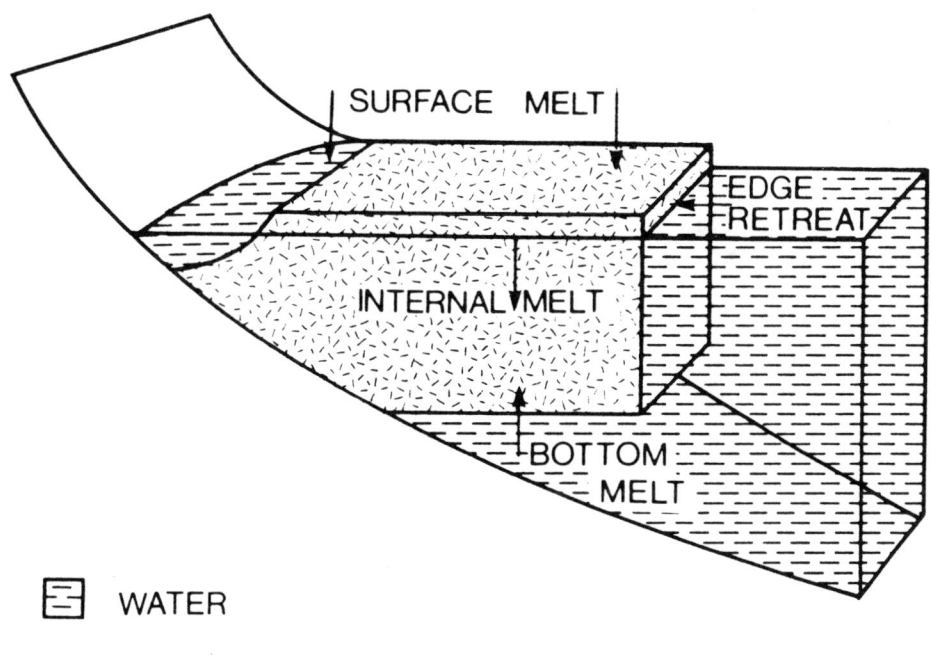

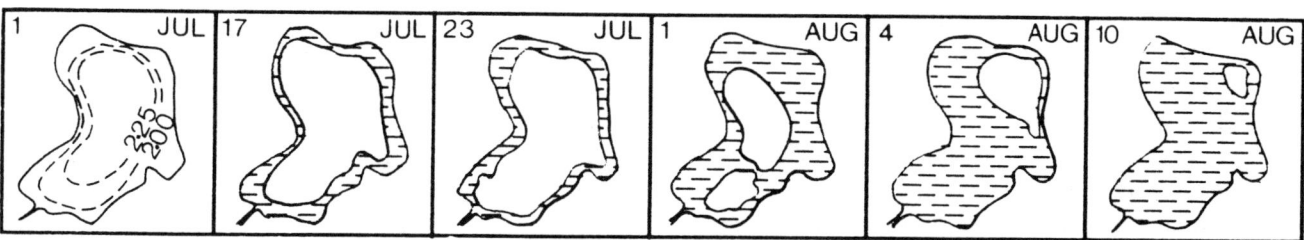

Figure 4  Ice melt components and the formation of a moat on Small Lake followed by ice fragmentation and disintegration during 1978.

Adams 1984). Bottom melt is produced by the contact of warm lake water with the base of the ice cover which thaws the ice. Where the ice is frozen to the lake bed, there is no bottom melt because the frozen ground is not a source of heat. Locally the lake ice may be covered with water from the hillslopes, from the ponding of meltwater, or from an upward seepage of lake water through major fissures in the ice. Then, direct surface melt as previously described is inhibited. Instead, if the surface water is kept warmer than the freezing point by radiative heating, the ice will be melted gradually by heat conducted from the water, and by radiation which penetrates the water. Lateral melting occurs only when the ice is fractured, where the warmer lake water that is in contact with the edge of the ice floe can thaw the ice.

The relative contribution of several melt components to the decay of lake ice may be illustrated by the information for Small Lake located about 5 km northwest of Resolute. In both 1980 and 1981 surface melt accounted for about 40% of total ablation. Internal melt represented about 50% and the remaining 10% was attributed to bottom melt.

Snowmelt often proceeds rapidly in spring, yielding considerable meltwater to the lakes before ice melt is complete (Woo et al. 1981). Snow meltwater from the basin slopes and from the ice cover soon floods the lake edges where the ice is often frozen to the bed. This creates a moat on the ice. Figure 4 shows a typical moat developed on the ice of Small Lake, during the course of a summer (1978). Some of the ponded water can drain through the ice via cracks and vertical holes (Williams 1968) to raise the lake water level. Being frozen to the bed along the edges, the ice will be arched by this rising lake level until the ice fractures near the hinge line or until enough heat is transmitted to the bottom-fast zone to release the ice from the bed. After this, the ice will be able to float freely on the lake (Fig. 5).

Freely floating ice is subject to fragmentation and attrition. This is facilitated by prolonged internal melting that etches micro-scale channels around individual ice crystals until the previously solid ice mass becomes a loose agglomeration of elongated, hexagonal crystals

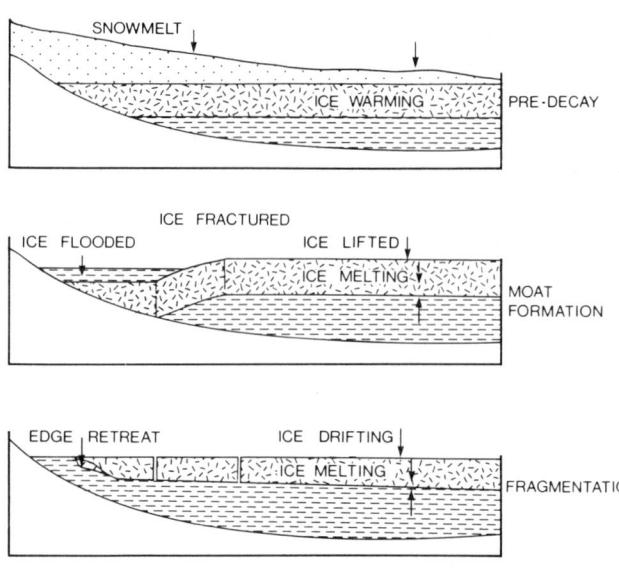

Figure 5 Stages in the melting, flooding and detachment of bottom-fast ice at the lake margin. Arrows indicates direction of ice decay.

known as candle ice. This ice crumbles easily when attacked by wave action, when driven against the shore or when the ice floes grind against each other. At this stage, ice edge retreat of as much as 12 m/d has been observed.

The processes of ice melt and mechanical disintegration continue until the ice disappears or until the summer ends. Any residual ice not melted completely will then be incorporated into the freshly formed ice cover. Whether an incomplete ice cover remains at the end of summer depends upon the coolness of the summer months, and upon the spatial disposition of the lake. A survey was carried out in September 1979 to determine the percentage of lake ice cover at the end of summer. Parts of Cornwallis and Devon Islands were flown over to determine the residual ice coverage (Fig. 6). Results indicate that ice remained on small lakes located at high altitudes because of the more frequent cloud cover and lower summer temperatures at the high elevations. Large lakes at low elevations also had residual ice floes because there was insufficient time to destroy completely the more extensive ice sheet. It is therefore not uncommon

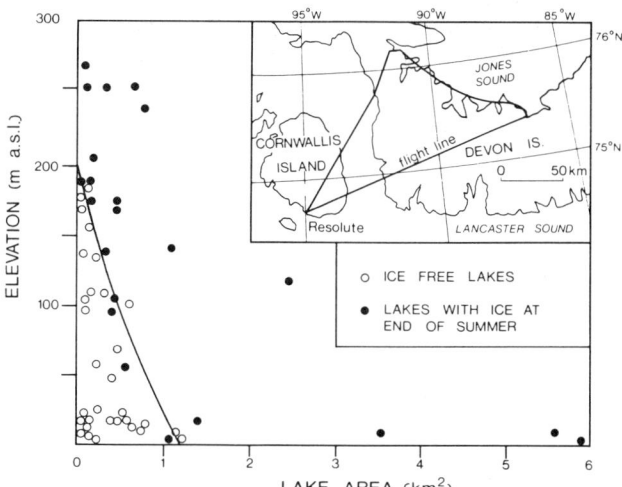

Figure 6   Relationship between lake area, lake elevation and residual ice cover at the end of summer, 1978, based on a flight over Cornwallis and Devon Islands.

to encounter multi-year ice on the lakes of Queen Elizabeth Islands, particularly in the eastern sector where the land is high.

## Discussion

The growth of ice in small Arctic lakes is a relatively straightforward process, involving mainly the cooling of water due to heat conduction. Ice grows continuously for 8 months or more in each year, with the maximum thickness attained not long before the break-up. Break-up processes are more complex, involving both thermal and mechanical actions.

One popular approach to predict ice growth and decay has been the use of degree day methods:

$$\Delta H/\Delta t = a(T_o - T_a)\Delta t \qquad (3a)$$

and

$$\Delta M/\Delta t = b(T_a - T_o)\Delta t \qquad (3b)$$

Here, $\Delta H/\Delta t$ and $\Delta M/\Delta t$ are the ice growth and ice decay rates, $T_a$ is mean air temperature for the period $\Delta t$, $T_o$ is a reference temperature above which ice decays and below which ice growth occurs. The values of a and b are empirically derived. This method is often successful in predicting ice growth (Bilello 1961) because it uses the same variable (air temperature) as the more meaningful Stefan's equation that has a physical basis. It may be argued that the Stefan's equation is preferable if snow data are available because the physically based equation is as easy to use as eq. (3a); but it is not site specific (i.e., not restricted by the empirical coefficient whose numerical value varies with location).

For break-up, eq. (3b) has been used (Bilello 1980; Ashton 1983) but not as satisfactorily because a wide assemblage of processes are indexed by air temperature alone. This approach is particularly unreliable for large lakes where mechanical action plays a significant role but cannot be accounted for by the temperature. However, although it is desirable to use the physically-based equations to predict break-up, a substantial meteorological data base has to be available. Thus, one has to consider the trade-off between the less accurate degree-day method and the superior but more demanding (and therefore more costly) process oriented approach.

## Acknowledgements

Financial support for this study was provided by a grant from the Natural Sciences and Engineering Research Council of Canada and by the Northern Training Grant. The Polar Continental Shelf Project offered generous logistical support for the research programme and the late Dr. F. Rigler made available to us the ice data from Char Lake.

## References

Abels, G.
1892   Measurements of snow density at Ekaterinburg during the winter of 1890-1891. Contribution to Vol. XLX of their memoirs of the Akademia Mauk.

Ashton, G.D.
1983   Lake ice decay. Cold Regions sci. and Technol. 8, 83-86.

Bilello, M.A.
1961    Formation, growth and decay of sea-ice in the Canadian Arctic archipelago. Arctic 14, 2-24.
1980    Maximum thickness and subsequent decay of lake, river and fast sea ice in Canada and Alaska. Cold Regions Research and Engineering Laboratory, Report 80-6, 160 p.

Bird, J.B.
1967    The Physiography of Arctic Canada. Johns Hopkins Press, Baltimore, Maryland, 336 p.

Fisheries and Environment Canada
1978    Hydrological Atlas of Canada, Department of Supply and Services, 38 maps.

Hobbie, J.E.
1973    Arctic limnology: a review. in Britton M.E. (ed), Alaska Arctic Tundra, Technical Paper No. 25, Arctic Institute of North America, 127-168.

Holtzmark, B.E.
1965    Insulating effect of a snow cover on the growth of young sea ice. Arctic 8, 60-65.

Muguruma, J. and K. Kikuchi
1963    Lake ice investigation at Peters Lake, Alaska. J. Glaciol. 4, 689-708.

Rigler, F.H.
1978    Limnology in the high Arctic: a case study of Char Lake. Verh. Internat. Verein. Limnol. 20, 127-140.

Roulet, N.T. and W.P. Adams
1984    Illustration of the spatial variability of light entering a lake using an empirical model. Hydrobiologia 109, 67-74.

Schindler, D.W., H.E. Welch, J. Kalff, G.J. Brunshill and N. Kritsch
1974    Physical and chemical limnology of Char Lake, Cornwallis Island (75 N Lat.). J. Fish. Res. Board Can. 31, 585-607.

Williams, G.P.
1968    Freeze-up and break-up of fresh water lakes. Ice Pressures Against Structures, Proc. of a conference at Laval University, 1966. National Research Council of Canada Technical Memorandum 92, 203-212.

Woo, M.K., R. Heron and P. Steer
1981.   Catchment hydrology of a High Arctic lake. Cold Region Sci. Technol. 5, 29-41.

# Biological Processes in Northern Freshwater Systems

The physical processes which operate in northern systems markedly affect the living organisms which are found there. For most of the year water temperatures are very low, depressing the rate at which life processes can occur in aquatic organisms. In addition days are short and light intensities are low during the long winters. This results in a very short time each year in which reproduction, growth and biological production can occur. In general organisms which live in northern freshwater systems have low rates of production relative to those in the south and the organisms which live in freshwater habitats in the north generally have low growth rates compared to their southern counterparts. Nevertheless organisms which live in northern freshwater have many unique adaptations to northern systems.

A common problem faced by freshwater animals in the north is low oxygen availability, particularly during the winter. Low oxygen levels are a result of oxygen consumption due to decay of organic matter in the sediments under the ice. In addition the long periods of low water temperatures during the winter severely limits the metabolism and growth of freshwater organisms.

Northern biological communities tend to be simple with a small number of species relative to their southern counterparts. This is true in both the terrestrial and freshwater environments. In general there are fewer species at all trophic levels in northern communities than in southern ones. Factors which determine what species are found in particular water bodies may be both biological, such as competition and predation or physical such as low oxygen levels, low temperatures or high turbidity at some time during the year.

Disease is a common feature of life at all latitudes. Some fish diseases such as infectious pancreatic necrosis is wide spread and could have strong negative impact on fish species which are important to people in northern communities.

# Limnology of Arctic Lakes

## Summarized from Presentation of Dr. H.E. Welch

The limnology of northern freshwater has been studied in several locations in northern Canada. The most detailed studies have been done at Char Lake near Resolute on Cornwallis Island (Rigler, 1978. Schindler et al., 1974), in the Saquaqjuac region of eastern Keewatin as well as at Southern Indian Lake in northern Manitoba and the Experimental Lakes Area (ELA) in northwestern Ontario. In both Saqvaqjuac and ELA experimental fertilization experiments were carried out to determine the response of lakes in these areas to increased nutrient inputs.

Seventeen percent of the surface area of the Saqvaqjuac region in the northeastern NWT is covered by freshwater. Northern lakes receive minimal organic matter loading. Typically most of the runoff occurs in May and June in dry years but during wet years discharge may occur all summer depending on rain fall. Salt input is a function of when discharge occurs. In dry years phosphorous input is largely from the atmosphere. The concentration of phosphorus in runoff is constant through the year. In a dry year almost all phosphorus enters lakes in the spring runoff. In a wet year input of phosphorus and runoff can occur over the entire summer.

Silica is a product of weathering and undergoes a twenty fold change in concentration over the summer season. The concentration of silica in runoff increases as the active zone (non-frozen layer above the permafrost) enlarges during the summer months, hence silica input to northern lakes is skewed to later in the season and coincides with storm events.

Freeze-up concentrates salts in lakes as the salt freezes out during ice formation. During early melt runoff enters lakes, passes under the ice and out of the lake again without mixing with the total water volume. Arctic lakes have higher salt concentration than inflowing water. At Saqvaqjuac lake water was 60% more dense than the inflowing water. Depending on the timing of run-off, water flowing into lakes may not mix well with lake water. Consequently the amount of salt retained in the lake depends on when discharge occurs.

Low water temperatures may slow down processes but they do not place limits on the production of chlorophyll. Northern freshwater systems appear to use phosphorous efficiently during the summer months. When one lake in the Saqvaqjuac region, known as P&N Lake, was fertilized with both phosphorous and nitrogen the chlorophyl production doubled.

A large portion of the total lake production in the Saqvaqjuac lakes at least is benthic. After fertilization a large proportion of production occurred during the open water season. In most arctic lakes a very large proportion of the total primary production occurs under ice in spring.

In the Saqvaqjuac region actual surface irradiance is maximal before summer solstice because cloud cover after summer solstice reduces solar input. Radiant energy does not penetrate the water of lakes in this region until mid June as a result of snow and ice cover.

At latitude 75°N there is about 23% as much radiant energy input as in the tropics and production is about 23% of the values further south. Therefore production is probably not temperature limited. There is enormous production in the Arctic Ocean which experiences even lower water temperatures than those in freshwater.

Food chains in arctic freshwater ecosystems are much more simple than in the south. Where generation times might be 5 to 7 days in temperate climates they are 1 to 3 years in arctic lakes.

Lakes in the arctic are more efficient than those further south. The Saqvaqjuac lakes produced more chironomid biomass per unit area than the ELA lakes which were much further south.

Arctic lakes are clear and nutrient input is low. Benthic production in these systems is much more important than in southern lakes. One reason for this is the nature of silica cycling in these lakes.

Even withing six weeks of fertilization there was an increased emergence of chironomids at Saqvaqjuac. Amphipods also responded rapidly to fertilization but caddis flies did not respond until the third year after fertilization. This slow response appears to be due to their long life cycle at this latitude.

Saqvaqjuac lakes had populations of land-locked lake trout, which grew very large after they became cannibals. These fish grew slowly to a certain size and then became piscivorous, which in these lakes was cannibalistic since there were no other species of fish. The cannibals grew very quickly and behaved like another species in the lake. In these systems lake trout spawned at 15 to 20 years of age. One cannibalistic lake trout was 63 years old. Arctic charr, which are anadromous, do not live so long and grow somewhat faster than lake trout. Charr responded to fertilization better than lake trout in terms of improved condition factor. Char respond best to fertilization in terms of increased numbers. Lake trout responded to fertilization in 1979 but not in 1982.

Arctic and temperate lakes differ quantitatively but not quantitatively. They also differ in ice cover (thickness and duration) and in being located on permafrost dominated water sheds.

## References

Rigler, F.H.
1978 Limnology of the high Arctic: a case study of Char Lake. Verh. Internat. Verein. Limnol. 20: 127-140

Schindler, D.W., H.E. Welch, J. Kalff, G.J. Brunshill and N. Kritsch
1974 Physical and chemical limnology of Char Lake, Cornwallis Island (75° N Lat.). J. Fish. Res. Board Can. 31: 585-607.

# Ecology of Pill Clams (Pisidium, Bivalvia) with Focus on Adaptations to Northern Winters. A Short Review of Studies in Scandinavian Lakes and Rivers.

Ismo J. Holopainen
Department of Biology, University of Joensuu
P.O.Box 111, SF-80101 Joensuu, Finland

## Abstract

Of the 21 European species of *Pisidium* 18 are found in Scandinavia at latitudes north of 60 degrees; at least six of them are common at the same latitudes in Canada.

The dispersal of these clams by passive means (floating or carriage by waterfowl etc.) is generally considered effective.

One or two species at least are present in most Scandinavian lakes and rivers and assemblages of five to ten sympatric species are not uncommon.

The most probable food source for these clams which live in the bottom mud is the interstitial suspension of microorganisms.

Population densities of up to 1000 individuals per square meter can be found in profundal and up to 3000 in littoral zones of oligotrophic lakes in Scandinavia (a maximum of 6000 is reported from the eutrophic Lake Esrom, Denmark).

Because of their small size, the biomass of *Pisidium* is low, less than 1 g ash-free dry weight per $m^2$, and so are the production values since annual turnover rates are approximately 1.

A wide inter- and intraspecific variation and flexibility in life history events (time of egg laying and parturition, number of litters per parent, longevity etc.) exist probably as an adaptation to the seasonal environment and variable food concentrations.

Some reports suggest an impoverished pisidiid fauna in South Norway because of acid rain.

A considerable capacity for anaerobiosis is suggested to be an important adaptation for both passive dispersal and overwintering in the littoral zone of northern lakes and rivers. Cases of overwintering inside ice or frozen sediment in natural waterbodies are reviewed.

## Introduction

Pisidiidae is a family of small (2-20 mm shell length), mainly infaunal bivalve molluscs with a cosmopolitan and ubiquitous distribution in fresh waters.

Most species belong to the genus *Pisidium* (commonly known as pill clams or pea cockles), which have a smaller size but wider ecological amplitude than the other genera (*Sphaerium*, *Musculium*, or fingernail clams) and are morphologically distinct from them (e.g. Odhner 1929). Pisidiidae have a highly specialized reproductive system with facultative autogamy (capability for self-fertilization) and ovoviviparity (giving birth to young clams), and they show much inter- and intraspecific variation in many life history traits like timing of reproductive events, longevity etc. (Holopainen and Hanski 1986).

Of the 21 European species of *Pisidium*, most (18) are found in Scandinavia at latitudes north of 60 degrees. Almost equal numbers of species are found in North America at the same latitudes (e.g. Clarke 1981). At least the following six *Pisidium* species are widely distributed and common in both Scandinavia and Canada, *P. conventus*, *P. casertanum*, *P. subtruncatum*, *P.milium*, *P.nitidum* and *P. lilljeborgi*.

Studies on freshwater molluscs (including Pisidiidae or Sphaeriidae as it was previously called) have long traditions in Scandinavia starting from Odhner (e.g. 1923, 1929, 1951) and Valle (1927). Later on, Koli (1961, 1964), Aho (1966), Hinz (e.g. 1974, 1976), Ökland (1971, 1980), Jonasson (1972) and Holopainen (e.g. 1979, 1986) have contributed to our knowledge of the ecology of Pisidiidae. Russian studies on freshwater bivalves were recently reviewed by Alimov (1981).

Astonishingly the dispersal capacity of these sluggish sediment dwelling clams is thought to be fairly good. This is because their tiny size allows the use of passive means (floating or carriage by flying aquatic insects, waterfowl or amphibians, see e.g. Mackie 1979, Prezant and Chalermwat 1984, Holopainen 1986) and their colonization success is greatly enhanced by their capacity for anaerobiosis (Holopainen 1986) together with autogamy and ovoviviparity.

*Mode of life, food and feeding*

Most species of *Pisidium* live inside the soft surface sediments of fresh waters (Fig. 1.). They may burrow down to the oxic-anoxic boundary usually a few centimeters deep in the sediment, but commonly they are found only a few millimeters below the sediment surface (Meier-Brook 1969). Typically they turn umbo down and filter-feed on water-born particles drawn from the sediment and sorted by the gills and labial palps. Several potential food sources from dissolved organic compounds (Efford and Tsumura 1973) to sediment deposits (Hornbach et al., 1984) have been considered; recent findings suggest, however, feeding on interstitial suspensions (suspended microorganisms) with bacteria probably as the main food source (Holopainen 1985, Lopez and Holopainen 1986). Life among vegetation or on hard bottoms requires other adaptations which are not considered here. The amount of interstitial bacteria in sediments of even oligotrophic freshwater bodies appears to be high enough (up to $2 \times 10^9$ cells/cm³ (Lopez and Holopainen 1986) for nutritional requirements of these tiny molluscs even at their low water pumping rate in filtration.

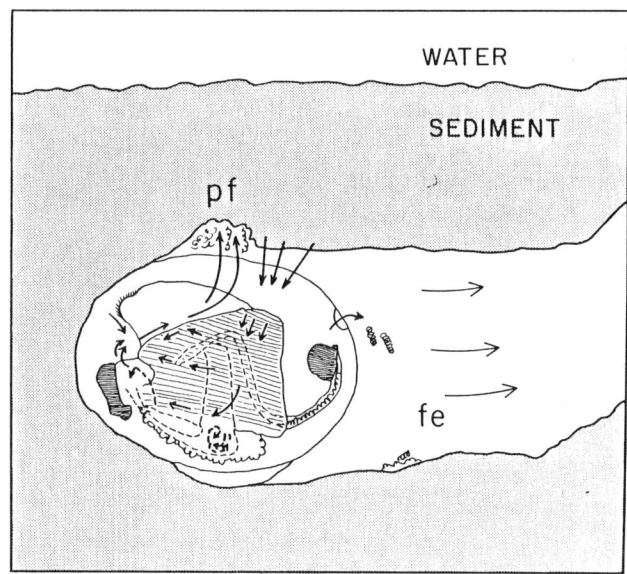

Figure 1  Feeding position of *P. conventus* inside surface sediment. fe = faeces; pf = pseudofaeces. (adapted from Meier-Brook 1969 and Holopainen 1985).

Studies on feeding have concentrated on gut analysis or filtering rates, both of which can be criticized, the former because of studying waste materials (after absorption) and the latter because of indirect methods using unnatural food substitutes (Holopainen 1985). Results on filtering rate show large variation probably because of methodical problems, but the rates of filtration in *Pisidium* seem to be lower than in the other genera.

*Species number and population densities*

The number of *Pisidium* species in Scandinavian lakes is variable, often only a few species are found (e.g. Ökland 1980) but lakes with 5 to 10 coexisting species in the littoral zone are common (Valle 1927, Odhner 1929, Aho 1966, Bagge 1968, Hinz 1974, 1976, Holopainen 1979).

The population densities of *Pisidium* show wide bathymetric, spatial and temporal variation as is the case in most other benthic groups. In general, the highest densities are found at one to two meters depth and the profundal densities are low with some exceptions e.g. in case of the cold stenothermic species *P. conventus*, which can have densities of up to 1000 individuals per m². Yet the highest densities in Scandinavia (up to 6000 per m²) were recorded in the mid-fifties from the profundal zone (20 m) in the well studied, eutrophic Lake Esrom in Denmark (Holopainen and Jonasson 1983). The longest series of samples for temporal variation (21 years) is from this same lake. In littoral areas total densities of 2000 to 4000 are not uncommon (Hinz 1974, 1976, Holopainen 1979) and densities up to 2000 per m² have been reported even from the subarctic regions (Hinz 1976)

*Biomasses and production/biomass ratios*

Because of their small size, the biomasses of *Pisidium* stay low, less than one gram ash-free dry weight per m² even in case of the highest densities recorded. The same is true with production in Scandinavia, where turnover rates or P/B ratios of approximately 1 are commonly reported (Table 1, Holopainen and Jonasson 1983 and references therein). In North America higher turnover rates of 3-4 have been given for some populations (e.g. Gillespie 1969, Hamill et al. 1979).

*Respiration and energy budgets*

In his recent review on metabolism of Pisidiidae, Hornbach (1985) revealed intergeneric differences in the weight-specific metabolic rates with members of the genus *Pisidium* having lower rates than in the other genera. With equal production efficiency this suggests lower P/B ratios which are probably mainly caused by the lowered reproductive capacity in this genus (one clutch developing at a time vs. several in other genera).

The deep or cold water specialist, small sized arctic and alpine species *P. conventus* was shown to have lower metabolic costs (respiration rate) and consequently higher growth efficiency in its stable environment than does the shallow water generalist *P. casertanum* in littoral areas (Fig.2.; Holopainen and Hanski 1979).

*Reproduction and life history*

*Pisidium* gives birth to a clutch of miniature adults. Only one clutch (one marsupium or brood sac in each demibranch) is developed at a time and the length of newborn is approximately 1 mm, except for in the very smallest and very largest species. In contrast, the clutch size varies

Table 1 Production (P) and annual production bio-mass (P/B) ratios in Pisidiidae

| Species | P kJ m$^{-2}$ yr$^{-1}$ | P/B | depth m | water body and locality | author |
|---|---|---|---|---|---|
| P. Virginicum | 342.26 | | 0.2 | Root Spring, USA | Teal 1957 |
| P. Compressum | 50.17 | 4.3 | 1 | Madison River, USA | Gillespie 1969 |
| P. crassum | 0.88 | 1.3 | 0-4 | Lake Krugloe, USSR | Alimov 1970 |
| S. suecicum | 61.59 | 1.5 | 0-4 | —"— | —"— |
| Sphaeriidae (several species) | 5.0-10.0 | 1.2-1.5 | 5-30 | Great Lakes, Canada | Johnson and Brinkhurst 1971 |
| P. casertanum | 1.4-1.8 | | 1.4 | Upton Broad, England | Mason 1977 |
| —"— | 3.93 | 1.3 | 2 | Lake Pääjärvi, Finland | Holopainen 1979 |
| P. conventus | 1.0 | 1.0 | 25 | —"— | —"— |
| P. casertanum | 0.4-3.7 | 3.8 | 2-8 | Ottawa River, Canada | Hamill et al. 1979 |
| —"— | 0.9-8.2 | 0.8-1.1 | 20 | Lake Esrom, Denmark | Holopainen and Jonasson 1983 |
| P. subtruncatum | 0.4-2.6 | 0.8-1.2 | 20 | —"— | —"— |
| P. amnicum | 2.4 | 1.4 | 1 | St. Lawrence River, Canada | Vincent et al. 1981 |

considerably within and among species and is clearly constrained by the parent size, the range can be from 1 to 40 within one species.

The number of eggs laid is usually greater than the number of young reaching birth size (Meier-Brook 1970, 1977, Holopainen and Jonasson 1983) which gives a neat mechanism to fine-tune reproductive output according to environment. Also the time of egg-laying is species specific but the time of birth can be adjusted to fit the habitat: in Lake Esrom *P. casertanum* always lays its eggs in spring but growth of the embryos at 20 m depth is soon retarded by oxygen depletion during the summer stratification and the birth of young does not take place until two months after the autumn overturn (in November). In years with a late overturn, however, birth is further delayed until the next spring. At 11 m in the same lake (and at 2 m in Lake Pääjäärvi, see Holopainen 1979), with higher temperatures and better oxygen availability, parturition takes place in July-August (Fig.3; Holopainen and Jonasson 1983). So the potential 2-3 months embryonic development in the brood sac can be prolonged up to 12 months by adverse physical environment.

*Water quality requirements*

In his study of more than 30 small lakes in southern Finland, Aho (1966) found that the following water quality criteria correlated positively with the number of pisidiid species present: total hardness (calcium content), pH, alkalinity (hydrocarbonate content) and conductivity. A negative correlation was found with water colour (humus content) and chemical oxygen demand — these factors were also positively correlated with each other.

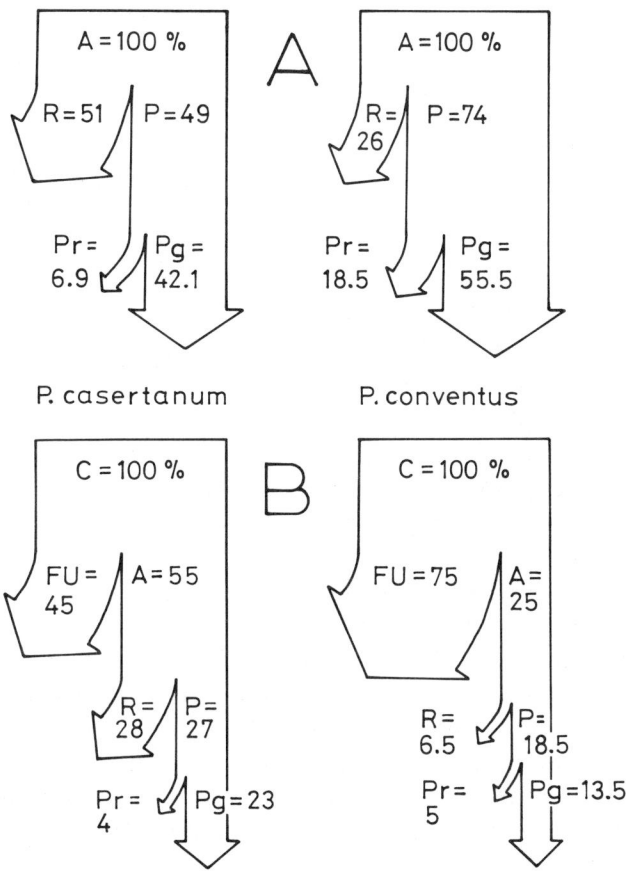

Figure 2  The energy allocation in populations of *P. casertanum*, a shallow water generalist and *P. conventus*, a cold-stenotherm deep water specialist in an oligotrophic lake in southern Finland. C = food energy, A = assimilation (P+R), P = production, R = respiration, FU = faeces plus excreta, Pr = reproductive production, Pg = growth production (Holopainen 1978).

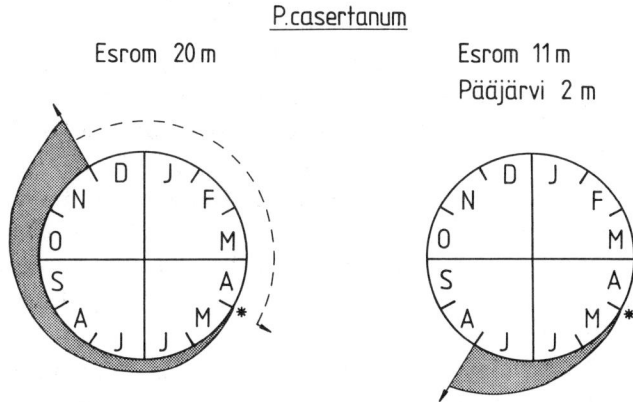

Figure 3  The timing of egg-laying (asterisk) and birth (arrow) in different populations of *P. casertanum* in Scandinavia. At 20 m the birth takes place 2 months after the autumn overturn with late overturn birth is postponed to the next spring.

Hinz (1976) observed that the densities of Pisidiidae were several times higher in Northern Scandinavia than in Southern Norway and hypothesized that acid rain was responsible for the low numbers in south.

Ökland (1980) investigated the distribution of Pisidiidae (number of species) and their relation to pH and calcium content (total hardness) in 660 Norwegian localities of which 515 were lakes. In 151 of the 159 squares (50x 50 km) searched, one or more species were present (20 species altogether). Ten commonly found species could be divided into three groups according to their tolerance of low pH and low calcium. Acidification was reported to have strong effects at two levels: firstly a pH change from 6.0 to pH 5.7 wiped out six species and then at pH 5.0 the most tolerant four species (*P. hibernicum, P. obtusale, P. lilljeborgii* and *P. casertanum*) were exterminated.

*Anaerobiosis or life without oxygen*

Numerous water bodies including small lakes and ponds in boreal and subarctic areas commonly experience seasonal anoxia starting from the bottom sediments (Nagell and Brittain 1977, Salonen et al. 1984). Consequently the capacity for facultative anaerobiosis is especially common in benthic animals (e.g., Eggleton 1931, Lindeman 1942) including both marine and freshwater molluscs (e.g. De Zwaan 1987, Gäde 1983). Several reports exist on anoxia survival of *Pisidium* (literature from Juday 1908 onwards is reviewed by Burky 1983 and Holopainen 1986). Representatives of both *Pisidium* and *Sphaerium* are experimentally shown to tolerate several months of total anoxia at low temperatures (below 5°C, Holopainen 1986).

The common features of behaviour and physiology of molluscs in anoxia include: 1) inactivity with metabolic suppression down to 10% of aerobic values in order to save energy, 2) use of alternative metabolic pathways to increase energy (ATP) gain and to avoid harmful end products and 3) accumulation and/or excretion of succinate, acetate or propionate instead of lactate (e.g. De Zwaan 1983).

The ecological consequences of this are obvious and important: these molluscs can survive not only in anoxic water but during aestivation in drying mud, while overwintering inside ice, or during aerial exposure while being passively carried (dispersed) by waterfowl or flying aquatic insects (Fig. 4. Bleck and Heitkamp 1980, McKee and Mackie 1979).

Many molluscs, including Pisidiidae, are able to survive winter inside ice or frozen sediment. This ability is of special value for slow-moving animals in shallow shore areas and water bodies with fluctuations in water level, like rivers and regulated lakes. The overwintering abilities of pill clams and many other benthic invertebrates in ice has long been known (Nordenskiöld 1897, Grimås 1961, Holmqvist 1973) but the quantitative importance of it has been only recently understood (Olsson 1981).

Wintering in ice requires cold-hardiness even with the insulation of snow and ice. For example in the case of *P. amnicum* (Holopainen 1986) probably more than half of the population is susceptible to freezing. In March 1985 this species was melted from the ice of the small river Siilaisenpuro (Fig.5) in eastern Finland (and found to be alive) after an exceptionally cold weather, which must have lowered the temperature in ice well below freezing point (mean monthly temperatures in the preceding January and February were -21.2 and -19.8°C, respectively). However, Olsson (1981) has shown experimentally that 57% of *Pisidium* survive 4 months at -4°C. Ice is thought to provide a refuge from predation which at least in the case of some species may more than compensate for the risk of fatally freezing.

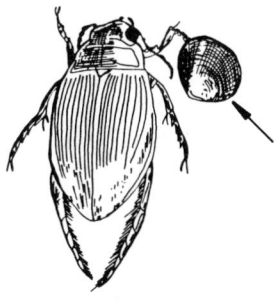

A
Insect

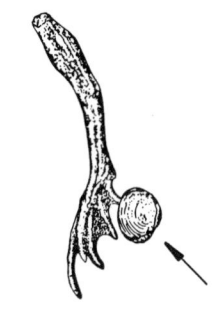

B
Amphibian

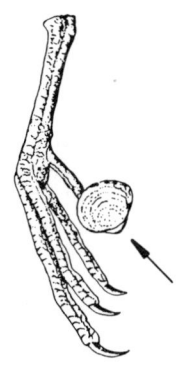

C
Waterfowl

Figure 4  The passive dispersal of *Pisidium* is accomplished by floating with floods or by sticking to various aquatic insects (A), amphibians (B) or waterfowl (C). A=redrawn from Kew (1893); B and C redrawn from Guerne (1893).

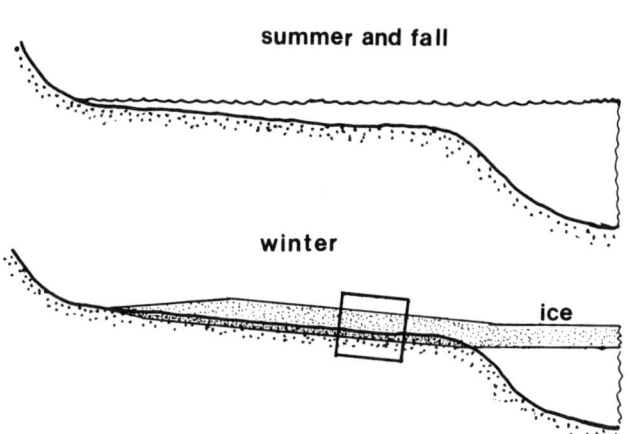

Figure 5  A drop of water level in winter may cause freezing of shallow water sediments and the invertebrates in them. Here an example from eastern Finland, where a population of *Pisidium amnicum* (ca. 100 inds.per $m^2$) overwintered inside the ice (Holopainen 1986).

## References

Aho, J.
1966  Ecological basis of the distribution of the littoral freshwater molluscs in the vicinity of Tampere, South Finland. — Ann. Zool. Fennici 3: 287-322.

Alimov, A.F.
1970  Potok energii cherez populyatsiu mollyuskov (Na primere Sphaeriidae). — Gidrobiol. Zhurnal 6: 63-71.
1981  Funktsionalnaja ekologiya presnovodnykh dvustvorchatykh mollyuskov. — Trud. Zool. Inst. AN SSSR 96: 1-248.

Bagge, P.
1968  Ecological studies on the fauna of subarctic waters in Finnish Lapland. — Ann. Univ. Turku AII: 28-79.

Bleck, V. and U. Heitkamp
1980 Ökophysiologische Untersuchungen an *Pisidium personatum* Malm, 1855 und *Pisidium obtusale* (Lamarck 1818) (Bivalvia, Sphaeriidae). — Zoologische Anzeiger 205: 162-180.

Burky, A.
1983 Physiological ecology of freshwater Bivalves. In: W.D. Russel-Hunter (ed.). The Mollusca. Vol.6: 281-327. Academic Press.

Clarke, A.H.
1981 The freshwater molluscs of Canada. 446 pp. National Museum of Natural Sciences, Canada.

De Zwaan, A.
1977 Anaerobic energy metabolism in bivalve mclluscs. — Oceanogr. Mar. Biol. Ann. Rev. 15:103-187.
1983 Carbohydrate catabolism in Bivalves. In: Hochachka, P.W. (ed.). The Mollusca. Vol. 1: 138-175. Academic Press.

Efford, I.A. and K. Tsumura
1973 Uptake of dissolved glucose and glycine by *Pisidium* , a freshwater bivalve. — Can. J. Zool. 51: 825-832.

Eggleton, F.E.
1931 A limnological study of the profundal bottom fauna of certain freshwater lakes. — Ecol. Monogr. 1(3): 231-331.

Gillespie, D.M.
1969 Population studies of four species of molluscs in the Madison river, Yellowstone National Park. — Limnol. Oceanogr. 14: 101-114.

Gnaiger, E.
1983 Heat dissipation and energetic efficiency in animal anoxibiosis: Economy contra power. — The Journal of Experimental Zoology 228: 471-490.

Grimås, U.
1961 The bottom fauna of natural and impounded lakes in northern Sweden (Ankarvattnet and Blåsjön). — Institute for Freshwater Research Drottningholm Report. 42 183-237.

Guerne, J. de
1893 Dissemination des Pelecypodes d'eau douce par les Vertebres. — Extr. Comp. rend. hebdom. Soc.Biol. Ns. V: 1-3.

Gäde, G.
1983 Energy metabolism of Arthropods and Molluscs during environmental and functional anaerobiosis. — The Journal of Experimental Zoology 228: 415-429.

Hamill, S.E., S.U. Qadri and G.L. Mackie
1979 Production and turnover ratio of *Pisidium casertanum* (Pelecypoda: Sphaeriidae) in the Ottawa River near Ottawa-Hull, Canada. — Hydrobiologia 62: 225-230.

Hinz, W.
1974 Molluskenfauna und -siedlungsdichten in einigen Gebirgsgewässern der umgebung von Dombås (Südnorwegen). — Norw. J. Zool.22: 221-229.
1976 Siedlungsdichten limnischer Mollusken in Nordskandinavien und in Sudnorwegen. — Norw. J. Zool. 24: 205-223.

Holmquist, C.
1973 Some arctic limnology and the hibernation of invertebrates and some fishes in sub-zero temperatures. — Archiv für Hydrobiologie 72: 49-70.

Holopainen, I.J.
1978 Ecology of *Pisidium* (*Bivalvia, Sphaeriidae*) populations in an oligotrophic and mesohumic lake. — Publ. Univ. Joensuu B2,(9): 1-12.
1979 Population dynamics and production of *Pisidium* species (Bivalvia, Sphaeriidae) in the oligotrophic and mesohumic lake Pääjärvi, southern Finland. — Arch. Hydrobiol. Suppl.54(4): 466-508.
1986 Seasonal variation of survival time in anoxic water and the glycogen content of *Sphaerium corneum* and *Pisidium amnicum* (Bivalvia, Pisidiidae). — American Malacological Bulletin (in press)

Holopainen, I.J. and I. Hanski
1979  Annual energy flow in populations of two *Pisidium* species (Bivalvia, Sphaeriidae), with discussion on possible competition between them. — Arch. Hydrobiol. 86: 338-354.
1986  Life history variation in *Pisidium* (Bivalvia:Pisidiidae). — Holarctic Ecology 9: 85-98. Hornbach, D.J. 1985. A review of metabolism in the Pisidiidae with new data on its relationship with life history traits in *Pisidium casertanum.*— Amer. Malacol. Bulletin 3(2): 187-200.

Holopainen, I.J. and P. Jonasson
1983  Long-term population dynamics and production of *Pisidium* (Bivalvia) in the profundal of Lake Esrom, Denmark. — Oikos 41: 99-117.
1985  Feeding biology of Pisidiidae (Bivalvia) with special emphasis on functional morphology of the digestive tract. — Lammi Notes 12: 5-9.

Hornbach, D.J.
1985  A review of metabolism in the Pisidiidae with new data on its relationship with life history traits in *Pisidium casertanum*. Amer. Malacol. Bulletin 3(2): 187-200.

Hornbach, D.J., E.M. Way, T.E. Wissing and A.J. Burky
1984  Effects of particle concentration and season on the filtration rates of the freshwater clam, *Sphaerium striatinum* Lamarck (Bivalvia, Pisidiidae). — Hydrobiologia 108: 83-96.

Johnson, M.G. and R.O. Brinkhurst
1971  Production of benthic macroinvertebrates of Bay of Quinte and Lake Ontario. — J. Fish. Res. Bd. Canada 28: 1688-1714.

Juday, C.
1908  Some aquatic invertebrates that live under anaerobic conditions. — Trans. Wisconsin Acad. Sci., Arts and Letters 16: 10-16.

Kew, H.W.
1893  The dispersal of shells. Kegan Paul. London.

Koli, L.
1961  Die Molluskenfauna des Brackwassergebietes bei Tvärminne, Südwestfinnland. — Ann. Zool. Soc. Vanamo 22(5): 1-22.

Koli, L. and E. Turkia
1964  Über die Wassermollusken im Südteil des Saimaa-Sees in Südostfinnland. — Ann. Zool. Fennici 1: 81-88.

Lindeman, R.L.
1942  Experimental simulation of winter anaerobiosis in a senescent lake. — Ecology 23(1): 1-13.

Lopez, G.R. and I.J. Holopainen
1986  Interstitial suspension-feeding by *Pisidium* spp.(Pisidiidae: Bivalvia): a new guild in the benthos. — Amer. Malacol. Bull. (in press).

Mackie, G.L.
1979  Dispersal mechanisms in Sphaeriidae (Mollusca: Bivalvia). — Bulletin of American alacological Union, Inc. 45: 17-21.

Mason, C.F.
1977  Populations and production of benthic animals in two contrasting shallow lakes in Norfolk. — J. general feature of ponds in cold temperate region.- Int. Rev. Ges.Hydrobiol.62(6): 821-824.

McKee, P.M. and G.L. Mackie
1980  Desiccation resistance in *Sphaerium occidentale* and *Musculium securis* (Bivalvia: Sphaeriidae) from a temporary pond. — Canadian Journal of Zoolong 58: 1693-1696.

Meier-Brook, C.
1969  Substrate relations in some Pisidium species (Eulamellibranchiata: Sphaeriidae). — Malacologia 9: 121-125.
1970  Untersuchungen zur Biologie einiger *Pisidium* — Arten (Mollusca. Eulamellibranchiata, Sphaeriidae). — Arch. Hydrobiol. Suppl. 38: 73-150.
1977  Intramarsupial suppression of fetal development in Sphaeriid clams. — Malac. Rev. 10: 53-58.

Nagell, B. and J.E. Brittain
1977  Winter anoxia — a general feature of ponds in cold temperate region. — Int. Rev. Ges. Hydrobiol. 62(6): 821-824.

Nordenskiöld, E.
1897  Några iakttagelser rörande våra vanligaste sötvattenmolluskers lif under vinter. — Öfversigt af Kongliga Vetenskaps-Akademiens Förhandlingar, Stockholm 1897, 2: 77-85.

Odhner, N.H.
1923  Mollusca. *Pisidium* conventus Clessin (P. clessini Surbeck, partim). Rep. Norwegian Exp. Novaya Zemlya 1921, No 6.
1929  Die Molluskenfauna des Tåkern. — Sjön Tåkerns Fauna och Flora (Stockholm) 8: 2-239.
1951  Swedish high mountain mollusca. In: Brinck, P. and Wingstrand, K.G. (eds.), The mountain fauna of the Virihaure area in Swedish Lapland. — Lunds Univ. Årsskr. N. F. (avd. 2) 46: 26-50.

Ökland, K.A.
1971  On the ecology of Sphaeriidae in a high mountain area in South Norway. — Norw. J. Zool. 19: 133-143.
1980  Småmuslinger (Sphaeriidae) i ferskvann i Norge utbredelse, okologi og relasjon til forsuring. — SNSF prosjekt, IR 61/80.Oslo.

Olsson, T.I.
1981  Overwintering of benthic macroinvertebrates in ice and frozen sediment in a North Swedish river. — Holarctic Ecology 4: 161-166.

Prezant, R.S. and K. Chalermwat
1984  Flotation of the Bivalve *Corbicula fluminea* as a Means of Dispersal. — Science 225: 1491-1493.

Salonen, K., L. Arvola and M. Rask
1984  Autumnal and vernal circulation of small forest lakes in Southern Finland. — Verh. Int. Ver. Limnol.22: 103-107.

Teal, J.M.
1957  Community metabolism in a temperate cold spring. — Ecol. Monogr. 27:283-302.

Valle, K.J.
1927  Ökologisch-limnologische untersuchungen über die boden- und tiefenfauna in eingien Seen nördlich vom Ladoge-see.I. — Acta Zool. Fennica 2: 1-179.

Vincent, B., G. Vaillancourt and N. Lafontaine
1981  Cycle de developpement, croissance et production de *Pisidium amnicum* (Mollusca: Bivalvia) dans le Saint-Laurent (Quebec). — Can J. Zool. 59: 2350-2359.

# Growth, Feeding and Reproductive Biology of Freshwater Fish in Northern Canada

W.C. Mackay
Department of Zoology
University of Alberta
Edmonton, Alberta T6G 2E9

## Introduction

Only a small number of species of freshwater fish have successfully adapted to the severe environmental conditions which exist in northern lakes and streams. Many of the conspicuous fish found in this region are temperate zone species whose northern range extends into the arctic. These species include yellow perch, walleye, northern pike and lake trout. Other species including inconnu, burbot, lake whitefish, round whitefish, broad whitefish and arctic grayling are widely distributed over arctic and subarctic areas and are well adapted to life in freshwater habitats which are ice covered for periods of eight to ten months each year. For many of these species the center of their geographic distribution is in the Northwest Territories.

This review will focus on large, freshwater species which are important to the subsistence of northern people. Anadromous species such as salmon and char which periodically migrate to the ocean will not be included.

Growth and metabolism of northern freshwater fish is most directly affected by the abiotic conditions which exist in northern freshwater. Abiotic factors such as the long period of low (<4°C) water temperature during the winter, rapid warming associated with break-up, relatively high summer water temperatures in shallow arctic water bodies, and the fluctuations in flushing associated with break-up are all significant factors acting on northern freshwater fish. In addition northern freshwater systems are generally much less productive than their southern counterparts.

The period of ice cover on northern lakes varies considerably depending on conditions such as surface area, depth, size of inflowing streams, and latitude. Break-up in the large northern lakes is delayed compared to small, shallow lakes nearby. Similarly freeze-up is delayed although water temperature drops to low levels (< 4°C) quickly in the fall but freeze-up doesn't occur until December or January. The effective summer period is only 10 weeks on Great Bear Lake, 12 weeks on Great Slave Lake, and 18 weeks on Lake Athabasca (Rawson, 1947b). Lake Athabasca is south of Great Slave and it is relatively shallow compared to the other two lakes (Larkin, 1948).

Annual temperature regimes in northern lakes are highly variable. Water temperatures in the main body of large lakes such as Great Slave and Great Bear remain low (<13°C) throughout the summer months but in shallow bays of these lakes water temperatures may reach 25°C in the summer (Miller, 1947). In Great Bear Lake mid summer water temperatures in shallow areas are 11.5 to 15.5°C while in Great Slave Lake they are 13.5 to 17°C (Larkin, 1948). In the shallow western basin of Lake Athabasca water temperatures reach 16 to 19°C in August (Rawson, 1947b). In shallow arctic lakes water temperatures approximately track average daily air temperature over the previous several days. Thus water temperatures during the open water season can be calculated with reasonable accuracy from meteorological data.

Annual temperature regimes in rivers can vary considerably, even for rivers at the same latitude. The Mackenzie river breaks up around the end of May and is ice covered again by mid-October while the Coppermine River at the same latitude breaks up around mid June and is ice-covered by early October (Muth, 1969). Maximum summer water temperatures in the Mackenzie reach 15.5°C in July and August while in the Coppermine they only reach 10°C (Muth, 1969).

## Coregonids

Coregonids or whitefishes are wide spread in northern Canada and there is a rich diversity of coregonid species, particularly in the western arctic (McPhail and Lindsey, 1970). The two species which are most wide spread and most abundant in the North are the lake whitefish *Coregonus clupeaformis* (Mitchill) and the cisco or lake herring, *Coregonus artedii* (Le Sueur). In Great Slave Lake they represent over 75% of the fish caught in gill nets (Rawson, 1951). Lake whitefish appear to be restricted to continental North America and are not reported from the arctic islands. The distribution of arctic cisco extends to the northern end of Baffin Island (Ellis, 1962).

Whitefish are harvested by commercial and domestic fisheries over much of the north making them the most important commercial species in northern freshwater. Both whitefish and cisco show good growth rates at high latitudes although lake whitefish have a more extensive northern range than cisco (Scott and Crossman, 1973). Whitefish and cisco feed on invertebrates, both bottom dwelling and planktonic. Cisco tend to feed more on zooplankton than whitefish in most habitats (Clements et al. 1944). They are more planktivorous than lake whitefish in lakes such as Great Bear where both species are found (Kennedy, 1949).

Whitefish and cisco are the intermediate host for the tapeworm, *Triaenophorus,* the adult phase of which is found in northern pike (Lawler and Scott, 1954). The density of *Triaenophorus* cysts in the muscle of many whitefish and cisco populations is so high that these fish are unsuitable for human consumption.

## Lake Whitefish

Lake whitefish are a cold water species well adapted to life in arctic lakes. They are wide spread in large northern rivers and are known to migrate from lakes up major rivers in the fall (late October for fish in the Slave River) to spawn (RL&L/EMA, 1985) although lake spawning is the normal mode for this species. Spawning occurs in the fall; in Lac la Ronge in northern Saskatchewan they spawned between late October and mid November (Qadri, 1968) and in the Yukon from early November to mid December (Bryan and Kato, 1975). Lake whitefish spawn at night (Bryan and Kato, 1975).

Studies using experimental gill netting indicate that whitefish are pelagic, the smaller fish being found in the upper few meters of the water column while the larger fish are uniformly distributed throughout the upper 20 meters, at least in deep, fairly oligotrophic lakes (Godfrey, 1955). In Great Slave Lake whitefish are common to a depth of 75 m (Rawson, 1951). In Lac la Ronge, Saskatchewan whitefish appear to be concentrated at depths below 15 m for most of the year but in the early summer they appeared to move into shallow water (Qadri, 1961).

Examination of stomach contents reveals a wide range of diet both within and between lakes. Under some conditions lake whitefish feed primarily on bottom dwelling organisms such as insect larvae and small molluscs while in other situations they feed primarily on planktonic crustaceans (Godfrey, 1955). In Great Slave Lake whitefish are bottom feeders consuming shrimp (*Pontoproeia*), insect larvae, snails, and clams (Rawson, 1948). *Potoproeia* are the major source of food (85%) for whitefish which live in deep water (between 25 and 100 m) in large, deep lakes such as Great Slave and Lake Athabasca (Larkin, 1948, Rawson, 1947b). Whitefish in Babine Lake feed mainly on benthic organisms, those in Morrison Lake feed on zooplankton (Godfrey, 1955). In Great Bear Lake Kennedy (1949) found that whitefish feed on both benthic (molluscs) and planktonic (amphipods, copepods and *Mysis*) invertebrates. In Lac la Ronge, Saskatchewan which is a large shallow lake whitefish are primarily bottom feeders with from 40 to 60% by of their food by volume being chironomid larvae while two other benthic taxa, sphaerids and caddisfly larvae were also important (Qadri, 1961). In one large deep arm, Hunter Bay, amphipods were the dominant food organism comprising 44 to 90% by volume of their food during both summer and winter (Qadri, 1961). Planktonic organisms comprised only 15% of the food items of whitefish in the main body of Lac la Ronge (Qadri, 1961).

In Great Slave Lake whitefish are relatively sedentary with an average movement of about 10 km over an average time period of 8 months (Keleher, 1963). However whitefish tagged and released in the fall (Oct.) moved more than those tagged and released earlier (June and Sept). (Keleher, 1963). Gill net catches suggest that whitefish are more active at night than during the day, however low day time catches may simply be a result of net avoidance during the day (Qadri, 1961).

Whitefish are intermediate hosts of the cestode parasite, *Triaenophorus* which form cysts in the body musculature. Northern pike are the host of the adult tapeworm so that the incidence of *Triaenophorus* cysts in whitefish muscle is often high in lakes where the density of pike is high. The distribution fo *Triaenophorus* extends from the lower St. Lawrence River to Alberta and north to Great Bear Lake (Lawler and Scott, 1954). Whitefish are infected by the larvae of *Triaenophorus* to such a high extent in many northern lakes including Athabasca (Rawson, 1947b) that they are unsuitable for human consumption.

Whitefish growth is highly variable. Healey (1975b) reviewed the growth rate of 16 populations of whitefish from the Northwest Territories and concluded that growth rate of whitefish from the NWT is in the high end of the range of growth rates reported in the literature. Lake whitefish reach weights of up to 11.8 kg in southern waters (van Oosten, 1946) and a 10 kg specimen has been reported from Great Slave Lake (Keleher, 1961). Whitefish show a wide range of growth rates in northern Canada and the best growth rates recorded in the NWT are equal to the best growth rates observed much further south (Kennedy, 1963). Although there is no apparent relationship between latitude and whitefish growth rate (Tables 1 and 2) they grow more slowly in large, deep lakes than in shallow ones.

Growth of whitefish in Great Slave Lake occurs between late June or early July and December with about 90% of total annual growth occurring between the end of June and the end of August (Kennedy, 1953). Further south at Lac la Ronge, Saskatchewan, growth started in late May for sexually immature fish and in early June for sexually mature fish (Qadri, 1968) and continued until September with 90% of annual growth occurring in May, June and July. The longer growing season may account for the more rapid growth in Lac la Ronge than that reported for Great Slave Lake.

Whitefish in Lac la Ronge reached sexual maturity at age 8. Most males were mature at a fork length of 36 cm and most females at 40 cm (Qadri, 1968). In Great Bear Lake they reach sexual maturity at age 7+ and 8+ when they are about 40 cm long and weigh about 850 g (Kennedy, 1949). In Lake Superior they start to mature at 37 cm total length (age 3) and all are mature at 44 cm (age 8) (Bailey, 1963). Healey (1975b) reported a range in age and size at sexual maturity of from 3 to 10 years and from 20 to 40 cm fork length for nine populations from the NWT. There is no evidence of differential growth between males and females (Kennedy, 1949, Qadri, 1968).

Lake whitefish in some cold deep lakes may not spawn every year. Kennedy (1953) found that female whitefish from Great Slave Lake which were large enough to be sexually mature apparently spawned every other year. Parallel data could not be obtained for males.

The fecundity of a 45 cm (fork length) whitefish was between 25,000 and 30,000 for fish from four small lakes near Yellowknife (Healey, 1978) and between 18,000 and 59,000 for fish of 45 cm (standard length) from northern Alberta (Healey and Dietz, 1984). Exploitation of whitefish populations appears to result in significant year to year variation in fecundity (Healey, 1978, Healey and Dietz, 1984), significant decrease in the age at sexual maturity and a significant increase in growth rate (Healey, 1975a).

Table 1  Growth of whitefish in northern lakes

| Age | Length in mm | | | | | | |
|---|---|---|---|---|---|---|---|
| | Babine Lake | Morrison Lake | Great Bear | Great Slave | Hudson Bay | Lac la Ronge | Superior |
| 1 | | | | | | 152 | 150 |
| 2 | 248 | 207 | | | | 178 | 241 |
| 3 | 307 | 264 | | | 203 | 216 | 323 |
| 4 | 365 | 307 | | | 241 | 244 | 376 |
| 5 | 384 | 321 | 279 | | 260 | 279 | 429 |
| 6 | 394 | 329 | 292 | 256 | 273 | 307 | 472 |
| 7 | 419 | 344 | 373 | 287 | 318 | 338 | 516 |
| 8 | 449 | 366 | 411 | 309 | | 363 | |
| 9 | | | 455 | 355 | | 391 | |
| 10 | | | 478 | 383 | | 419 | |
| 11 | | | 493 | 410 | | 439 | |
| 12 | | | 521 | 427 | | 462 | |
| 13 | | | 528 | 454 | | 483 | |
| 14 | | | 551 | 450 | | | |
| 15 | | | 561 | 457 | | | |

\* data for Great Slave Lake recalculated from Kennedy, 1953
Great Bear Lake recalculated from Kennedy, 1949
Hudson Bay from Dymond, 1933
Lac la Ronge from Qadri, 1968
Babine and Morrison Lakes from Godfrey, 1955
Superior from Dryer, 1963

Table 2  Growth of whitefish

| Age | Weight (g) | | |
|---|---|---|---|
| | Nueltin | MacDonald | MacEwen |
| 4 | | | |
| 5 | | | 726 |
| 6 | | | 946 |
| 7 | | | 1188 |
| 8 | | | 1320 |
| 9 | 682 | 572 | 1540 |
| 10 | 814 | 660 | 1672 |
| 11 | 858 | 748 | |
| 12 | 924 | 814 | |
| 13 | 968 | | |
| 14 | 1144 | | |

\* data from Nueltin, MacDonald, and MacEwen Lakes from Kennedy, 1963

## Cisco

The cisco, or lake herring, *Coregonus artedii* (Le Sueur) is wide spread in northern Canada and Alaska. They are much smaller than whitefish, typically attaining weights of about 500 g (Table 3). Cisco of 793 g and 383 mm fork length are reported from Hudson Bay (Dymond, 1933). Males and females have similar growth rates but males appear to live longer than females (Kennedy, 1949). Cisco become sexually mature in their fifth year at a length of about 25 cm in Great Bear Lake (Kennedy, 1949)

Cisco are commonly planktivorous (Clemens et al., 1944) and in deep lakes are common to depths of 75 m (Rawson, 1951). Like whitefish cisco are fall spawners but they appear to spawn earlier than whitefish (Dymond, 1933).

Cisco occupy an important role in the food chain of the large deep lakes in which they are found. They are usually the dominant plaktivore

Table 3  Growth of Cisco in northern lakes

| Age | Length (mm) Great Bear | Length (mm) Hudson Bay | Weight (g) Great Bear |
|---|---|---|---|
| 1 | | | |
| 2 | | 202 | |
| 3 | | 236 | |
| 4 | | 309 | |
| 5 | 254 | 317 | 227 |
| 6 | 284 | 335 | 255 |
| 7 | 315 | 354 | 268 |
| 8 | 320 | 367 | 397 |
| 9 | 333 | | 453 |
| 10 | 351 | | 510 |
| 11 | 356 | | 510 |

Ref. 1  Great Bear — Kennedy, 1949
Hudson Bay — Dymond, 1933

in such lakes. In Great Slave Lake cisco feed on copepods, *Mysis* and some insect larvae, copepods comprise about 60% of their diet and *Mysis* about 30% (Rawson, 1951). Cisco are usually the major prey species of lake trout (Rawson, 1949).

## Inconnu

Inconnu, *Stenodus leucichthys* (Guldenstadt), are found in the Yukon and Mackenzie River systems as far east as the Anderson River (128°W) (Dymond, 1943). It is a truly northern freshwater fish with a circumpolar arctic distribution, its range extending to just below 60°N in Teslin Lake, B.C., Canada (Clemens et al., 1944). Inconnu are well known from the Mackenzie River drainage and extend as far upstream in that system as Fort Smith where further southern migration appears to be prevented by rapids in the Slave River (Fuller, 1955).

Inconnu are large predaceous coregonids which are well adapted for piscivory, they have a long head, pointed anteriorly and a large mouth for a whitefish. They are the only piscivorous whitefish, feeding on fish up to about 10 cm long (Fuller, 1955) including other coregonids such as cisco (Clemens et al. 1944; Alt, 1969). The inconnu Alt (1969) studied fed on cisco of up to 30 cm and 200 g early in the open water season but later they shifted to smaller (15 cm) cisco.

The inconnu is the largest of the whitefish, reaching a weight of over 28 kg and a length of 1.5 m (Dymond, 1943). Growth appears to take place between June and September and there is no difference in growth rate between males and females (Fuller, 1955). Growth is fairly uniform over the range of locations for which data are available (Table 4). Fuller found that inconnu grow much more quickly than lake whitefish and reach a greater ultimate size. Inconnu also grow slightly more quickly than lake trout in northern waters thus it is well adapted to arctic habitats.

Inconnu which are normally resident in lakes, such as Great Slave, undergo spawning migrations up major rivers in mid August (RL&L/EMA, 1985) and return to the lakes where they over winter in late September and early (Fuller, 1955) to mid (RL&L/EMA, 1985) October. In some Alaska rivers upstream migration begins in June but spawning does not occur until late September (Alt, 1969). Males become sexually mature at about 55 cm standard length while females mature at about 65 cm (Fuller, 1955). Spawning occurs at discrete locations in rivers (RL&L/EMA, 1985). Downstream movement after spawning appears to take place at night (Fuller, 1955).

Spawning occurs in swift flowing water in discrete areas of rivers which are sites of active erosion, such as the outside of bends (RL&L/EMA, 1985). Substrates used for spawning have a roughened texture such as gravel and cobble (Alt, 1969)

## Broad Whitefish

Broad whitefish, *Coregonus nasus* are found in the Mackenzie Delta and northwestern NWT including the Coppermine River west of Bathurst Inlet (109°W) (Muth, 1969). They grow much more slowly in the Coppermine than in the Mackenzie River probably the result of a shorter growing season and lower summer water temperatures in the Coppermine than in the Mackenzie River (Table 5),(Muth, 1969).

Table 4  Rate of growth of Inconnu

| Age | Length (mm) | | | | Weight (g) |
|---|---|---|---|---|---|
| | Great Slave | Upper Yukon R. | Chatanika River | Lobuk River | Great Slave |
| 1 | 146 | 113 | 148 | 130 | 54 |
| 2 | 247 | 195 | 246 | 217 | 200 |
| 3 | 312 | 265 | 326 | 280 | 395 |
| 4 | 403 | 322 | 406 | 341 | 375 |
| 5 | 473 | 380 | 485 | 397 | 1360 |
| 6 | 529 | 442 | 539 | 451 | 1978 |
| 7 | 572 | 501 | 582 | 506 | 2549 |
| 8 | 610 | 540 | 634 | 561 | 3234 |
| 9 | 657 | 586 | 671 | 612 | 3769 |
| 10 | 688 | | 717 | 656 | 4423 |
| 11 | 727 | | 760 | 700 | 5012 |
| 12 | | | | 746 | |
| 13 | | | | 793 | |
| 14 | | | | 833 | |
| 15 | | | | 877 | |
| 16 | | | | 913 | |
| 17 | | | | 966 | |
| 18 | | | | 1026 | |

* Great Slave — Fuller, 1955
  Upper Yukon River, Alaska — Alt, 1969
  Chatanika River, Alaska — Alt, 1969
  Kobuk and Lobuk Rivers, Alaska — Alt, 1969

Table 5  Growth of broad whitefish in northern waters

| Age | Length (mm) | | Weight (g) | |
|---|---|---|---|---|
| | Coppermine River | Mackenzie River | Coppermine River | Mackenzie River |
| 1 | 94 | 126 | | |
| 2 | 129 | 190 | | 85 |
| 3 | 167 | 255 | | 185 |
| 4 | 203 | 316 | 113 | 444 |
| 5 | 232 | 363 | 279 | 640 |
| 6 | 268 | 398 | 297 | 783 |
| 7 | 293 | 428 | 338 | 1060 |
| 8 | 320 | 442 | 408 | 1279 |
| 9 | 348 | 469 | 501 | 1656 |
| 10 | 366 | 487 | 691 | 1595 |
| 11 | 400 | 497 | 672 | 1869 |

* Coppermine and Mackenzie River — Muth, 1969

## Round Whitefish

Round whitefish, *Prosopium cylindraceum* Pallas, are found in the Northwest Territories, Labrador and the Great Lakes. They are much smaller than lake whitefish commonly reaching a weight of 500 g (Mackay and Power, 1968). The maximum size reported for round whitefish is 2.3 kg (Keleher, 1961) and 40 to 50 cm in length (Mackay and Power, 1968). They live to twelve years or more in cold water (Table 6).

Some round whitefish mature at 20 cm and all of both sexes have matured by the time they reach about 25 cm (age 7 for males and age 6 for females) in the Ungava region (Mackay and Power, 1968). In the Yukon they spawned in November during the day (Bryan and Kato, 1975). The eggs of round whitefish are 3.1 to 3.4 mm in diameter which is slightly larger than those of lake whitefish (2.4 – 2.6 mm diameter) from the same habitat (Bryan and Kato, 1975). Male round whitefish mature at a smaller size (180 mm total length) and a younger age (5 years) than females (220 mm and 6 years) in Lake Superior (Bailey, 1963). However the size at sexual maturity appears to vary from lake to lake. In Lake Michigan round whitefish mature at 300 to 380 mm but males mature at a smaller size (300 mm) than females (330 mm) (Mraz, 1964). In Lake Michigan spawning occurs before mid December (Mraz, 1964).

Round whitefish are invertebrate feeders in Great Slave Lake where their diet consisted largely of caddis fly larvae and small gastropods but they also ate chironomid and tabanid larvae, terrestrial beetles, amphipods and sphaerid clams.

**Table 6  Growth of round whitefish**

| Age | Great Bear | Koksoak River | Lake Michigan (north) | Lake Michigan (central) | Lake Superior | Great Slave |
|---|---|---|---|---|---|---|
| 1 |  | 61 | 117 | 134 | 86 | 102 |
| 2 |  | 97 | 229 | 255 | 152 | 160 |
| 3 |  | 136 | 312 | 346 | 211 | 215 |
| 4 |  | 170 | 363 | 396 | 262 | 247 |
| 5 |  | 201 | 396 | 436 | 307 | 285 |
| 6 | 328 | 230 | 427 | 460 | 340 | 315 |
| 7 | 338 | 256 | 455 | 481 | 366 | 347 |
| 8 | 353 | 279 | 480 |  | 389 | 365 |
| 9 | 368 | 300 |  |  | 406 | 392 |
| 10 | 422 | 318 |  |  | 427 | 410 |
| 11 |  | 337 |  |  | 439 |  |
| 12 |  | 355 |  |  | 457 |  |

Ref 1. Great Bear Kennedy, 1949
Koksoak River — Mackay and Power, 1968 (also Lake Michigan and Lake Superior — Isle Royale)
Great Slave — Rawson, 1951
Lake Superior — Bailey, 1963
Lake Michigan (north) — Mraz, 1964
(central) — Armstrong et al., 1977

## Lake Trout

Lake trout, *Salvelinus namaycush* (Walbaum), are found throughout the northern continental portion of North America and some of the arctic Islands including Victoria, King William, Southampton (Walters, 1955) and possibly Baffin Island (Ellis, 1962). They are absent from Newfoundland and do not extend into Siberia. Their distribution may be explained, in part at least, by their vulnerability to lamprey predation (Lindsey, 1964). The geographic center of lake trout distribution is in the southern Northwest Territories in western North America but in the east they extend southward to the Great Lakes (Scott and Crossman, 1973).

Lake trout are an important, much sought after, cold adapted species which grows to a large size and lives in freshwater lakes away from estuaries. They can reach a size of 40 kg, in Great Slave Lake they reach 30 kg (Keleher, 1961). Specimens weighing 15 kg are often caught in some northern lakes (Rawson, 1961).

Lake trout spawn on shallow rocky regions of lakes in the fall. In Lac la Ronge, Saskatchewan spawning occurs during the first week of October when water temperature is 9 to 10°C (Rawson, 1961) and as one moves further north spawning occurs at progressively earlier dates, mid September in Great Slave Lake and mid August in Great Bear Lake (Miller and Kennedy, 1948a).

Lake trout grow more slowly in northern lakes than in southern ones (Martin, 1951). Lake trout grow only during the summer months, June to September, in Great Slave with about half the annual growth occurring in July (Kennedy, 1954). In large lakes growth rate can differ in different regions of the lake. In Great Slave Lake for example lake trout grow more quickly in the western than in the eastern half of the lake (Kennedy, 1954). This may be due to differences in nutrient levels (food available) in the two regions since the major rivers flow into and out of the western portion of the lake. Growth in Great Slave Lake was similar to some southern populations (Kennedy, 1954), however growth in Great Bear Lake is very slow (Miller and Kennedy, 1948a). Where growth rates are slow, such as Great Bear Lake lake trout live for more than 30 years. It is interesting to note that growth in Lac la Ronge, Saskatchewan which is at 55°N is significantly faster than that in Redrock lake (45°N) in Algonquin Park, Ontario (Table 7).

The growth rate of male and female lake trout was similar in Lac la Ronge (Rawson, 1961).

There is a north-south gradient in spawning frequency of lake trout. Mature female lake trout in Great Bear Lake appear to spawn once every two or three years (Miller and Kennedy, 1948a) while sexually mature females in Great Slave Lake spawn every second year (Kennedy, 1954) so that only half of the population of mature lake trout spawn in any one year. In Lac la Ronge, the southern most of these lakes more than 90% of the sexually mature female lake trout spawn every year (Rawson, 1961). In Great Slave Lake some trout reach sexual maturity in their seventh year, 50% are mature in their eighth year and by age eleven all have reached sexual maturity (Kennedy, 1954). In Great Bear Lake where growth rates are slower fish first mature in their thirteenth year and all the fish are mature by age 17 (Miller and Kennedy, 1948a). In Lac la Ronge, Saskatchewan lake trout mature at between 5 and 8 years (Rawson, 1961). Sexual maturity is closely related to size with virtually all fish greater than 51 cm fork length and 1.4 kg body weight being sexually mature (Rawson, 1961). There is no difference between males and females in the age at sexual maturity in Great Bear Lake (Miller and Kennedy, 1948a). Adequate data have not been gathered to determine whether or not males spawn annually in Great Bear or Great Slave Lakes.

Lake trout are relatively sedentary in large lakes such as Great Bear (Miller, 1947), Great Slave (Keleher, 1963) and Lac la Ronge (Rawson, 1961) with average movements of less than 8 km over about 8 months in Great Slave Lake (Keleher, 1963). In Lac la Ronge lake trout were generally found in water of less than 10°C (Rawson, 1961).

Lake trout have been reported to feed on cisco and whitefish, as well as other lake trout, pike, burbot, and sculpins in Teslin Lake in northern British Columbia (Clemens et al., 1944). Lake trout are mainly found in shallow areas near shore in Great Bear Lake, under these conditions terrestrial insects were important (33.5% of fish stomachs) in the diet in addition to various fish species (44.3% of fish stomachs), particularly cisco and sculpin (Miller and Kennedy, 1948a) but they also feed on bottom dwelling invertebrates (25% of stomachs) and plankton (25.2% of stomachs) (Miller, 1947). In Great Slave Lake, where they are found down to 300 m and are common to 100 m (Rawson, 1951) lake trout feed almost entirely on fish, cisco being the most important single species (Rawson, 1947). The diet of lake trout differs between the deep eastern portion of Great Slave Lake and the more shallow western basin. A much high proportion of the diet is fish (90% vs 62%) in the western basin, whereas crustaceans comprise a higher proportion (38% vs 10%) in the deep eastern basin (Rawson, 1951). In Lac la Ronge large trout (>400 mm) were almost completely piscivorous with cisco being the most important prey species (50% by volume) followed by whitefish (15%) and eight other fish species (30%) with invertebrates comprising only 5% of their diet (Rawson, 1961). Small trout (<400 mm) also ate fish, particularly ciscoes, sculpins and sticklebacks which comprised approximately 80% of their diet by volume however they made more extensive use (29% of diet) of the crustaceans *Mysis* and *Pontoporeia* than did large trout (Rawson, 1961).

**Table 7 Growth of lake trout in northern waters**

| Age | Length (mm) | | | |
|---|---|---|---|---|
| | Great Slave | Great Bear | Lac la Ronge | Redrock |
| 0 | | 28 | | |
| 1 | | 63 | | |
| 2 | | 98 | 267 | 147 |
| 3 | | 134 | 376 | 188 |
| 4 | | 180 | 427 | 277 |
| 5 | | | 511 | 335 |
| 6 | | | 544 | 401 |
| 7 | 548 | 293 | 589 | 452 |
| 8 | 574 | 320 | 612 | 493 |
| 9 | 596 | 354 | 643 | 538 |
| 10 | 627 | 372 | 660 | 635 |
| 11 | 660 | 412 | 691 | 729 |
| 12 | 695 | 412 | 709 | 749 |
| 13 | 724 | 420 | 754 | |
| 14 | 767 | 440 | 787 | |
| 15 | 798 | 487 | 813 | |
| 16 | | 515 | 833 | |
| 17 | | 556 | | |
| 18 | | 574 | | |
| 19 | | 607 | | |
| 20 | | 626 | | |
| 21 | | 656 | | |
| 22 | | 700 | | |
| 23 | | 698 | | |

\* Great Slave Lake data from Kennedy, 1954
Great Bear Lake data from Miller and Kennedy, 1948.
Lac la Ronge data from Rawson, 1961 (fork length)

## Grayling

The grayling, *Thymallus arcticus* (Walbaum) is found in the western arctic of North America and eastern Siberia (Scott and Crossman, 1973). It is an important sports species in northern streams where it is found during the summer months (Clemens et al., 1944). In streams they feed primarily on aquatic insect larvae and some adult terrestrial insects which fall into the water (Clemens et al., 1944). In large lakes such as Great Slave and Great Bear grayling are found along rocky shores and near the mouths of streams (Miller, 1946; Rawson, 1951). In Great Slave Lake their diet consisted of terrestrial insects (28%), aquatic insects (21%) and amphipods (43%) (Rawson, 1951). The food of grayling in and near streams in Great Bear Lake is mainly terrestrial insects (75% of diet, 93% of all stomachs) which fall into the water but they also eat planktonic invertebrates (26.5% of stomachs), benthic invertebrates (21.6% of stomachs), and fish (10.8% of stomachs) (Miller, 1946, Miller, 1947).

Grayling reach weights of up to about 2.3 kg in Great Slave Lake (Keleher, 1961). The largest grayling reported is a 2.69 kg fish caught in the Northwest Territories (Scott and Crossman, 1973). Growth of grayling is remarkably similar between lakes (Table 8). In Great Bear Lake they commonly reach one kg in weight with a length of 280 to 380 mm at 4 or 5 years of age (Miller, 1947). A twelve year old fish from Great Bear weighed 1.4 kg and was 462 mm long (Miller, 1947). There is no evidence of sexual dimorphism in growth rate of grayling (Miller, 1947).

Grayling reach sexual maturity during their fourth year in Great Bear Lake where some individuals may spawn every other year (Miller, 1946). Grayling spawn in gravel substrate in streams (Kratt and Smith, 1977, Kratt, 1981). Their eggs are adhesive for a short time following spawning (Bishop, 1971). Spawning has been reported to occur in late May and early June in the Fond du Lac River, Saskatchewan (59°N) (Kratt and Smith, 1977).

**Table 8  Growth of grayling in northern waters**

| Age | Fork length (mm) | | |
|---|---|---|---|
| | Great Bear | Great Slave | Athabasca |
| 1 | 93 | 104 | 112 |
| 2 | 155 | 186 | 191 |
| 3 | 231 | 254 | 254 |
| 4 | 285 | 314 | 304 |
| 5 | 325 | 362 | 349 |
| 6 | 353 | | |
| 7 | 378 | | |
| 8 | 399 | | |
| 9 | 410 | | |
| 10 | | | |

\* All data from Miller, 1946

## Northern Pike

The relationship between latitude and growth rate of northern pike, *Esox lucius* L., that growth rate decreases with increased latitude, appears to be well established in the literature (eg Scott and Crossman, 1973). This was first suggested by Miller and Kennedy (1948b) who reported data on the growth rate of pike from three northern lakes (Great Slave, Great Bear and Lake Athabasca). They found essentially no difference in growth rate of pike from these three lakes. Miller and Kennedy (1948b) went on to compare the growth rates they found to data in the literature for several southern lakes, Lesser Slave in northern Alberta, Waskesiu in southern Saskatchewan and Mendota in Wisconsin. Their general conclusions with regard to latitude were that pike from northern lakes grew more slowly than pike from the more southerly lakes; that pike from northern lakes lived longer than their southern counterparts and; that pike from northern lakes did not reach as great an ultimate size as those from southern lakes. However the lakes used for these comparisons differed in morphology as well as latitude. The southern lakes were small, shallow, and eutrophic while the northern lakes were large, oligotrophic and two of the three (Great Slave and Great Bear) were deep.

I collected pike from four lakes in central Alberta (Lac Ste. Anne, Narrow, Seibert and Tucker) located between latitudes 53 and 55°N;

two lakes in the southern Northwest Territories (Kakisa and Great Slave) located between latitudes 61 and 62°N and four lakes on or near the Mackenzie River Delta (Campbell, Shell, and two unnamed lakes on the Mackenzie Delta) between latitudes 68 and 69°N. Growth rates were determined by back calculation from the cleithra.

The patterns of growth were similar for pike from shallow lakes in Central Alberta and the southern NWT (Table 9). However at any age pike from Great Slave Lake were only about 75% as large as those from the lakes in central Alberta or from Kakisa Lake which is a large shallow lake at the same latitude and near (<40 km) Great Slave Lake. The growth rates I recorded for Great Slave Lake fish differed from those reported by Miller and Kennedy (1948b). The growth rates I determined were greater than those reported by Miller and Kennedy (1948b) for young fish (<6 yrs) and less than those of Miller and Kennedy for older fish (>11 yrs).

The overall patterns of growth by pike from 68°N were similar to those of pike from southern lakes (Fig. 1). The average length at age was less in pike from the northern lakes than in those from southern lakes. During the first three years of life variations in length at age at any single latitude were greater than the differences between latitudes 54 and 68°N (Table 9). However length at age of pike from 54 and 68°N diverged with increasing age and fish older than 3 years from the northern lakes were consistently smaller than those from the south. Thus near the limits of their range, latitude (length of growing season, degree days) has a significant effect on growth rate but there is still considerable variation in growth rate due to other environmental parameters including biotic factors such as the number and size of prey species available and perhaps abiotic factors such as depth and rate of warming.

Pike from some lakes (eg Campbell) showed a biphasic pattern of growth (Fig. 2). In these populations body length approached one asymptote in young fish and a markedly higher asymptote in older fish. The length at which the inflection occurred corresponded to the length at which the pike in these lakes switched to coregonids as a major prey species.

The ice-free season of the lakes I examined ranges from approximately 26 to 13 weeks. The magnitude of the difference in number of degree days (sum of the amount water temperature exceeds 4°C over the number of days water temperature exceeded 4°C) would be even larger than this two fold difference in open water season.

The relative independence of growth rate and latitude could be explained by a low optimum temperature for growth in pike or that pike are able to feed and grow even at low water temperatures and at high latitudes a large portion of their total annual growth occurs under ice cover in the winter.

I have found that when one compares growth rates of northern pike in lakes of similar morphometry that the range of growth rates observed at 54 and 68°N overlap. However the average growth rate at 68°N is slower than that seen in the south.

Table 9 Standard length (back calculated) for northern pike from central Alberta (54°N), the southern Northwest Territories (61°N) and the northern NWT (68°N).

|  | Standard Length (mm) Age (years) | | |
|---|---|---|---|
|  | 3 | 4 | 5 |
| 54°N | | | |
| Lac Ste. Anne | 426 | 478 | 514 |
| Tucker Lake | 380 | 413 | 449 |
| Narrow Lake | 288 | 363 | 411 |
| 61°N | | | |
| Kakisa Lake | 349 | 418 | 450 |
| Great Slave Lake | 245 | 313 | 372 |
| 68°N | | | |
| Shell Lake | 368 | | |
| Reindeer Station | 282 | 336 | 361 |
| Campbell Lake | 269 | 319 | 358 |

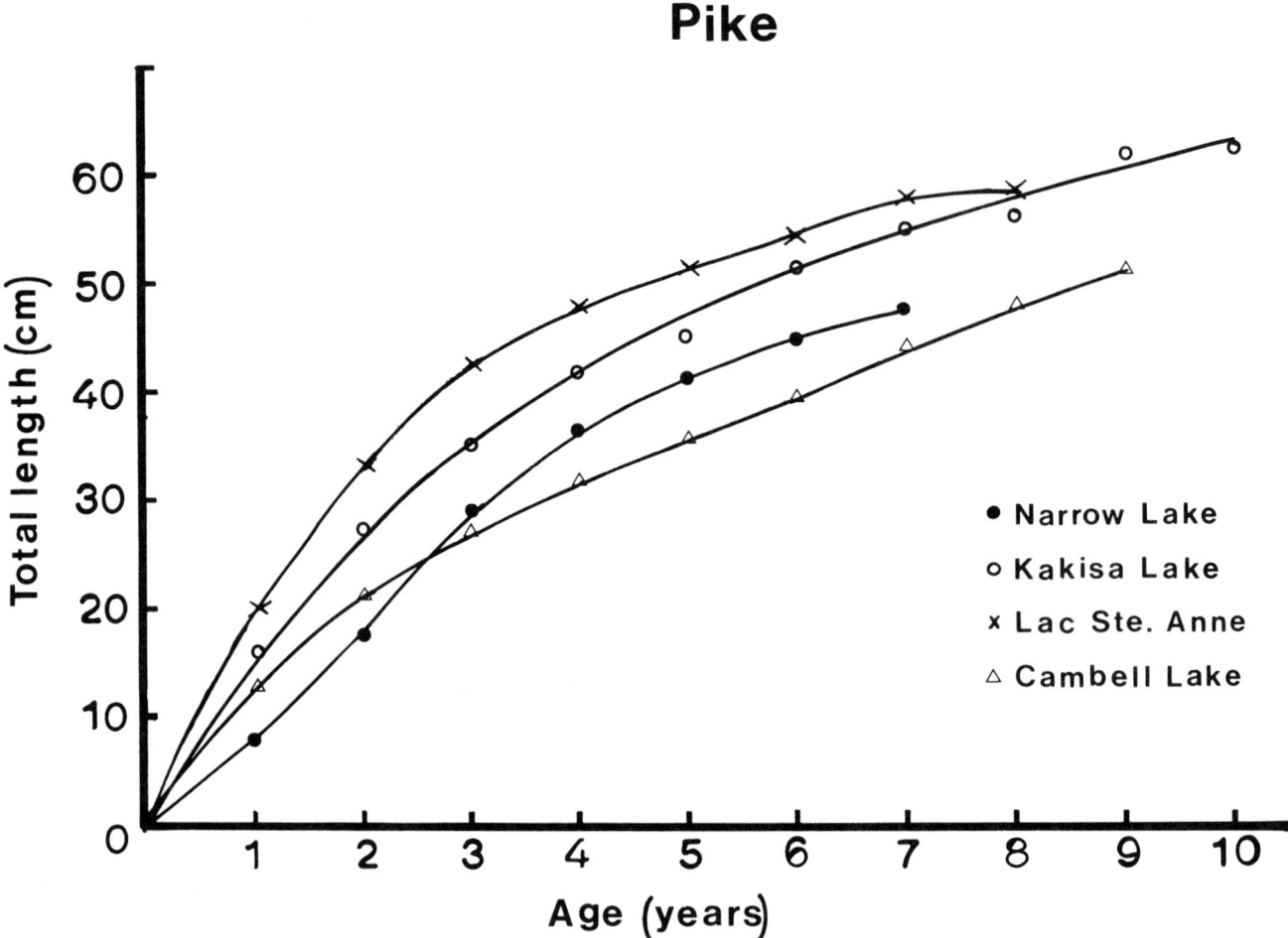

Figure 1  Comparison of growth curves for northern pike from two lakes (Lac Ste. Anne and Narrow) at 54°N, one lake (Kakisa) at 61°N and one (Cambell) at 68°N.

## Burbot

The growth and biology of burbot, *Lota lota L.*, are relatively poorly studied even though burbot have a circumpolar distribution. Little is known about the growth of burbot because they are often difficult to catch using conventional sampling techniques (gill nets). However, they can be caught in traps and by angling during the winter and by seine and electrofishing at night in the summer.

Burbot are a cold water species which grow well in the north. Burbot weighing 27 kg with a length of 1.5 m have been reported from Alaska (Chen, 1969). Burbot often reach weights of 4 to 5 kg and lengths of close to a meter in northern lakes and rivers. Growth is quite variable between water bodies and even between subpopulations within a single large water body (Table 10).

Female burbot become sexually mature at between 550 and 700 g and males at between 850 and 1000 g in Lake Winnipeg (Hewson, 1955). In Lake Winnipeg spawning occurs in early February when water temperature was 1°C (Hewson, 1955).

There are seasonal changes in the size of both the liver and gonad of mature burbot. Liver weights reach a maximum size in males early in the fall and in females in mid winter. In both cases live weight decreases during the period of rapid gonad growth (Chen, 1969).

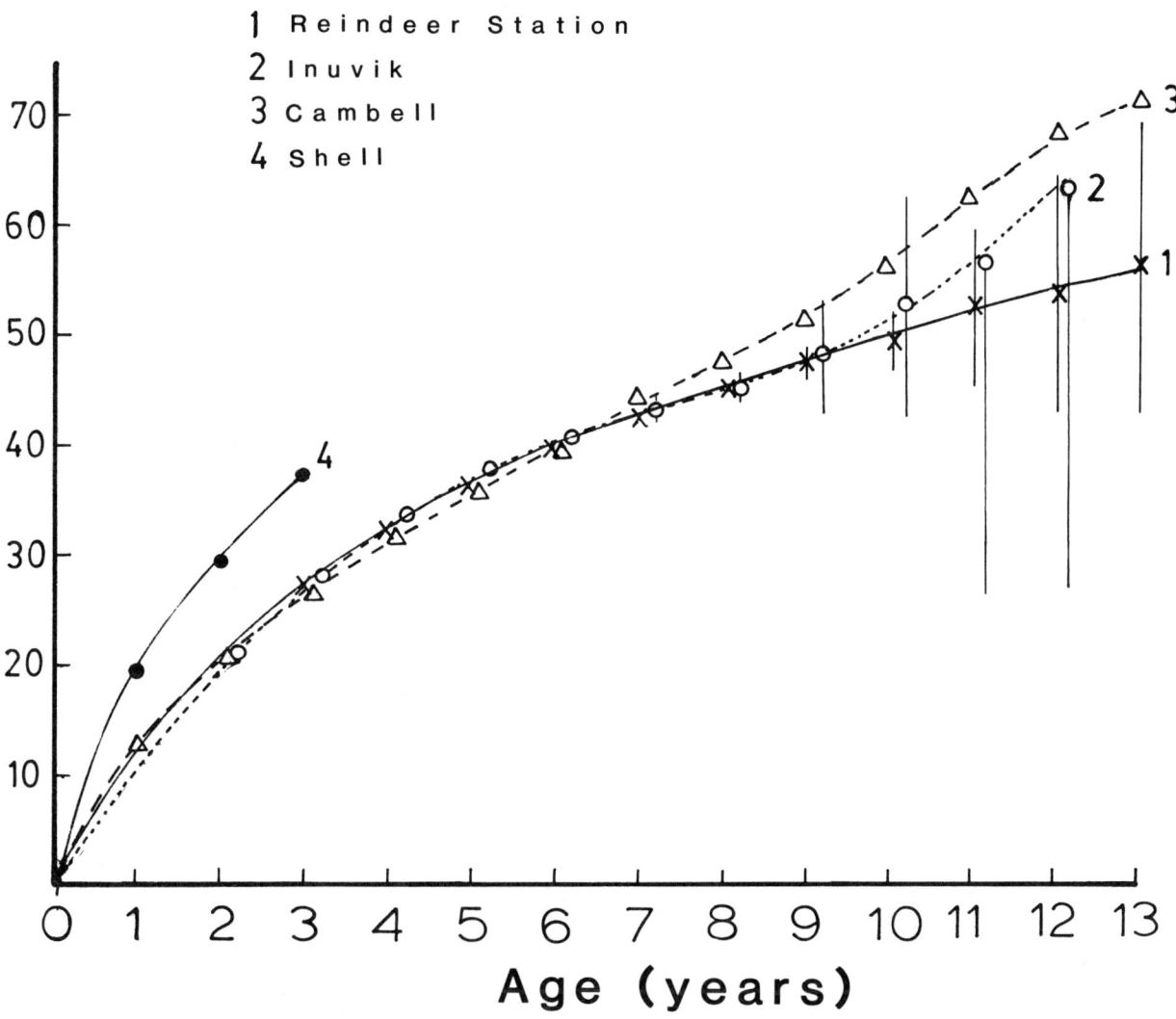

Figure 2  Growth of northern pike from four water bodies at 68°N. Inuvik and Reindeer Station designated fish were collected from lakes in the Mackenzie River Delta. Cambell Lake is also connected by a short channel to the Mackenzie River. Shell is a small shallow lake that drain into the Mackenzie River but fish passage between the river and lake is prevented by an outlet structure on the lake

In some areas of the NWT there is a domestic fishery for burbot in the late fall and winter (Cunningham Landing/Salt River — RL&L/EMA, 1985). The liver and sometimes the eggs are used for human consumption (RL&L/EMA, 1985).

Burbot are piscivorous feeding primarily on whitefish and cisco, as well as lake trout, pike and sculpins in northern British Columbia (Clemens et al., 1944) and primarily on cisco and crayfish in Lake Winnipeg (Hewson, 1955).

Burbot have been reported to migrate into the Slave River from Great Slave Lake in late fall (RL&L/EMA, 1985, Keleher, 1963).

### Catastomidae

Suckers, particularly longnose, *Catostomus catostomus* Forster, and white, *Catostomus commersoni* Lacèpéde, are common in northern freshwater.

Table 10 Growth of burbot in northern waters

| | Length (mm) | | | | |
|---|---|---|---|---|---|
| Age | Lake Winnipeg (south end) | Lake Winnipeg (north end) | Yukon River (Alaska) | Tananak River (Alaska) | Heming Lake (Manitoba) |
| 1 | | | 109 | 110 | 147 |
| 2 | | | 174 | 175 | 246 |
| 3 | 411 | 373 | 239 | 236 | 279 |
| 4 | 490 | 460 | 300 | 294 | 323 |
| 5 | 526 | 511 | 355 | 352 | 366 |
| 6 | 531 | 566 | 408 | 405 | 399 |
| 7 | 554 | 615 | 450 | 457 | 429 |
| 8 | 587 | 676 | 497 | 507 | 465 |
| 9 | 632 | 719 | 537 | 546 | |
| 10 | 668 | | 575 | 585 | |
| 11 | 721 | | 614 | | |
| 12 | 782 | | 643 | | |
| 13 | 795 | | 678 | | |
| 14 | | | 712 | | |
| 15 | | | 750 | | |
| 16 | | | 814 | | |
| 17 | | | 834 | | |
| 18 | | | 868 | | |
| 19 | | | 931 | | |
| 20 | | | | | |

\* Lake Winnipeg north and south from Hewson, 1955
Yukon and Tananak River from Chen, 1969

| | Weight (g) | |
|---|---|---|
| Age | Lake Winnipeg (south) | Lake Winnipeg (north) |
| 1 | | |
| 2 | | |
| 3 | 591 | 318 |
| 4 | 1000 | 818 |
| 5 | 1090 | 1136 |
| 6 | 1182 | 1545 |
| 7 | 1318 | 2091 |
| 8 | 1682 | 2727 |
| 9 | 2227 | 3909 |
| 10 | 2227 | 3818 |
| 11 | 3000 | |
| 12 | 3545 | |
| 13 | 3818 | |
| 14 | 3364 | |

\* Lake Winnipeg north and south from Hewson, 1955
Heming Lake, Manitoba from Lawler, 1963

The longnose sucker is plentiful to the arctic ocean (Ellis, 1962) and reaches 3.3 kg and 64 cm fork length in Great Slave Lake (Keleher, 1961). In Great Slave Lake longnose suckers are very abundant and are found to depths of 30 m (Rawson, 1951). Their growth rate appears to have been determined only in Great Slave Lake where they grow faster on the southern than the northern side of the lake (Table 11). The growth rates reported by Rawson (1951) for Great Slave Lake are similar to those reported by Harris (1962) for the northern part of the same lake. Males and females grow at the same rate but females live longer (19 years) than males (16 years) and thus ultimately become larger than males (Harris, 1962).

In Great Slave Lake longnose suckers may compete with whitefish as bottom feeders but the whitefish are far more abundant than the suckers (Rawson, 1951). Their diet in Great Slave Lake consisted of amphipods (63% by volume), chironomid larvae (15%), caddis fly larvae (11%) and sphaerids (9%) (Rawson, 1951). Longnose suckers mature at between 7 and 9 years in Great Slave Lake (Harris, 1962).

## Table 11 Growth of longnose suckers

| Age | Great Slave* Lake | Great Slave Lake† north side | south side |
|---|---|---|---|
| 1 | 110 | | |
| 2 | 150 | 152 | 179 |
| 3 | 190 | 170 | 203 |
| 4 | 225 | 253 | 239 |
| 5 | 270 | 290 | 306 |
| 6 | 300 | 314 | 308 |
| 7 | 330 | 330 | 363 |
| 8 | 360 | 372 | 412 |
| 9 | 390 | 403 | 479 |
| 10 | 425 | 433 | 496 |
| 11 | 450 | 465 | 496 |
| 12 | 480 | 499 | 517 |
| 13 | | 510 | 530 |
| 14 | | 518 | 541 |
| 15 | | 547 | 557 |
| 16 | | 527 | 575 |
| 17 | | 579 | 586 |

* Rawson, 1951
† Harris, 1962

## White Suckers

White suckers, *Catostomus commersoni* Lacépède, have a more southerly distribution than longnose suckers being found north of 60°N only in the western NWT as far north as the Mackenzie River delta and in Ungava and Labrador (Scott and Crossman, 1973). They reach a size comparable to long nose suckers, about 3 kg in both northern (Keleher, 1961) and southern (Webster, 1942) waters. In Great Slave Lake they are found primarily in shallow bays where they feed on chironomid larvae (32% of diet by volume), amphipods (30%), caddis fly larvae (17%), gastropods (11%) and sphaerids (9%) (Rawson, 1951).

Suckers are bottom feeders (Clemens et al. 1944). In Great Slave Lake the shrimp *Pontoporeia* is an important food organism for both *C. commersoni* and *C. catostomus* (Larkin, 1948).

## Walleye

Walleye *Stizostedion vitreum* extend through the boreal forest but not far into the arctic. Preble (1908) reported them as far down the Mackenzie as Fort Rae and Fort Providence. In Great Slave Lake they are found primarily in shallow bays and in rivers and small lakes connected to the lake (Rawson, 1951). Where they do occur they are an important commercial and subsistence species. Walleye are abundant in the west end of Lake Athabasca and form the basis of an important local fishery. However their potential as a sports or commercial species is severely limited in the North because growth and production is slow compared to southern populations.

In Great Slave Lake walleye reach a length of 22 cm at the end of 5 years and about 40 cm at 10 years of age (Rawson, 1951). This is an extremely slow growth rate for this species and likely marks what can be expected at the northern limits of its range.

Walleye feed mainly on trout perch and stickleback in Lake Athabasca (Rawson, 1947b). The walleye in Lake Athabasca were an important intermediate host for cysts of the tapeworm *Diphyllobothrium latum* which infects humans and dogs (Rawson, 1947b).

## Perch

Perch *Perca flavescens* extend through the boreal forest but like their close relative the walleye, the growth of perch populations in northern freshwater is much slower than the growth reported for this species from populations in the southern part of their range.

## Goldeye

Goldeye, *Hiodon alosoides* (Rafinesque) are particularly abundant in the region of Lake Athabasca and the Slave River but is rare in Great Slave Lake (Rawson, 1951). Preble (1908) reported goldeye from as far north as Fort Norman where they were rare. They are also found in Great Slave Lake but are not abundant there.

Growth rate of goldeye decreases with increased latitude (Rawson, 1947b). In Lake Athabasca they feed on aquatic and terrestrial insects with the larger individuals taking some small fish such as trout perch and sticklebacks (Rawson, 1947b) while in Great Slave Lake they feed on aquatic and terrestrial insect (Rawson, 1951).

## Bibliography

Alt, K.T.
1969   Taxonomy and ecology of the inconnu, *Stenodus leucichthys nelma* in Alaska. Univ. Alaska Biol. Pap. No. 12:63pp.

Armstrong, J.W., C.R. Liston, P.I. Tack, and R.C. Anderson
1977   Age, growth, maturity and seasonal food habits of round whitefish, *Prosopium cylindraceum*, in Lake Michigan near Ludington, Michigan. Trans. Am. Fish. Soc. 106:151-155.

Bailey, M.M.
1963   Age, growth and maturity of round whitefish of the Apostle Islands and Isle Royale regions, Lake Superior. Fish. Bull. U.S. Fish Wildlife Serv. 63:63-75.

Bishop, F.G.
1971   Observations on spawning habits and fecundity of Arctic grayling. Progr. Fish-Cult. 33(1):12-19.

Bryan, J.E. and D.A. Kato
1975   Spawning of lake whitefish, *Coregonus clupeaformis*, and round whitefish, *Prosopium cylindraceum*, in Aishihik Lake and East Aishihik River, Yukon Territory. J. Fish. Res. Board Can. 32:283-288.

Chen, Lo-Chai
1969   The biology and taxonomy of the burbot, *Lota lota leptura*, in interior Alaska. Biol. Pap. Univ. Alaska No. 11 53 pages.

Clemens, W.A., R.V. Boughton and J.A. Rattenbury
1944   A preliminary report on the fishery survey of Teslin Lake, British Columbia. Rept. British Columbia Fisheries Dept. 1944:M70-75.

Dryer, W.R.
1963   Age and growth of the whitefish in Lake Superior. Fishery Bull. 63:77-94.

Dymond, J.R.
1933   Biological and oceanographic conditions in Hudson Bay 8. The coregonine fishes of Hudson and James Bays. Contrib. Can. Biol. and Fish. 8:1-12.
1943   The coregonine fishes of northwestern Canada. Trans. Roy. Can. Inst. 24:171-231.

Ellis, D.V.
1962   Observations on the distribution and ecology of some arctic fish. Arctic 15:179-189.

Fuller, W.A.
1955   The inconnu (*Stenodus leucichthys mackenziei*) in Great Slave Lake and adjoining waters. J. Fish. Res. Bd. Canada. 12:768-780

Godfrey, H.
1955   On the ecology of Skenna River whitefishes, *Coregonus* and *Prosopium*. J. Fish. Res. Board Can. 12:499-542.

Harris, R.H.D.
1962   *Catostomus catostomus* (Forster), in Great Slave Lake. J. Fish. Res. Bd. Canada 19:113-126.

Healey, M.C.
1975a  Dynamics of exploited whitefish populations and their management with special reference to the Northwest Territories. J. Fish. Res. Board Can. 32:427-448.
1975b  Production in unexploited lake whitefish populations in northern Canadian lakes. Verh. Internat. Verein. Limnol. 19: 2371-2377.
1978  Fecundity changes in exploited populations of lake whitefish (*Coregonus clupeaformis*) and lake trout (*Salvelinus namaycush*). J. Fish. Res. Board Can. 35: 945-950.

Healey M.C. and K. Dietz
1984  Variation in fecundity of lake whitefish (*Coregonus clupeaformis*) from Lesser Slave and Utikuma lakes in northern Alberta. Copeia 1984(1): 238-242.

Hewson, L.C.
1955  Age, maturity, spawning and food of burbot, *Lota lota*, in Lake Winnipeg. J. Fish. Res. Bd. Canada. 12:930-940.

Keleher, J.J.
1961  Comparison of largest Great Slave Lake fish with North American records. J. Fish. Res. Bd. Canada. 18:417-421.
1963  The movement of tagged Great Slave Lake fish. J. Fish. Res. Board Can. 20:319-326.

Kennedy, W.A.
1949  Some observations on the coregonine fish of Great Bear Lake, N.W.T.. Bull. Fish. Res. Bd. Can. 82:1-10
1953  Growth, maturity, fecundity and mortality in the relatively unexploited whitefish, *Coregonus clupeaformis*, of Great Slave Lake. J. Fish. Res. Bd. Can. 10:413-441.
1954  Growth, maturity and mortality in the relatively unexploited lake trout, *Cristivomer namaycush*, of Great Slave Lake. J. Fish. Res. Bd. Canada. 11:827-852.
1963  Growth and mortality of whitefish in three unexploited lakes in northern Canada. J. Fish. Res. Bd. Canada. 20:265-272.

Kratt, L.F.
1981  Evidence of Arctic Grayling (*Thymallus arcticus*) spawning in a highway culvert. Can. Field-Nat. 95:358.

Kratt, L.F. and R.J.F. Smith
1977  A post-hatching sub-gravel stage in the life history of Arctic Grayling, (*Thymallus arcticus*). Trans. Am. Fish. Soc. 106:241-243.

Larkin, P.A.
1948  *Pontoporeia* and *Mysis* in Athabaska, Great Bear and Great Slave Lake. Bull Fish. Res. Bd. Can. 78:1-33

Lawler, G.H.
1963  The biology and taxonomy of the burbot, *Lota lota*, in Heming Lake, Manitoba. J. Fish. Res. Bd. Canada 20:417-433

Lawler, G.H. and W.B. Scott
1954  Notes on the geographical distribution and the hosts of the cestode genus *Triaenophorus* in North America. J. Fish. Res. Bd. Canada 11:884-893.

Lindsey, C.C.
1964  Problems in zoogeography of the lake trout, *Salvelinus namaycush*. J. Fish. Res. Bd. Canada. 21:977-994.

Mackay, I. and G. Power
1968  Age and growth of round whitefish (*Prosopium cylindraceum*) from Ungava. J. Fish. Res. Bd. Canada 25:657-666.

Martin, N.V.
1951  A study of the lake trout *Salvelinus namaycush* in two Algonquin Park, Ontario, lakes. Trans. Am. Fish. Soc. 81:111-137.

McPhail, J.D. and C.C. Lindsey
1970  Freshwater fishes of northwestern Canada and Alaska. Fish. Res. Bd. Canada. Bull. 173. 381pp.

Miller, R.B.
1946  Notes on the Arctic grayling, *Thymallus signifer* Richardson, from Great Bear Lake. Copeia 1946(4):227-236.
1947  Great Bear Lake. Bull. Fish. Res. Bd. Can. 72:31-44.

Miller, R.B. and W.A. Kennedy
1948a  Observations on the lake trout of Great Bear Lake. J. Fish. Res. Bd. Canada. 7(4):176-189
1948b  Pike (*Esox lucius*) from four northern Canadian lakes. J. Fish. Res. Board Can. 7:190-199.

Mraz, D.
1964 Age and growth of the round whitefish (*Prosopium cylindraceum*) in Lake Michigan. Trans. Am. Fish. Soc. 93:46-53

Muth, K.M.
1969 Age and growth of broad whitefish, *Coregonus nasus* in the Mackenzie and Coppermine Rivers, N.W.T. J. Fish. Res. Bd. Canada. 26:2252-2256.

Preble, E.A.
1908 A biological investigation of the Athabasca- Mackenzie Region. pp 502-515. IN: North American Fauna No. 27.

Qadri, S.U.
1961 Food and distribution of lake whitefish in Lac la Ronge, Saskatchewan. Trans. Amer. Fish. Soc. 90:303-307.
1968 Growth and reproduction of the lake whitefish, *Coregonus clupeaformis*, in Lac la Ronge, Saskatchewan. J. Fish. Res. Bd. Canada. 25:2091-2100.

Rawson, D.S.
1947a Great Slave Lake. Bull. Fish. Res. Bd. Can. 72:45-68
1947b Lake Athabasca. Bull. Fish. Res. Bd. Can. 72:69-85.
1949 Estimating the fish production of Great Slave Lake. Trans. Am. Fish. Soc. 77:81-92
1951 Studies of the fish of Great Slave Lake. J. Fish. Res. Bd. Can. 8:207-240.
1961 The lake trout of Lac La Ronge, Saskatchewan. J. Fish. Res. Board Can. 18: 423-462.

RL&L/EMA
1985 Fall fish spawing habitat survey, 1983 - 1985. Prepared for the Slave River Hydro Study Group.

Scott, W.B. and E.J. Crossman
1973 Freshwater fishes of Canada. Fish. Res. Bd. Canada. Bull. 184. 966 pp.

van Oosten, J.
1946 Maximum size and age of whitefish. The Fisherman 14(8):17-18.

Walters, V.
1955 Fishes of western arctic America and eastern arctic Siberia: taxonomy and zoogeography. Bull. Amer. Mus. Nat. Hist. 106:255-368

Webster, D.A.
1942 The life histories of some Connecticut fishes. IN A fishery survey of important Connecticut lakes. Bull. State Geol. Nat. Hist. Sur., No. 63, pp. 122-127.

# Fish Assemblages in Small Boreal Lakes

W.M. Tonn and C.L.K. Robinson
Department of Zoology
University of Alberta
Edmonton, Alberta T6G 2E9

## Introduction

The boreal forest biome of North America and Scandinavia contains an immense number of small lakes that are potentially suitable for fishes. From this natural abundance of freshwater habitats arises an intriguing ecological question: must we study the fish assemblages of each lake one-by-one, as unique individuals, or are there patterns of fish assemblage structure among groups of lakes that will aid our understanding of these systems and be useful for predictive or management purposes? More specifically, are the numbers and kinds of fish species found in a boreal lake merely a random sample from among all the species present in the local region or are they determined by specific characteristics of the lake, including its abiotic features and its inhabitants?

Objectives of this review are to:
1. describe a general approach taken by ecologists in their search for, and evaluation of, patterns of assemblage structure.
2. review three classes of factors that are important in organizing fish assemblages in small boreal lakes:
   a. factors related to colonization (e.g., lake isolation and age)
   b. factors related to maintenance of a species population in a lake or to its local extinction following colonization (e.g., lake size, habitat diversity, habitat severity)
   c. biotic interaction (e.g., competition, predation)
3. compare boreal lake fish assemblages, and the factors that structure them, in similar regions of North America (northern Wisconsin) and northern Europe (Finland).

## A Community Analysis Approach

Most ecologists recognize that boundaries separating communities are frequently indistinct (e.g., Whitaker 1975), but because lakes and ponds are themselves usually discreet, it is not unreasonable to consider their fish assemblages as separate entities. A local assemblage is the product of local and regional environmental characteristics, attributes of individual species available to colonize an area, species interactions, historic events, and chance (Ricklefs 1987). Thus, within a region, composition of a local assemblage might be predictable if the influence of the first three factors are more important than those of the last two.

Fisheries biologists have long been aware of the fact that certain fish species occur together in certain types of lakes. Until recently, it has been difficult to translate this knowledge, developed through experience, into a quantitative and objective framework. However, with the development of multivariate analysis, "effective, efficient, and appropriate" methods are available to summarize complex community-level data sets and reveal structural patterns (Gauch 1982). Multivariate community analyses mathematically measure similarities and differences among assemblages or lakes based on their species composition and environmental characteristics. This provides an objective way to examine whether or not groups of similar assemblages exist that are distinct from other groups.

Multivariate analyses can also assist in ecological interpretation by determining which species are important contributors to assemblage-level patterns or which environmental factors are most closely associated with different assemblage types. Conducting controlled manipulative experiments is often not feasible at the assemblage level. However, comparative studies, together with multivariate analyses, are frequently able to detect patterns, generate and test hypotheses that assess the importance of different processes, and ultimately produce acceptable explanations for community-level problems (Tonn et al. 1983; Diamond 1986). Gauch (1982) and Pielou (1984) provide overviews of general principles and explanations of some uses of multivariate analyses in community ecology; Green and Vascotto (1978), Tonn et al. (1983) and Rice (1985) provide applications of multivariate analyses to aquatic community studies.

## Colonization Events

Colonization by fish of lakes within a boreal watershed may be considered analogous to species colonization of oceanic islands (Magnuson 1976). Geographical ecologists have identified several characteristics of islands that influence the number and kinds of species that can colonize them (MacArthur and Wilson 1967). A number of these characteristics have been examined relative to post-glacial dispersal (e.g., Crossman and McAllister 1986) and subsequent development of fish assemblages in boreal lakes (e.g., Stewart and Linsey 1983).

### Lake Isolation

According to the theory of island biogeography, lakes more isolated from a source of species (e.g., a large lake or river) will have lower assemblage diversity than lakes closer to the source. It is expected that after moving into a new watershed, a species' dispersal becomes limited by physical barriers (e.g., waterfalls) and/or the filtering nature and potential seasonal instability of connecting waterways (Barbour and Brown 1974; Browne 1981).

Various measures of lake isolation (e.g., presence/absence of an outlet, size of the outlet's watershed, distance and gradient from a source of colonists) are significantly related to fish assemblage richness and composition (Tonn and Magnuson 1982; Rahel 1984; Tonn et al. MS; C. Robinson, unpublished data). For example, seepage lakes in Finland contain, on average, only 55% as many species as similarly-sized drainage lakes (Tonn et al. MS).

Dispersal mechanisms used by fishes to enter isolated lakes may include the ability to move through small and temporary quantities of surface runoff (J. Kitchell, pers. comm.), wind transport (Bajkov 1949), underground streams (Nelson and Paetz 1974), past connections (Nordqvist 1903), and man (Rahel 1984). The first three dispersal mechanisms support the observation that most isolated lakes contain small bodied fish species (e.g., minnows and sticklebacks). Man represents an important and often overlooked selective dispersal factor (e.g. Magnuson 1976).

### Lake Age

Another "colonization" variable that contributes to the relatively depauperate diversity in northern lakes is the age of these systems (Barbour and Brown 1974). Northern watersheds in glaciated regions are generally too young to have evolved endemic species or to have allowed all potential species the chance to reach otherwise suitable habitats (Magnuson 1976). However, the history of each region must be considered before broad generalizations are appropriate. Post-glacial Fennoscandia was covered by several large water bodies that submerged existing smaller lake basins. So although the regional ichthyofauna as a whole is depauperate because of its youth and regional isolation from glacial refuges, it is believed that most fish present at the time of Lake Ancylus (ca. 8800 ybp) had access to all smaller basins (Nordqvist 1903; Svardson 1970). Thus, fish assemblages present today within the region may primarily result from differential extinction rather than colonization (Tonn et al. MS).

## Extinction Events

As colonization of boreal lakes proceeds, events related to local extinction of fish species within a lake influence assemblage structure. Theoretically, one expects an interaction between colonization and extinction events such that at some point an equilibrium number of species is maintained within a lake (MacArthur and Wilson 1967; Magnuson 1976). Three important extinction-related variables are lake size (and/or habitat heterogeneity), other limnological factors (e.g., habitat severity), and biotic factors (predation and competition).

*Lake size and habitat heterogeneity*

Larger lakes should contain a greater variety of habitats than small ponds. Therefore, larger lakes should have an increased number of sites for reproduction, a greater diversity of vegetation for cover, etc., and thus should be able to support more fish species. Eadie and Keast (1984) found for boreal lakes in Ontario that fish species diversity was significantly and positively related to both surface area and several measures of habitat complexity (plant species diversity, substrate diversity). Similarly, Tonn and Magnuson (1982) determined that species richness in Wisconsin lakes was correlated with lake area and vegetation diversity, which in turn, were correlated with each other. It has not been established that species richness in boreal lakes is related to area independent of habitat diversity, as predicted (MacArthur and Wilson 1967) and found elsewhere (Simberloff 1976).

Specific habitat characteristics of small boreal ponds may contribute to reduced assemblage diversity. For example, small boreal lakes in Alberta tend to be shallow and frequently have accumulated detrital material, which reduces the occurrence of hard-bottomed areas and potentially blocks outlets (C. Robinson, personal observation). Either or both of these habitats are required by some species for spawning (e.g., white sucker, *Catostomus commersoni*, and walleye, *Stizostedion vitreum*; Balon 1975).

*Environmental severity*

Studies of adaptations of fish species to chemical conditions in small boreal lakes have focussed on responses to low pH and low dissolved oxygen concentrations, two common features of these ecosystems. These studies have found that the distribution and abundance of species among lakes with different chemical conditions are related to the physiological tolerances of these species.

*pH*

Several studies have shown that pH is one of the most important environmental characteristics distinguishing boreal lakes that contain different types of fish assemblages. This is especially true in continental shield regions, where many poorly-buffered lakes have pH values near or below tolerance levels for many fish species (Rahel 1984; Wales and Beggs 1986). Because of the strong correlation between species richness and pH, Henderson (1984) suggested that fish assemblages of acidic waters are not unique combinations of species but rather are simply reduced forms of assemblages found at higher pH levels. However, because of the close correspondence among rankings of species occurrence with minimum pH in naturally acidic lakes (northern Wisconsin), occurrence in lakes affected by acid precipitation (Ontario), and rankings based on survival during laboratory exposure to low pH, Rahel and Magnuson (1983) suggested that low pH is directly responsible for the absence of many minnows and darters from lakes with pH below 6.

Another factor complicating an evaluation of the effects of pH on boreal fish assemblages is the fact that many other environmental characteristics covary with pH. Boreal lakes with naturally low pH tend to be small, isolated, and have low alkalinites and limited habitat diversity, all of which may reduce species richness in a selective manner. Indeed, Rahel (1986) observed that low-alkalinity lakes (pH > 5.0.) had fewer species than high-alkalinity lakes and added species at a slower rate as lake size increased. Rahel (1984) also concluded that a sequential loss of fish species occurs in isolated dystrophic lakes as bog mat development decreases lake size and eliminates the littoral zone, as well as acidifying the water. Still, Rago and Wiener (1986), using analysis of covariance and a blocked comparison test to remove effects of lake area, found that Ontario and Wisconsin lakes with low pH (<6.0) contained significantly fewer species than lakes with high pH (> 6.0).

From these studies we can conclude that: (1)

naturally low pH, common to many boreal lakes, can prevent establishment and maintenance of fish populations due primarily to reduced reproduction and increased mortality of eggs and larvae (e.g. Rask 1983, 1984), and (2) environmental covariates of low pH also affect fish species richness and composition. Thus, although pH is not the only factor influencing the structure of fish assemblages, it is usually an excellent empirical predictor of species richness and presence or absence of individual species.

*Low Dissolved Oxygen*

Extreme depletion of dissolved oxygen is frequent in small boreal lakes during winter. Because of the high sediment surface: water volume ratio of shallow lakes, the amount of dissolved oxygen consumed by processes of decomposition can approach the total amount of oxygen dissolved in the water. During the long boreal winter, a continuous cover of ice and snow can severely reduce the amount of light entering a lake, preventing the generation of fresh oxygen from photosynthesis. As the ice thickens from the surface downward, an anaerobic layer develops along the bottom and expands upwards (Magnuson and Karlen 1970). As living space decreases, the lake may experience a fish kill. Behavioral adaptations of fishes in response to increasing anoxia may include redistribution to aerobic refuges within the lake or emigration from the lake (Magnuson et al. 1985). Physiological adaptations associated with small body size and "air-breathing" may also allow certain fishes to survive winter hypoxia (Casselman and Harvey 1975; Klinger et al. 1983; Magnuson et al. 1983). As a result, winterkill is a selective mortality factor that can alter the composition of fish assemblages in small boreal lakes.

Tonn and Magnuson (1982) were able to separate fish assemblage types in northern Wisconsin lakes based on a combination of winter oxygen concentration and lake isolation. In more isolated lakes experiencing hypoxia, assemblages dominated by central mudminnows (*Umbra limi*) and minnows (*Cyprinidae*) occurred whereas in lakes with outlets, or in deeper lakes having sufficient oxygen supplies, assemblages were characterized by northern pike (*Esox lucius*), largemouth bass (*Micropterus salmoides*), and other centrarchids. Tonn and Magnuson concluded that mudminnows and cyprinids could persist in shallow isolated lakes because of physiological/behavioral adaptations allowing survival under low oxygen conditions and that these physically harsh habitats in turn offered refuges from piscivorous predators. A different refuge was available to pike; as winter conditions proceeded they apparently emigrated from the lakes and survived in outlet stream refugia, returning to the lake in the spring. By exploiting this refuge, pike were able to avoid the harsh abiotic lake environment and exclude the predation-intolerant mudminnow and cyprinids.

*Lake Productivity*

Relations between species composition and correlates of lake productivity (alkalinity, phosphorous concentration, total dissolved solids, etc.) have been useful predictors of boreal fish assemblages. Theoretically, more productive habitats should maintain more fish species as a result of increases in prey abundance/diversity. For example, Gascon and Leggett (1977) found that diversity of the littoral fish community within Lake Memphremagog (Quebec-Vermont) was positively correlated with a nutrient production gradient.

Correlations between prey abundance/diversity and fish species diversity may be a result of fish and prey responding independently to physical environmental parameters. Harvey (1975) found a strong correlation between the number of zooplankton species and fish species in a group of Ontario lakes, but concluded that this correlation was due to independent correlations with physical/chemical features of the environment rather than cascading actions between trophic levels.

Differences in assemblage diversity between lakes of northern and southern Ontario also support the diversity/productivity theory. Less productive lakes in northern Ontario tend to have lower vegetation and invertebrate prey abundance/diversity than southern lakes and a corresponding reduction in fish species number

(Eadie and Keast 1984). However, as with pH, assigning cause-and-effect in productivity/fish assemblage relations is difficult, because several alternative factors, e.g., habitat diversity, covary with productivity gradients.

## Biotic Interactions

Prediction of fish assemblage composition would be relatively straightforward and accurate if only abiotic variables operated as determinant factors. Although abiotic conditions clearly limit their distribution and occurrence, fish species are often absent from seemingly suitable and accessible habitats. Biotic interactions, in the form of competition or predation, may be equally or more important than abiotic factors in structuring assemblages.

### Competition

At a time when competition was gaining prominence among theoretical and terrestrial vertebrate ecologists (e.g., Lack 1954; Hutchinson 1957, 1959), Larkin (1956; p. 327) wrote that "there is relatively little literature which deals directly with the subject of interspecific competition in freshwater fish." Since then, a considerable number of studies, based on varied types of evidence, have focussed on the effects of interspecific competition in boreal fish assemblages (e.g. Svardson 1976; MacLean and Magnuson 1977; Keast 1978; Werner 1986). Although they differ in approach (experimental, comparative, observational), most of these studies compare some measure of a species' population performance (e.g., resource use, growth rate, density) in the presence and absence of a potential competitor.

Patterns of resource partitioning among sympatric species are frequently interpreted as evidence of the importance of interspecific competition in communities (Schoener 1974; Ross 1986). Keast (1978; p. 7) found that fishes in Ontario lakes "differ in body size, morphology, abundances, habitats, diurnal and seasonal habitat utilization patterns, diets, dietary changes with age, reproductive strategies, and population turnover rates...that, by channeling their owners towards alternative resources, permit species to co-occur." Similar segregation was found among coexisting minnows in a northern Minnesota lake (Moyle 1973) and Lake Memphremagog (Gascon and Leggett 1977). Although suggestive, resource partitioning studies by themselves cannot provide strong support for the competition hypothesis if alternative processes have not been ruled out.

Stronger evidence is available when resource use patterns of species are observed to differ in the presence or absence of a potential competitor. Although still indirect, the interpretation of such "niche shifts" can be relatively straightforward in the simplified fish assemblages of boreal lakes (Svardson 1976). Several lakes in a region may contain a pair of fish species whereas other lakes contain just one of the pair. In these systems, the species often have similar patterns of habitat use, food habits, and/or growth when allopatric, but distinct patterns when they coexist (Nilsson 1965; Nilsson and Northcote 1981; Magnan and FitzGerald 1982; Tonn and Paszkowski 1987). In addition, differences in foraging behavior between species have been confirmed in laboratory experiments (Nilsson 1963; Schutz and Northcote 1972; Paszkowski 1985; Magnan and FitzGerald 1984; Tonn et al. 1986). Simplicity, natural replication, and supporting laboratory studies consistently point to a role for competition.

In another use of the natural experiment approach, Tonn (1985) documented density responses to interspecific interactions. In a two-species system containing yellow perch (*Perca flavescens*), central mudminnows contributed only 10% of the total fish biomass, whereas in similar lakes lacking perch, mudminnow densities increased to the extent that total fish density was similar in one-species and two-species lakes. This phenomenon of increased abundance in the absence of interacting species is termed density compensation. Sumari (1970) quantified a similar strong negative relation between densities of Eurasian perch (*P. fluviatilis*) and roach (*Rutilus rutilus*) in small Finnish lakes, although complete compensation did not always occur.

A powerful approach for examining competition is the manipulative field experiment, in which a potential competitor is added or removed and responses (niche shifts, changes in growth rates, density compensation) are quantified. Although the potential for undertaking such studies is relatively high for studies of small lake fish assemblages due to fisheries management practices, there are few well-documented studies in the ecological literature.

Fraser (1978) examined angler return, food habits, and growth rates of three salmonids stocked into a small lake in Algonquin Park, Ontario both before and after introduction of yellow perch. Yields of salmonids declined to 13% of pre-perch values, growth rates of the three species were significantly reduced, and the proportion of large food items (fish, leeches, Odonata nymphs) also declined following perch introduction. Fraser also noted that these significant competitive effects contrasted with the situation in nearby larger lakes, in which yellow perch coexisted at equilibrium with lake and brook charr (*Salvelinus namaycush* and *S. fontinalis*), suggesting that simplified habitat features and/or fish assemblages in small boreal lakes intensifies the effects of competition.

To test an hypothesis of strong competition between perch and roach, Persson (1986) selectively reduced the population of roach in a Swedish lake by 40%. Persson documented niche shifts in use of food resources and habitat. He also observed that recruitment of young-of-the-year perch increased by 3.7 times, growth rates of four age-classes of perch increased by greater than 50%, and population size increased by 140%.

*Predation*

Selective predation can maintain relatively high local species diversity if it prevents dominant competitors from monopolizing food resources (Paine 1974). However, within the boreal fish community literature little evidence exists for this phenomenon. Rather, predators usually alter species composition through complete exclusion of predation-intolerant species. Tonn and Magnuson (1982) suggested that large piscivorous species (largemouth bass and/or northern pike) excluded most small-bodied species (e.g., minnows) from small lakes of northern Wisconsin.

Tolerance of predation by populations of small fishes is aided by combinations of behavioral, physiological, and morphological adaptations. One strategy is complete avoidance, i.e., residency in an environment unavailable or unsuitable to the predator. For example, Svardson (1976) suggested that a fish species that is easily preyed upon may develop tolerance for a severe abiotic environment where predation is low. As discussed above, many cyprinids and other small fishes are able to survive in lakes under severe conditions of winter hypoxia (e.g., Klinger et al. 1982; Magnuson et al. 1983, 1985; Holopainen and Hyvarinen 1985); in the absence of piscivores intolerant of these conditions, populations of these "fugitive" species thrive (Holopainen and Pitkanen 1985; Tonn and Paszkowski 1986).

Another behavioral strategy is the ability of small prey species to make use of vegetative cover (e.g., Tonn and Paszkowski 1987). Although use of such within-lake refuges may allow persistence of prey species with predators, this situation often results in reduced prey populations because of the limited abundance of suitable vegetation in small lakes (C. Robinson, per. obs.).

Morphological anti-predator strategies include general characteristics, such as body size, and specific characteristics like spines. Individual prey having a body size larger than the average predator gape will likely escape attack and thus maintain the population (Tonn and Paszkowski 1986). For example, golden shiners (*Notemigonus chrysoleucas*) appear to be better able to coexist with largemouth bass in Wisconsin lakes than other minnows because of their larger adult size (Rahel 1984).

Many species of centrarchids have well-developed dorsal spines and remain abundant within lakes containing pike and largemouth bass (Tonn and Magnuson 1982). Presence of pelvic spines on brook stickleback (*Culaea inconstans*) is also thought to reduce predation by northern pike (Reist 1980). Although this characteristic may only be an effective defense against juvenile pike, sticklebacks are able to coexist with pike to a much greater extent than similarly-sized, but spineless, cyprinids (C. Robinson, unpublished data).

## An Intercontinental Comparison

A question frequently debated among community ecologists is which factors are most important in structuring assemblages. It is clear from the above discussion that for fish assemblages in small boreal lakes, both biotic and abiotic factors contribute to assemblage composition. Furthermore, consistent interactions occur among biotic and abiotic factors which may result in repeatable and predictable patterns of fish assemblage structure. One can further examine the predictability of assemblage structure by investigating intercontinental community convergence. Are fish assemblage patterns in one boreal region similar to those in a second geographically distant region? If so, can community:environment relations in the first region be used to predict fish assemblage patterns in the second, even if the communities are composed of different species?

To address this question, Tonn et al. (MS) compared characteristics of fish assemblages from 114 small lakes in Finland with those from 56 limnologically similar lakes in northern Wisconsin, USA (Table 1). Regionally, northern Wisconsin contains twice as many fish species as Finland, yet similar numbers of species are present in the small lakes of both regions (Table 2). Largely due to historical factors, northern European fishes developed broad habitat use patterns, enabling many species to be successful in a wide variety of habitats, including small lakes (Mahon 1984). In contrast, North American species tend to be more specialized; only a small proportion of the regional fauna maintains populations in small lakes.

Species richness of individual lakes also did not differ between Finland and Wisconsin (Table 2). Similarities of present-day climate, habitat structure, and productivity levels can be associated with similar numbers of species in individual assemblages. In contrast, the effects of history (e.g., glaciation and the ecological characteristics and life-history adaptations of species in the two regions) appear more important in explaining the numbers of species in the regional pool and the proportion of this pool able to persist in small lakes.

Table 1 Environmental characteristics of the small boreal lakes in Finland (N=114) and Wisconsin (N=56) examined in the intercontinental comparison of Tonn et al. (MS)

| Environmental factor | Finland mean (range) | Wisconsin mean (range) |
|---|---|---|
| 1. Lake area (ha) | 9.5 (0.2-64.0) | 12.9 (0.2-86.7) |
| 2. Conductivity ($\mu$s @ 20°C) | 28 (3-96) | 26 (8-145) |
| 3. pH | 6.2 (4.3-7.5) | 5.9 (4.3-8.0) |
| 4. Maximum depth (m) | 9.6 (1.5-27.0) | 4.8 (1.2-10.0) |
| 5. % of lakes without outlets | 37 | 77 |
| 6. Gradient by water to next lake (m•km$^{-1}$) | 14.5 (0-88.6) | 1.9 (0-11.5) |

Table 2 Species richness, at three biogeographical scales, of the fish assemblages in Finland and Wisconsin studies by Tonn et al. (MS)

| Biogeographical scale | Finland | Wisconsin |
|---|---|---|
| 1. Freshwater fish fauna (# of species) | 37 | 73 |
| 2. Small forest lake fauna (# of species) | 20 | 23 |
| 3. Single-lake species richness (mean, range) | 3.7 (0-10) | 4.0 (0-11) |

Multivariate community analysis of the Wisconsin assemblages, based only on the presence and absence of fish species, identified three types of assemblages (Table 3). MUDMINNOW assemblages lacked specialized predators but were characterized by the presence of small and/or soft-rayed species such as the central mudminnow, northern redbelly dace (*Phoxinus eos*) and brook stickleback. Both BASS and PIKE assemblages contained specialized piscivores; in addition to largemouth bass or northern pike, both assemblage types were dominated by large and/or spiney-rayed fishes. Similar assemblage types have also been identified in Ontario (Harvey 1978, 1981).

Multivariate analysis of the fish assemblages in Finnish lakes using species presence and absence revealed a continuum based on an additive pattern of species richness and composition. Other analyses suggested that the continuum primarily resulted from similar, but graded, tolerance responses of individual species to abiotic conditions (Nordqvist 1903), rather than from biological co-adaptation (Zhakov 1974) or exclusion. When information on the relative abundance of each species in each lake was included, community analysis identified three assemblage types (Table 3); as in Wisconsin, environmental characteristics of the lakes of each assemblage type were relatively distinct.

Table 3 Composition of fish assemblage types in small forest lakes; these summaries present only the more common or abundant species

A. Relative occurrence frequency of eleven species, based on presence/absence, in PIKE, BASS, and MUDMINNOW assemblage types in northern Wisconsin lakes

| Species | Pike assemblages | Bass assemblages | Mudminnow assemblages |
|---|---|---|---|
| Yellow Perch (*Perca flavescens*) | 0.87 | 0.91 | 0.60 |
| Central Mudminnow (*Umbra limi*) | 0.12 | 0.43 | 0.90 |
| Largemouth Bass (*Micropterus salmoides*) | 0.25 | 0.78 | — |
| Bluegill (*Lepomis macrochirus*) | 0.38 | 0.52 | — |
| White Sucker (*Catostomus commersoni*) | 0.88 | 0.26 | 0.05 |
| Black Bullhead (*Ictalurus melas*) | 1.00 | 0.09 | 0.20 |
| Pumpkinseed (*Lepomis gibbosus*) | 0.75 | 0.30 | — |
| Northern Pike (*Esox lucius*) | 1.00 | 0.13 | — |
| N. Redbelly Dace (*Phoxinus eos*) | — | — | 0.30 |
| Brook Stickleback (*Culaea inconstans*) | — | — | 0.25 |
| Rock Bass (*Ambloplites rupestris*) | 0.50 | 0.04 | — |

**B. Mean relative abundance of nine species in ROACH, PERCH, and CRUCIAN CARP assemblage types in Finland**

| Species | Roach assemblages | Perch assemblages | Crucian Carp assemblages |
|---|---|---|---|
| Eurasian Perch (*Perca fluviatilis*) | 0.23 | 0.86 | 0.06 |
| Northern Pike (*Esox lucius*) | 0.18 | 0.06 | 0.08 |
| Roach (*Rutilus rutilus*) | 0.50 | 0.00[1] | 0.00[1] |
| Burbot (*Lota lota*) | 0.02 | 0.02 | — |
| Ruffe (*Gymnocephalus cernua*) | 0.02 | 0.04 | 0.00[1] |
| Crucian Carp (*Carassius carassius*) | 0.00[1] | 0.00[1] | 0.85 |
| Bream (*Abramis brama*) | 0.03 | 0.00[1] | — |
| Bleak (*Alburnus alburnus*) | 0.00[1] | 0.00[1] | — |
| Tench (*Tinca tinca*) | 0.00[1] | 0.00[1] | — |

[1] Present in at least one assemblage.

These community analyses revealed that the fish assemblage types on the two continents were distributed in similar ways along a number of environmental gradients. Characteristics of lakes containing ROACH, PERCH, and CRUCIAN CARP assemblages in Finland paralleled those of PIKE, BASS, and MUDMINNOW assemblages, respectively, in Wisconsin (Table 4). Tonn et al. were able to use fish assemblage:lake environment relations from one region to predict the type of assemblage occurring in lakes in the second region. From this procedure, they showed that analogous assemblage types were distributed in parallel ways on the two continents, suggesting community convergence.

Thus, fish assemblage structure in small lakes of Finland and Wisconsin are influenced by the same suite of environmental conditions, conditions that are common to Palearctic and Nearctic regions. Within the limited range of conditions present in small boreal lakes there may be a limited number of potential assemblage level responses. As a result, similarly-structured assemblages developed, even when derived from unrelated species pools in geographically distant lake districts.

Convergence of communities is not expected to be an all-or-nothing phenomenon. The richness, composition, and distribution of fish assemblages in small boreal lakes reflect the operation of many interacting factors, past and present, regional and local, biotic and abiotic. Nevertheless, for environmentally-similar small boreal lakes there has been significant convergence in some aspects of fish assemblage structure. Because of these and other parallel patterns among regions of the boreal biome, the study of fish assemblages in small boreal lakes can contribute to the development of community ecology as a predictive science.

Table 4  General distributions of analogous fish assemblage types in Finland and northern Wisconsin along gradients of five environmental factors.

| Environment factor | Fish Assemblage Type | | |
|---|---|---|---|
| | Finland: ROACH  Wisconsin: PIKE | PERCH  BASS | CRUCIAN CARP  MUDMINNOW |
| 1. Lake area | large | ——————————— | small |
| 2. pH | high | ——————————— | low |
| 3. Conductivity | high | ——————————— | low |
| 4. Maximum depth | shallow | ——→deep——— | shallow |
| 5. Lake isolation | low | ——————————— | high |

## References

Bajkow, A.
1949  Do fish fall from the sky? Science 109:402.

Balon, E.
1975  Reproductive guilds of fishes: a proposal and definition. J. Fish. Res. Bd. Can. 32:821-864.

Barbour, C. and J. Brown
1974  Fish species diversity in lakes. Amer. Nat. 108:473-488.

Browne, R.
1981  Lakes as islands: biogeographic distribution, turnover rates, and species composition in the lakes of central New York. Journal of Biogeography 8:75-83.

Casselman, J. and H. Harvey
1975  Selective fish mortality resulting from low winter oxygen. Verh. Int. Ver. Lim. 19:2418-2429.

Crossman, E. and D. McAllister
1986  Zoogeography of freshwater fishes of the Hudson Bay drainage, Ungava Bay, and the Arctic Archipelago. In: Hocutt, C. and Wiley, E. (eds.), The Zoogeography of North American Freshwater Fishes. John Wiley and Sons, New York, pp. 53-104.

Diamond, J.
1986  Overview: laboratory experiments, field experiments, and natural experiments. In: Diamond, J. and Case, T. (eds.), Community Ecology. Harper and Row, New York, pp. 3-22.

Eadie, J. and A. Keast
1984  Resource heterogeneity and fish species diversity in lakes. Can. J. Zoology 62:1689-1695.

Fraser, J.
1978  The effect of competition with yellow perch on the survival and growth of planted brook trout, splake and rainbow trout in a small Ontario lake. Trans. Amer. Fish. Soc. 107:505-517.

Gascon, D. and W. Leggett
1977  Distribution, abundance, and resource utilization of littoral zone fishes in response to a nutrient/production gradient in Lake Memphremagog. J. Fish. Res. Bd. Can. 34:1105-1117.

Gauch, H.
1982  Multivariate Analysis in Community Ecology. Cambridge University Press, Cambridge, England.

Green, R. and G. Vascotto
1978  A method for the analysis of environmental factors controlling patterns of species composition in aquatic communities. Water Research 12:583-590.

Harvey, H.
1975 Fish populations in a large group of acid stressed lakes. Verh. Int. Ver. Lim. 19:2406-2417.
1978 Fish communities of the Manitoulin Island Lakes. Verh. Int. Ver. Lim. 20: 2031-2038.
1981 Fish communities of the lakes of the Bruce Peninsula. Verh. Int. Ver. Lim. 21:1222-1230.

Henderson, P.
1984 An approach to the prediction of temperate freshwater fish communities with special reference to water acidification. Central Electricity Generating Bd., Surrey, Great Britain TPRD/L/2727/N84.

Holopainen, I. and H. Hyvärinen
1985 Ecology and physiology of crucian carp *Carassius carassius* (L.) in small Finnish ponds with anoxic conditions in winter. Verh. Int. Verein. Lim. 22:2566-2570.

Holopainen, I. and A. Pitkänen
1985 Population size structure of crucian carp *Carassius carassius* (L.) in two, small natural ponds in Eastern Finland. Ann. Zool. Fenn. 22:397-406.

Hutchinson, G.E.
1957 Concluding remarks. Cold Spring Harbour Symposium on Quantitative Biology 22:415-427.
1959 Homage to Santa Rosalia, or why are there so many kinds of mammals? Am. Nat. 93:145-159.

Keast, A.
1978 Trophic and spatial interrelationships in the fish species of an Ontario temperate lake. Env. Biol. Fish. 3:7-31.

Klinger, S., J. Magnuson, and G. Gallepp
1982 Survival mechanisms of the central mudminnow (*Umbra limi*), fathead minnow (*Pimephales promelas*), and brook stickleback (*Culea inconstans*) for low oxygen in winter. Env. Biol. Fish. 7:113-120.

Lack, D.
1954 The Natural Regulation of Animal Numbers. Clarendon Press, Oxford.

Larkin, P.
1956 Interspecific competition and population control in freshwater fish. J. Fish. Res. Bd. Can. 13:327-342.

MacArthur, R. and E. Wilson
1967 The Theory of Island Biogeography. Princeton University Press, N.J.

MacLean, J. and J. Magnuson
1977 Species interactions in percid communities. J. Fish. Res. Bd. Can. 34:1941-1951.

Magnan, P. and G. FitzGerald
1982 Resource partitioning between brook charr (*Salvelinus fontinalis* Mitchill) and creek chub (*Semotilus atromaculatus* Mitchill) in selected oligotrophic lakes of southern Quebec. Can. J. Zool. 60:1612-1617.
1984 Mechanisms responsible for the niche shift of brook charr, (*Salvelinus fontinalis* Mitchill), when living with creek chub, (*Semotilus atromaculatus* Mitchill). Can. J. Zool. 62:1548-1555.

Magnuson, J.J.
1976 Managing with exotics — a game of chance. Trans. Amer. Fish. Soci. 105(1):1-9.

Magnuson, J., A. Beckel, K. Mill and S. Brandt
1985 Surveying winter hypoxia: behavioral adaptations of fishes in a northern Wisconsin Lake. Env. Bio. Fish 14(4):241-250.

Magnuson, J. and D. Karlen
1970 Visual observations of fish beneath the ice in a winterkill lake. J. Fish. Res. Bd. Can. 27:1059-1068.

Magnuson, J., J. Keller, A. Beckel and G. Gallepp
1983 Breathing gas mixtures different from air: an adaptation for survival under ice of a facultative air-breathing fish. Science 220:312-314.

Mahon, R.
1984 Divergent structure in fish taxocenes of north temperate streams. Can. J. Fish. Awuat. Sci. 41(2):330-350.

Moyle, P.B.
1973 Ecological segregation among three species of minnows (Cyprinidae) in a Minnesota Lake. Tran. Amer. Fish. Soc. 102:794-805.

Nelson, J. and M. Paetz
1974 Evidence for underground movement of fishes in Wood Buffalo National Park, Canada, with notes on recent collections made in the park. Can. Field Nat. 88:157-162.

Nilsson, N.
1963 Interaction between trout and charr in Scandinavia. Trans. Amer. Fish. Soc. 92:276-285.
1965 Food segregation between salmonid species in North Sweden. Inst. Freshwater Res. Drottingham Rep. 46:58-78.

Nilsson, N. and T. Northcote
1981 Rainbow trout (*Salmo gairdneri*) and cutthroat trout, (*S. clarki*) interactions in coastal British Columbia lakes. Can. J. Fish. Aquat. Sci. 38:1228-1246.

Nordqvist, O.
1903 Some biological reasons for the present distribution of freshwater fish in Finland. Fennia 20(8):1-29.

Paine, R.
1974 Intertidal community structure. Experimental studies on the relationships between a dominant competitor and its principal predator. Oecologia 15:93-120.

Paszkowski, C.
1985 The foraging behavior of the central mudminnow and yellow perch: the influence of foraging site, intraspecific and interspecific competition. Oecologia 66:271-279.

Persson, L.
1986 Effects of reduced interspecific competition on resource utilization in perch (*Perca fluviatilis*). Ecology 67(2)-355-364.

Pielou, E.
1984 The Interpretation of Ecological Data. A Primer on Classification and Ordination. J. Wiley and Sons, New York.

Rago, P. and J. Wiener
1986 Does pH affect fish species richness when lake area is considered? Tran. Amer. Fish. Soc. 115:438-447.

Rahel, F.
1984 Factors structuring fish assemblages along a bog lake successional gradient. Ecology 65(4):1276-1289.
1986 Biogeographic influence on fish species composition of northern Wisconsin lakes with application for lake acidification studies.— Can. J. Fish. Aquat. Sci. 43(1):124-134.

Rahel, F. and J. Magnuson
1983 Low pH and the absence of fish species in naturally acidic Wisconsin lakes: inference for cultural acidification. Can. J. Fish. Aquat. Sci. 40:3-9.

Rask, M.
1983 Differences in growth of perch (*Perca fluviatilis*) in two small forest lakes. Hydrobiologia 101:139-144.
1984 The effect of low pH on perch (*Perca fluviatilis*). The effect of acid stress on different development stages of perch. Ann. Zool. Fennici 21:9-13.

Reist, J.
1980 Selective predation upon pelvic phenotypes of brook stickleback, *Culea inconstans*, by northern pike, *Esox lucius*. Can. J. Zoology 58(7):1245-1252.

Rice, J.
1985 A brief guide to ordination methods. In: Mahon, R. (ed.) Towards the inclusion of fishery interactions in management advice. Can. Tech. Rep. Fish. Aquat. Sci. No. 1347, pp. 119-131.

Ricklefs, R.
1987 Community diversity: relative roles of local and regional processes. Science 235:167-171.

Ross, S.
1986 Resource partitioning in fish assemblages: a review of field studies. Copeia 1986:352-388.

Schoener, T.
1974 Resource partitioning in ecological communities. Science 185:27-39.

Schutz, D. and T. Northcote
1972 An experimental study of feeding behavior and interactions of coastal cutthroat trout (*Salmo clarki clarki*) and Dolly Varden (*Salvelinus malma*). J. Fish. Res. Bd. Can. 29:555-565.

Simberloff, D.
1976 Experimental zoogeography os islands: effects of island size. Ecology 57:629-648.

Stewart, K. and C. Lindsey
1983 Postglacial dispersal of lower vertebrates in the Lake Agassiz region. In: Teller, J. and Clayton, L. (eds.), Glacial Lake Agassiz, Gobl. Assoc. Can. Spec. Pap., pp. 391-419.

Sumari, O.
1971 Structure of the perch populations of some ponds in Finland. Ann. Zool. Fennici 8:406-421.

Svärdson, G.
1970 Significance of introgression in coregonid evolution. In: Lindsey, C.C. and Woods, C.S. (eds.), Biology of Coregonid Fishes. University of Manitoba Press, Winnipeg, pp. 33-59.
1976 Interspecific population dominance in fish communities of Scandinavian lakes. Rep. Inst. Freshwater Res. Drott. 55:144-171.

Tonn, W.
1985 Density compensation in *Umbra-Perca* fish assemblages in northern Wisconsin lakes. Ecology 66:415-429.

Tonn, W. and J. Magnuson
1982 Patterns in the species composition and richness of fish assemblages in northern Wisconsin Lakes. Ecology 63(4):1149-1166.

Tonn, W., J. Magnuson and A. Forbes
1983 Community analysis in fishery management: An application with northern Wisconsin lakes. Tran. Amer. Fish. Soc. 112:368-377.

Tonn, W., J. Magnuson, M. Rask, and J. Toivonen
MS Intercontinental comparison of small lake fish assemblages: the balance between local and regional processes.

Tonn, W. and C. Paszkowski
1986 Size limited predation, winterkill, and the organization of *Umbra-Perca* fish assemblages. Can. J. Fish. Aquat. Sci. 43(1):194-202.
1987 Habitat use of the central mudminnow (*Umbra limi*) and yellow perch (*Perca flavescen*) in *Umbra-Perca* assemblages: the roles of competition, predation, and the abiotic environment. Can. J. Zool.: in press.

Tonn, W., C. Paszkowski, and T. Moermond
1986 Competition in *Umbra-Perca* assemblages: experimental and field evidence. Oecologia 69:126-133.

Wales, D. and G. Beggs
1986 Fish species distribution in relation to lake acidity in Ontario. Water, Air, and Soil Pollut. 30:601-609.

Werner, E.
1986 Species interactions in freshwater fish communities. In: Diamond, J. and Case, R. (eds.), Community Ecology. Harper and Row, New York, pp. 344-358.

Whittaker, R.
1975 Communities and Ecosystems. 2nd. ed. Macmillan, New York.

Zhakov, L.
1974 The composition of lake ichthyocoenoses in relation to the specific features of faunistic complexes of fishes. Journal of Ichthyology 14(2):208-218.

# Infectious Pancreatic Necrosis Virus in Arctic Char Populations in the Mackenzie Delta Region

T. Yamamoto
Department of Microbiology
University of Alberta
Edmonton, Alberta

## Introduction

Infectious pancreatic necrosis (IPN) is one of the most important infectious diseases of salmonids being widely disseminated in North America, Europe, Japan (reviewed by Hill 1982, McAllister 1983) and more recently has been found to infect eel, tilapia and trout in Asia (Hedrick et al. 1983, Chen et al. 1985). The disease has been reviewed by several authors (Hill 1982, McAllister 1983, Hedrick et al. 1983, Chen et al. 1985). The virus usually attacks young fry in hatcheries and mortalities can vary but mortalities greater than 90% have often been reported. The affected fish appear dark in color, with slightly bulging eyes and often have swollen bellies. Some fish show a characteristic whirling behavior. The name of the disease comes from the fact that the pancreatic tissue appears to be the primary target organ although the virus can be isolated from many other organs including the intestine, liver, spleen, kidneys, and reproductive products. Younger fish (one to two months old) are more susceptible to infection than older fish and survival rates increase with increasing age.

Many studies (Billie and Wolf 1969, Reno et al. 1978) have shown that fish surviving infection could become carriers for their lifetime. A study by Yamamoto and Kilistoff (1979) was able to show this clearly in an enclosed population of infected fish and that there was limited but definite transmission of infection to progeny under natural conditions.

The persistence of the virus in carrier populations appears to be continuous with a number of infected cells producing virus (Hedrick et al. 1987). The presence of defective interfering (DI) particles in the maintenance of the carrier state has been implicated in virus infected carrier lines *in vitro* (Macdonald and Yamamoto 1978, Hedrick et al. 1978) but its effect in the animal body is unknown since the presence of DI particles in infected fish is difficult to detect.

Control of IPN disease is by avoidance, namely the rearing of young fish from disease-free stock in waters that are free of virus. Epizootics occurring in hatcheries are dealt with by very strict measures of destruction of infected lots and sanitation of contaminated facilities. Egg transmission of IPN (Wolf et al. 1963) can be reduced by treatment with iodophors (Bullock et al. 1986).

In the province of Alberta IPN outbreaks became known in the late 1960's and early 1970's. The virus is thought to have been imported into hatcheries as contaminated eggs (Yamamoto 1974a), but to what extent it has been recirculated by carrier fish is unknown. The destruction of infected fish, use of clean water in hatcheries, and the introduction of fish health regulations that resulted in the importation of disease-free fish and eggs has been successful in the prevention of any recent IPN outbreaks in the province. Studies conducted in cooperation with Parks Canada (Yamamoto 1974b, 1978 and 1980) showed that carrier fish previously distributed into lakes and streams may eventually be diluted to extinction when combined with the policy of restrictive planting of disease-free fish, presumably due to the relatively low vertical transmission to progeny and the limited horizontal transmission in the wild (Yamamoto and Kilistoff 1979).

*Presence of IPN in Arctic Char in the Northwest Territories*

A study was undertaken to examine the health status of Arctic char in the Northwest Territories as part of a char survey conducted by the federal Fisheries Service. The presence of IPN in char was first detected in 1980 (Souter et al. 1984) and monitering was continued on an annual basis to 1985 (Souter et al. 1986) in order to determine the extent of the carrier state and possible yearly fluctuations that might occur in the presumed naturally established IPN virus carrier population. The studies showed that char in the western regions of the Mackenzie River delta were being maintained at the same high carrier rate that varied little from year to year. Over the five year period a total of 229 adult Arctic char were examined for virus and found to have an overall prevalence of 44%. This report is a review of those virus isolation data as well as some recent experimental studies by immersion infection of young salmonids which indicate that this char virus is as pathogenic to salmonids as other known virulent strains.

## Materials and Methods

*Fish Samples*

Fish were obtained by trapping or by angling. Tissues were aseptically removed either in the field or after shipment of the fish to the laboratory. The tissues were ground by mortar and pestle or homogenized with a Stomacher Lab Blender 80 (Seward Lab., England).

*Virus Detection*

The supernatant of the cell extracts was inoculated onto CHSE-214 cell monlayers in 6 well or 24 well cluster dishes and observed for the development of typical cytopathic effect. The cells were maintained in Minimal Essential Medium (Eagle) buffered with Hepes buffer and containing penicillin, streptomycin and 5% fetal bovine serum.

*Fish Infection Studies*

Experimental infection of young fingerlings was done by immersion of approximately 25 fish per lot for 1 hour in 1 liter of water containing approximately $10^4$ pfu/mL. The fish were then maintained in 2 liter plastic containers at temperatures ranging from 10°C to 14°C.

## Results

*Virus Isolations from Field Samples*

Arctic char were sampled for virus at three locations on the western tributaries of the Mackenzie Delta. These were Big Fish River, Fish Creek and Rat River. The locations are shown in Fig. 1. At Big Fish River, of 103 fish examined during 1982, 1983, 1984, and 1985, 43 were found to yield virus on cell culture giving an isolation rate of 41.8%. The data are shown in Table 1. Interestingly, 60 presmolts examined for virus in 1981 were negative for virus. At Fish Creek where virus was first detected in 1980 and sampled again in 1982 and 1983, 12 of 27 fish yielded virus to give 44.4% positive for virus. At Rat River samples taken during 1983, 1984 and 1985 gave 31 of 71 fish or 43.7% positives. These data give a grand total for the Mackenzie Delta region of 86/201 to give 42.8% yielding virus.

In addition a small number of fish were sampled from streams on the North Slope in the Yukon and the data are shown in Table 2. At Shingle point on the Arctic Ocean 3 of 7 fish were positive for virus. At Babbage River 5 of 11 were

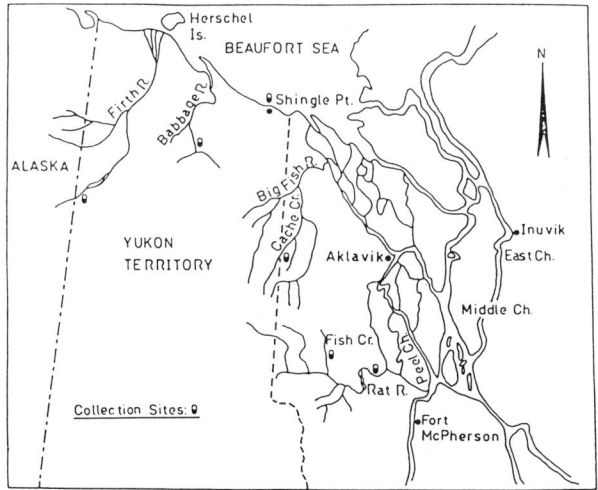

Figure 1  Map of the Mackenzie Delta Region and the Yukon North Slope showing the Arctic Char Collection sites.

positive and at Firth River 6 of 10 were positive. These give a total of 14 of 28 or 50.0% positive for virus. Analysis of Arctic char from regions to the east of the Mackenzie Delta and in regions to the North have shown that they are free of the virus.

Some limited testing of other species of fish in the Mackenzie Delta (where char have been found to have virus) indicate that they are not carriers of the virus. These included Arctic cisco, grayling and whitefish from Shingle Point, Big Fish River, Rat River and Fish Creek. The numbers of these fish sampled were comparatively small, but virus has not been isolated from fish species other than char.

*Virus Distribution in Carrier Fish*

It was of interest to determine whether the virus was present in many organs as is the case of other IPN infected animals. Of 18 char from Big Fish River sampled during 1983, whose organs were examined separately, the virus was most frequently isolated from the pyloric caeca and the kidneys. This organ-virus relationship for each fish is shown in Table 2. Similarly, of organs tested from 11 fish from Rat River the pyloric caeca and the kidneys appeared to yield virus most frequently. The data are shown in Table 3. These virologic findings indicate that the char virus is not different with respect to tissue affinity compared to IPN viruses infecting other species of salmonids.

*Pathogenicity of Arctic Char IPN for Salmonids*

Since it was determined that the char IPN virus was a distinctive strain (Macdonald et al. 1983), it was important to determine whether the char virus was pathogenic to young salmonids. Both young arctic char and brook trout fingerlings were subject to experimental infection by immersion in virus containing water for a period of 1 hour and observed for mortalities on a daily basis. Typical infection results are shown in Fig. 2 for brook trout fingerlings and in Fig. 3 for Arctic char fingerlings. For comparative infection standards we used the standard ATCC VR-299 IPN strain which is known to be relatively nonvirulent, and the West Buxton IPN virus known to have high virulence. The high mortalities observed in these experiments revealed that the Arctic char virus was highly pathogenic to young char as well as to other salmonid fishes. The infection was observed to cause the death of Arctic char beginning about 10 days following infection and increasing to about 50% within 25 days. In another study the char virus was found to be only slightly less pathogenic to brook trout fingerlings.

There are no data at the present time that would indicate whether the virus disease is adversely affecting the char population in those regions. The high carrier rate however shows that the disease, if infection were occurring early in life, could be an important factor in reducing the numbers of char surviving the fingerling stage.

**Table 1** **IPN virus isolations from Arctic char in the western tributaries of the Mackenzie delta**

| | Isolations/No. tested | % Yielding Virus |
|---|---|---|
| Big Fish River | | |
| 1981 (presmolts) | 0/60 | 0 |
| 1982 | 2/10 | 20.0 |
| 1983 | 8/18 | 44.4 |
| 1984 | 39/67 | 44.8 |
| 1985 | 3/8 | 37.5 |
| Total | 43/103 | 41.8 |
| Fish Creek | | |
| 1980 | 3/30 | (Pools; original detection of virus) |
| 1982 | 7/20 | 35.0 |
| 1983 | 5/7 | 71.4 |
| Total | 12/27 | 44.4 |
| Rat River | | |
| 1983 | 21/43 | 48.8 |
| 1984 | 3/5 | 60.0 |
| 1985 | 7/23 | 30.4 |
| Total | 31/71 | 43.7 |
| Grand Total | 86/20 | 42.8 |

Table 2   IPNV isolations from Arctic char in Big Fish River, August 1983

| Specimen | Pyloric-ceca | Kidneys | Spleen | Liver | Gonad |
|---|---|---|---|---|---|
| 1 | + | + | - | - | - |
| 2 | - | + | - | - | - |
| 3 | - | - | - | - | - |
| 4 | + | + | + | - | + |
| 5 | + | + | - | - | - |
| 6 | - | - | - | - | - |
| 7 | - | - | - | - | - |
| 8 | + | - | - | - | - |
| 9 | - | + | - | - | - |
| 10 | + | + | + | - | - |
| 11 | - | - | - | - | - |
| 12 | - | - | - | - | - |
| 13 | - | - | - | - | - |
| 14 | - | - | - | - | - |
| 15 | + | + | - | + | + |
| 16 | - | - | - | - | - |
| 17 | - | - | - | - | - |
| 18 | - | - | - | - | - |
| Total: 18 | 6/18 | 8/18 | 2/18 | 1/18 | 2/18 |
| Percentage: | 33 | 44 | 11 | 5 | 11 |

Total number of Big Fish River Arctic char positive for IPNV: 8/18; 44%

Table 3   IPNV isolations from Arctic char in Rat River, August 1983

| Specimen | Pyloric-ceca | Kidneys | Spleen | Liver | Gonad |
|---|---|---|---|---|---|
| 1 | + | + | + | + | - |
| 2 | - | - | - | - | - |
| 3 | + | + | + | - | - |
| 4 | + | + | + | - | - |
| 5 | + | + | + | + | + |
| 6 | - | - | - | - | - |
| 7 | + | + | + | - | - |
| 8 | + | + | - | - | - |
| 9 | - | - | - | - | - |
| 10 | - | - | - | - | - |
| 11 | - | - | - | - | - |
| Total: 18 | 6/11 | 6/11 | 5/11 | 2/11 | 2/11 |
| Percentage: | 54 | 54 | 45 | 18 | 18 |

Total number of Rat River Arctic char positive for IPNV: 6/11; 54%

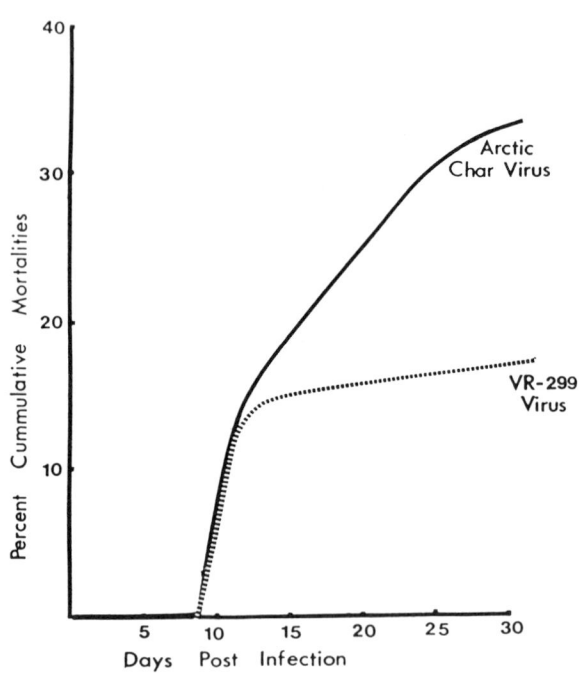

Figure 2  Pathogenicity of IPN Virus to Brook Trout

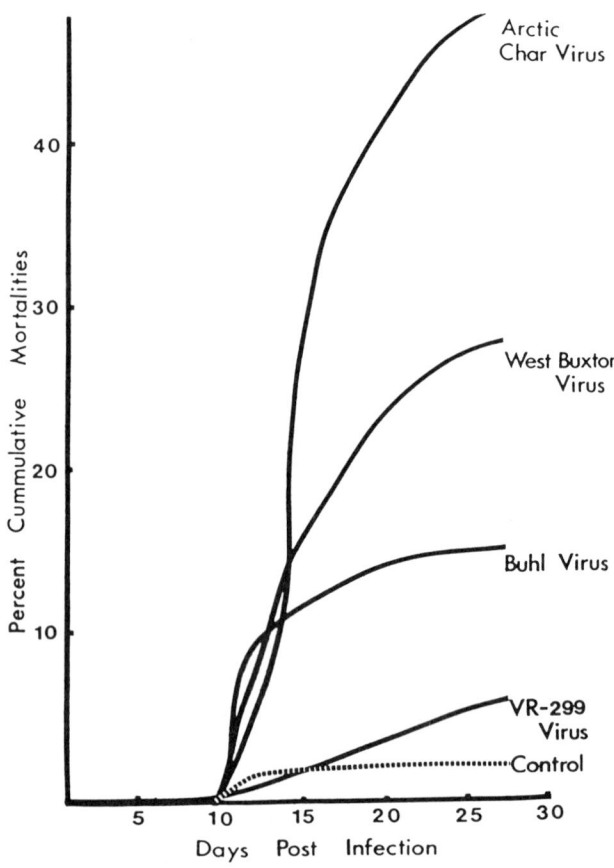

Figure 3  Pathogenicity of IPN Virus to Arctic Char

## Discussion

### Infection and Persistence of IPN Virus in Char

The high levels of char carrying virus in the western regions of the Mackenzie Delta and the Yukon north slope is unusual. As expressed by Souter et al. (1984) it is thought that these char populations are naturally infected since there has been no planting or farming of fish in the region. Just why it is present in the western regions and not on the eastern side is unknown. Since these fish are anadromous and migrate from the Mackenzie River out into the Arctic Ocean, one would think that the infection would spread to other populations of char that inhabit the same waters.

The high level of infection in the population could possibly be related to procedures in fish harvesting, cleaning and disposal of viscera, but there is no evidence for it. At the present time there is no information regarding the age of infection. Whether the char are infected at an early age, during their smolt stage, or out in the marine environment is unknown. Further studies are required to obtain information on the age and locale of virus infection and the mode of transmission, whether it occurs vertically or horizontally in the char populations.

### Implications for Future Salmonid Programs in Regions of IPN Persistence

Arctic char are a highly desired food resource that could be enhanced for production in the North. However the presence of IPN carriers in the western regions is a factor that should be considered for any future programs. Stocks of fish used for this purpose should be screened vigorously for virus and only fish and eggs taken from virus-free regions be used. Water used for the rearing of salmonids should be obtained from sources free of virus, namely waters not containing IPN carrier fish. The introduction of virus into populations of young fish in fish rearing facilities could be disastrous.

## Summary and Conclusions

1. This study showed that IPN infection is highly enzootic in char populations in the Western Mackenzie Delta region. The factors involved in the persistence of such high infection rates in this naturally infected carrier population is unknown and is quite different from the char populations east of the delta which have been uniformly negative for the virus.
2. Experimental data support the hypothesis that the char virus can be highly pathogenic to salmonids including Arctic char.
3. Future enhancement of salmonid production in IPN enzootic areas should be carefully considered in order to prevent epizootics and further spread of the virus.
4. Some attention should be paid to disposal of fish waste by burying instead of discarding it into the water. This practice may reduce the further spread of the virus and reduce the infection and resultant high carrier rate.

## Acknowledgement

For the field work I wish to acknowledge the participation of Brian Souter of the Freshwater Institute, Fisheries and Oceans, Winnipeg, and the assistance of Vic Gillman and his annual field assistants for providing the camp hospitality and trapping of fish at Rat River.

In my laboratory I wish to thank Lindsay Elmgren who assisted with the virologic testing as well as obtaining field specimens. I also wish to express my appreciation for the assistance of Rshmi Korhana who was a recipient of a scholarship from Women in Scholarship, Engineering, Sciences and Technology.

Funding for this project over the years was provided by Fisheries and Oceans, Ottawa; Natural Sciences and Engineering Research Council, Ottawa; Boreal Institute for Northern Affairs, Edmonton; and Central Research Funds, University of Alberta.

## References

Billie, J.L. and K. Wolf
1969    Quantitative comparison of peritoneal washes and feces for detecting infectious pancreatic necrosis (IPN) virus in carrier brook trout. J. Fish. Res. Board Can. 33:1197-1198.

Bullock, G.L., R.R. Rucker, D. Amend, K. Wolf and H.M. Stuckey
1976    Infectious pancreatic necrosis: transmission with iodine-treated and non-iodine treated eggs of brook trout (*Salvelinus fontinalis*). J. Fish. Res. Board Can. 33:1197-1198.

Chen, S.M., G.H. Kou, R.P. Hedrick and J.L. Fryer
1985    The occurrence of viral infections of fish in Taiwan. *In* Fish and Shellfish Pathology. A.E. Ellis, ed. pp. 313-319. Academic Press.

Hedrick, R.P., J.L. Fryer, S.N. Chen, and G.H. Kou
1983    Characteristics of four birnaviruses isolated from fish in Taiwan. Fish Pathol. 18:91-97.

Hedrick, R.P., J.C. Leong, and J.L. Fryer
1978    Persistent infections in salmonid fish cells with infectious pancreatic necrosis virus (IPNV). Fish Pathol. 1:297-308.

Hill, B.J.
1982    Infectious pancreatic necrosis virus and its virulence. *In* Microbial Disease of Fish. R.J. Roberts, ed. pp. 91-114. Academic Press.

McAllister, P.E.
1983    Infectious pancreatic necrosis (IPN) o salmonid fishes. U.F. Fish and Wildlife Service Fish Disease Leaflet No. 65.

Macdonald, R.D., A.R. Moore, and B.W. Souter
1983    Three new strains of infectious pancreatic necrosis virus isolated in Canada. Can. J. Microbiol. 39:137-141.

Reno, P.W., S. Darley and M. Savan
1978    Infectious pancreatic necrosis: experimental induction of the carrier state in trout. J. Fish. Res. Board Can. 35:1451-1556.

Souter, B.W., A.G. Dwilow, K. Knight and T. Yamamoto
1984 Infectious pancreatic necrosis virus: isolation from asymptomatic wild Arctic char (*Salvelinus alpinus*). J. Wildl. Dis. 20:338-339.
1986 Infectious pancreatic necrosis virus in adult Arctic char, *Salvelinus alpinus* (L.), in rivers in the Mackenzie delta region and Yukon territory. Canadian Technical Report of Fisheries and Aquatic Sciences. 1441:1-11.

Wolf, K., M.C. Quimby and A.D. Bradford
1963 Egg-associated transmission of IPN virus of trouts. Virol. 21:317-321.

Yamamoto, T.
1974a Infectious pancreatic virus occurrence at a hatchery in Alberta. J. Fish. Res. Board Can. 31:397-402.
1974b Investigations into the distribution and transmission of infectious pancreatic necrosis virus in the western National Parks, in particular in Jasper National Park. A report submitted to Parks Canada, Western Region, Dept. of Indian and Northern Affairs.
1978 Detection and identification of infectious pancreatic necrosis (IPN) virus carrier populations of fish in selected lakes in Jasper, Banff and Waterton Lakes National Parks. A report submitted to Parks Canada, Western Region, Department of Indian Affairs and Northern Development.
1981 Infectious pancreatic necrosis: persistence in resident populations of fish. Paper presented at the American Fisheries Society Meeting, Albuquerque, N.M.

Yamamoto, T. and J. Kilistoff
1979 Infectious pancreatic necrosis virus: quantification of carriers in lake populations during a 6-year period. J. Fish. Res. Board Can. 36:562-567.

# NEW BOOKS FROM THE BOREAL INSTITUTE FOR NORTHERN STUDIES

## ORDER FORM

Qty

| | |
|---|---|
| **Research and Monitoring in Circumpolar Biosphere Reserves**<br>*Norman Simmons, Milton Freeman, and Julian Inglis, Editors*<br>ISBN 0-919058-65-5, ISSN 0068-0303, Occasional Publication No. 20<br>softcover, 8 1/2"x11", 75 pages<br>A joint publication of UNESCO-MAB and the Boreal Institute for Northern Studies | $15.00 |
| **Knowing the North: Reflections on Tradition, Technology and Science**<br>*William C. Wonders, Editor*<br>ISBN 0-919058-66-3, ISSN 0068-0303, Occasional Publication No. 21<br>softcover, 8 1/2"x11", approximately 150 pages | $24.00 |
| **Northern Lakes and Rivers**<br>*William C. Mackay, Editor*<br>ISBN 0-919058-67-1, ISSN 0068-0303, Occasional Publication No. 22<br>softcover, 8 1/2"x11", approximately 120 pages | $25.00 |
| **Traditional Knowledge and Renewable Resource Management in Northern Regions**<br>*Milton Freeman and Ludwig Carbyn, Editors*<br>ISBN 0-919058-68-X, ISSN 0068-0303, Occasional Publication No. 23<br>softcover, 8 1/2"x11", approximately 150 pages | $24.00 |
| **Northern Environmental Disturbances**<br>*Peter Kershaw, Editor*<br>ISBN 0-919058-69-8, ISSN 0068-0303, Occasional Publication No. 24<br>softcover, 8 1/2"x11", approximately 70 pages | $15.00 |
| **Northern Communities: Prospects for Empowerment**<br>*Gurston Dacks and Ken Coates, Editors*<br>ISBN 0-919058-70-1, ISSN 0068-0303, Occasional Publication No. 25<br>softcover, 8 1/2"x11", 100 pages | $15.00 |
| **Health Care Issues in the Canadian North**<br>*David E. Young, Editor*<br>ISBN 0-919058-71-X, ISSN 0068-0303, Occasional Publication No. 26<br>softcover, 8 1/2"x11", 150 pages | $21.00 |
| **Kinship and the Drum Dance in a Northern Dene Community**<br>*Michael Asch*<br>ISBN 0-919058-73-6 (hardcover), 0-919-058-74-4 (softcover), ISSN 0838-133X<br>Circumpolar Research Series, Vol. I., Co-published with Academic Printing and Publishing<br>6"x9", approximately 140 pages | $27.95 hardcover<br>$12.95 softcover |
| **Small-Type Coastal Whaling in Japan:** Report of an International Workshop<br>ISBN 0-919058-75-2, ISSN 0068-0303, Occasional Publication No. 27<br>softcover, 8 1/2"x11", 120 pages | $20.00 |

Prices include postage and handling.
**10% discount for ordering Occasional Publication Nos. 21 to 26 inclusive**

Bill to: _____  Ship to: _____

Postal Code: _____

Date: _____  Shipping will be book rate mail, unless otherwise requested:

P.O.# _____

To order, send payment to:  The Boreal Institute for Northern Studies, CW 401, Biological Sciences Building
The University of Alberta, Edmonton, Alberta, T6G 2E9
(403) 432-4999 or 432-4512

## PREVIOUS PUBLICATIONS FROM THE BOREAL INSTITUTE FOR NORTHERN STUDIES

# ORDER FORM

Qty

| | |
|---|---|
| **Snow cover as an integral factor of the environment and its importance in the ecology of mammals and birds.** Occasional Publication No. 1. *A.N. Formozov.* 1964. Translated from original Russian edition (1946) by William Prychodko and William O. Pruitt, Jr. 141 pp., illustrations. | $5.00 |
| **Catastrophic advance of the Steele Glacier, Yukon, Canada. A report on surveys conducted on the Steele Glacier from August 20 to August 23, 1967.** Occasional Publication No. 3. *L.A. Bayrock.* 1967. 35 pp., illustrations. | $1.50 |
| **On the edge of the shield: Fort Chipewyan and its hinterland.** Occasional Publication No. 7. *John W. Chalmers, Editor.* 1971. 60 pp., illustrations. | $2.00 |
| **An interdisciplinary investigation of Fort Enterprise, Northwest Territories, 1970.** Occasional Publication No. 9. *Timothy C. Losey, et al., Editors.* 1973. Results of a five-week archaeological investigation carried out as part of the NWT's 1970 Centennial Year celebrations. | $4.00 |
| **Among the Chiglit Eskimos.** Occasional Publication No. 10. *Emile Petitot.* 1981. Translated from "Les grands Esquimeaux" (1887) by E.O. Höhn. 202 pp., illustrations. | $9.00 |
| **Settlements of Northern Canada: a gazetteer and index.** Occasional Publication No. 11. *Roy Jackson Fletcher.* 1975. 136 pp., illustrations. | $4.50 |
| **The land of Peter Pond.** Occasional Publication No. 12. *John W. Chalmers, et al.* 1974. Series of non-technical articles describing the oilsand area of northeastern Alberta, its people and its history. 131 pp., illustrations. | $4.50 |
| **Climate of Arctic Canada in maps.** Occasional Publication No. 13. *Roy Jackson Fletcher and G. Stanley Young.* 1976. 48 pp. | $4.00 |
| **Consequences of economic change in circumpolar regions.** Occasional Publication No. 14. *Ludger Müller-Wille et al., Editors.* 1978. Papers of the symposium on unexpected consequences of economic change in circumpolar regions at the 34th annual meeting of the Society for Applied Anthropology, 1975. 269 pp., illustrations. | $10.00 |
| **Wildlife of the Mackenzie Delta region.** Occasional Publication No. 15. *A.M. Martell, D.M. Dickinson, and L.M. Casselman.* 1984. Synthesizes information from published accounts with that of more recent papers in an annotated list of all invertebrate wildlife species that occur or have been reported in the Delta region. Also includes vegetation. 214 pp., maps. | $15.00 |
| **Between two worlds: the report of the Northwest Territories perinatal and infant mortality and morbidity study.** Occasional Publication No. 16. *D.W. Spady et al.* 1982. The health of infants born in the NWT in 1973-74 is analyzed with respect to the socio-economic and cultural environment, nutrition and health care. 271 pp. | $15.00 |
| **A time for burning.** Occasional Publication No. 17. *Henry T. Lewis.* 1982. The use of fire by native peoples of northern Alberta to transform and maintain their natural environment is examined. 62 pp. Complements the film *Fires of Spring.* | $5.00 |
| **Odyssey Northwest: a trilogy of poems on the Northwest Passage.** Occasional Publication No. 18. *Gerald St. Maur.* 1984. These poems deal with the explorations of Martin Frobisher, Henry Hudson and Sir John Franklin. 123 pp. | $15.00 hardcover $10.00 softcover |
| **Keeveeok awake: Mamngugsualuk and the rebirth of legend at Baker Lake.** Occasional Publication No. 19. 1986. Catalogue of 20 drawings, 5 prints and 1 wall hanging by Baker Lake artist Victoria Mamngugsualuk. Includes French translation insert. Jointly published by University Collections and the Boreal Institute. | $15.00 |

**Prices for these books do not include postage and handling.**